The Invincible Traveller

The Invincible Traveller

Edited by
RAJ THAPAR

Vikas Publishing House Pvt Ltd

VIKAS HOUSE, 20/4 Industrial Area, Sahibabad,
Distt. Ghaziabad, U.P. (India)

VIKAS PUBLISHING HOUSE PVT LTD
Regd. Office: 5 Ansari Road, New Delhi 110002
Head Office: VIKAS HOUSE, 20/4 Industrial Area, Sahibabad,
Distt. Ghaziabad, U.P.
Branches: Savoy Chambers, 5 Wallace Street, Bombay /
10 First Main Road, Gandhi Nagar, Bangalore / 8/1-B Chow-
ringhee Lane, Calcutta / 80 Canning Road, Kanpur

ISBN 0-7069-0828-7

1V2T1202

Printed at Indraprastha Press (CBT), New Delhi 110002

Preface

I have always wondered what preparations Hsuan Tsang must have made to set off on his journey to India over the Himalayas. And what happened to his family? Did they wither away with anxiety the years he was gone? Or was it an accepted part of life then, of the human condition some thirteen hundred years ago?

The scene is changing dramatically with technology, progress, time, call it what you will. Increasingly now, you race to an airport through unending traffic, fill up bits and pieces of irrelevant information on to cards which will finally be thrown into a computer or a waste paper basket, strap yourself on to a chair much the same as the chair you left at home, and caged in that plane you leave the earth in a burst of noise. Down to earth again, swallowed up by yet another cavernous airport, along with thousands of others you charge across the numerous corridors with their little card-receiving outposts to reach a hotel which could be much the same every place you go.

It all happens so quickly and yet seems to take so long, like playing a game with time. There seems little occasion for that brush with another culture, another terrain, another people. One can hardly conceive of sitting in peace to sketch for instance. Krishen Khanna, Abu Abraham and Amena Jayal have done that for us in their travelogues, but what of the others? Have they the time that Rousselet and Torrens had, who punctuated their narratives with visuals of what they saw and the fun they had?

Judging from the meticulousness of the earlier accounts, even language seems to have been less of a barrier than it is today. The traveller had to learn it; there was no alternative. Actually, speed cuts out much of the excitement, much of life. One is filled with a vicarious nostalgia for those winding caravan journeys over parched deserts, for the monsoon-tossed voyages to Java and beyond, even for the traumas of the lone individualists who set out on foot, undaunted by the possible encounters with strange men and stranger beasts.

Very few in our generation could write off a few years of their lives just for a journey—as people certainly did in the past. And they must have had to suffer for it in physical terms far more agonizing than we can imagine. To transcend the heat and the snow and sea sickness and what have you, the urge to travel must have been awesome.

In a sense, this travelogue was born out of such an urge, but for different reasons. Our rather serious magazine, *Seminar,* was closed down during the Emergency. To keep the office functioning, we decided on a publications programme. What better than a random collection of travel in India through the ages. It is incomplete in every sense. The Rousselet, Torrens, and Seely accounts have been severely edited from the originals and vast stretches of the country have not been covered at all. Even so, we hope the reader will be nudged a little, just enough to read some more or, hopefully, even to take to the road.

I would like to thank H.K. Kaul of the India International Centre library for his generous assistance, and Tejbir Singh for his photographs of Ladakh (plates 34, 35 and 37-42) and his patient photographic coverage of the etchings reproduced here. I am also grateful to the National School of Design, Ahmedabad for providing the photographs for plates 44 and 45, and to Jyoti Bhatt for his photograph for plate 46. Plates 10, 12, 13, 14, 16 are Daniell etchings, while plates 3, 9, 11, 24, 43 are taken from Philip Baldaeus' book, *A true and exact description of the most celebrated East India Coasts of Malabar and Coromandel,* Henry Lintot and John Oborn, 1672.

RAJ THAPAR

Contents

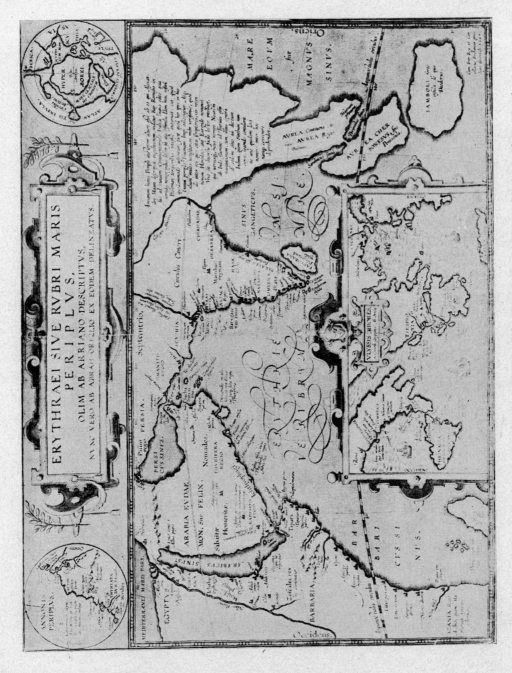

Map prepared in 1597 on the basis primarily of information contained in the Periplus of the Erythrean Sea (a navigational guide relating to the Red Sea and the Arabian Sea) and the Geography of Ptolemy as well as the descriptions contained in the accounts of Arrian—all dating to the first and second centuries A.D.

Once Upon a Time

ROMILA THAPAR

The Indian has been an inveterate traveller for many millennia. Merchants, traders, pilgrims, monks, religious mendicants and the emissaries of royal courts were all on the move. For some, travelling became a full time occupation with virtually no capital investment, and continues to be so, as in the case of the wandering *sadhus*. Traders and monks are, however, the most visible both in numbers and in impact from these early descriptions, for the incentives from trade and the mission to preach took people long distances. Among outsiders, the vision of India remained fairly constant. Images were born from the accounts of visitors to the country and possibly confirmed by Indians settled outside where, like many settlers, the land they had left behind probably took on in time the contours of a utopia. But in the earlier centuries it was curiosity that encouraged visits to India.

The earliest traces of connections between India and the outside world are the scattered traces of Harappan seals and weights, part of the baggage of merchandise, which turn up at sites along the Gulf and in some Mesopotamian cities of the third millennium B.C. Sumerian texts speak of the land of Meluhha which many historians now identify with the Indus civilisation. Not only did ships dock in Mesopotamian ports bringing timber, copper and stone from Meluhha, but the Meluhhans had to have their own interpreters. It was the same genius for trade which took Indians to other parts of Asia in later centuries and which today finds them even in the remotest parts of the world.

From the late first millennium B.C. trade fanned out into other interests. Some were linked to diplomacy and some to the major missionary religion which arose in India—Buddhism. Thus, the emissaries of the Mauryan emperor, Ashoka, were despatched in the third century B.C. to various parts of Asia contiguous with the empire and to the eastern Mediterranean. In their wake came the Buddhist missions taking the religion to Khotan, Yarkhand, Miran, Tun-

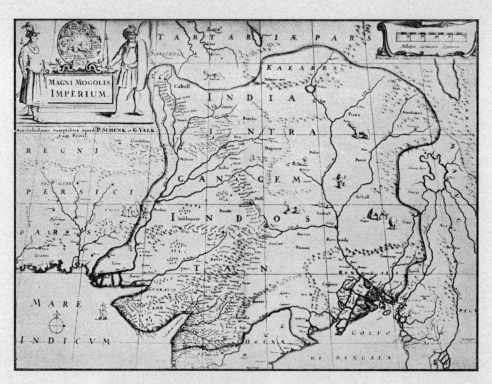

1. Part of a seventeenth century map of the Mughal empire.

huang—towns set in the oases scattered across the central Asian deserts—and on to China in the early centuries of the Christian era. Buddhist teachers acted as catalysts in the central Asian towns introducing a new cultural milieu to the area.

The establishment of Buddhism in China led to a number of Chinese Buddhists coming to the "holy land". They braved the almost impenetrable snow country of the high mountains and finally breathed the sanctity of the birth-place of the Buddha. Monks and brahmans went together to South-East Asia where the latter, in spite of the ban on crossing the oceans, were to establish themselves not only in commerce but even in politics. There is the charming story of the brahman, Kaundinya, who married the Princess Willow-leaf and founded a kingdom in Cambodia.

The initial and the most continuous coming and going has been between India and the Gulf. But, with the dissemination of information regarding the monsoon winds, there was a burst of activity between the Red Sea, southern Arabia and the coasts of peninsular India. Greek texts of the early centuries A.D. maintain that Hippalus "discovered" that the south-west monsoon winds could be used to sail ships on a mid-ocean route directly from southern Arabia to the west coast of India in the summer months, and in winter the north-east monsoon could be used for the return journey. Whether this was a discovery or merely the unlocking of an earlier secret of maritime navigation, the result was dramatic. Over a hundred Roman ships were said to sail each year from the Red Sea to the ports of south India, bringing amphorae of oil and wine, pottery of the finest Arretine ware, lamps, and glassware for the wealthy, and taking back with them textiles (produced to Roman fashion), spices, precious stones and occasionally apes and peacocks for the villas of the patricians. The Roman paid for these items in good gold coin, and Pliny, the Roman historian, lamented that this trade was a serious drain on the finances of the Roman empire.

At the same time, the north Indian traders were tapping the overland routes. Some went through Afghanistan, Persia and the eastern Mediterranean to Rome. In the opposite direction, Indian merchants were also involved in the silk trade from China and followed the "silk route" through central Asia. This was the route which was used by Buddhist monks as well. When the Chinese interest dwindled in later times, the central Asian connection with India was strengthened. Roman sources record the coming of Indian merchant embassies to the court of Augustus and of later emperors up until the fifth century A.D. According to the account of Florus, one of the Indian missions brought elephants as well as precious stones and pearls as gifts and spent four years on the journey. He adds that their complexion proved that they came from beneath another sky, one directly under the sun.

Later, in Islamic times, this Indo-Roman trade formed the bedrock of Arab concern in trying to capture the supply of Indian goods to Europe. This not only necessitated Arab settlements in Indian maritime areas but ultimately took the Arabs to south-east Asia to tap a further source of some of the more lucrative commodities such as spices. Islam travelled to Indonesia from the west coast of India. What enhanced the Arab trade was that the Mongol migrations and invasions through central Asia at the turn of the first millennium A.D. gradually disrupted the traditional trade which turned seawards and increasingly into the hands of the Arabs. And, in turn, it was to bypass the Arab traders that Italian merchant missions set out, such as the family of Marco Polo, taking the initiative in trying to establish direct trade with Asian centres. This was to culminate in the European search for a route to Asia in the fifteenth century, one that would avoid Arab ports and territories—a search which landed

Amerigo Vespucci and Colombus in America.

Indian involvement in the commerce of south-east Asia was of such consequence that the Chola kings took a deep interest in this trade. It is thought that Chola naval power moved in to clear the sea for Indian merchants. Later, towards the end of the eleventh century a large mission of Indian merchants from south India visited China. Commercial links with southern China prospered in later periods and by the nineteenth century the traders of Gujarat and Canton had very close ties.

Throughout the medieval period, Indian traders maintained their earlier links and in some areas went further afield. Thus, Indian merchants visiting Persia travelled into the borders of Russia. But with the arrival of the Portuguese and, later, with the setting up of East Indian Trading Companies by many European states—the English, French and Dutch for example—the ventures of the Indian merchant

2. The Dutch enter Cochin.

were curtailed. Later, the encroaching of colonial authority on the Indian economy slowed down enterprise abroad, except of course

4   *The Invincible Traveller*

where it suited colonial needs. Over the last hundred years or so there has been an exodus of Indians to various corners of the British empire and elsewhere. Some went as indentured labour to work on the plantations of other British colonies, for example in South Africa, the Caribbean (Trinidad and the Guyanas), and Malaysia. Others went as traders to accelerate commercial enterprise where it was barely in existence, as in east Africa. A handful went as political exiles, mainly to the west coast of Canada and the United States.

There is now a vast Indian diaspora in every region of the world. Large settlements of Indians form minority communities fighting for rights or dominant groups vying for political power. Lesser settlements boast of Indians participating in commerce and a wide range of technical professions. Perhaps the numbers are greater now than they were in the pre-colonial period. Yet, one has the impression that the Indian diaspora has always existed.

A curious and almost inexplicable aspect of this distribution and migration of Indians is that the information on them comes from the people and the sources of the lands where they travelled and worked. Not a single one among them ever thought of writing an account of his or her travels, until recent times. We hardly know them as individuals, for their names and their biographies have for the most part gone unrecorded. Very infrequently there may be some stories about distant places and adventures as in the *Dasakumaracharita* (The Tale of the Ten Princes) where references are made to lands beyond India, but so fictionalised as to be almost fables. This apparent lack of interest in an alien environment takes on the dimensions of an Indian trait. Was this due to an alienation with the new environment to a point where it does not impinge on one's life or, alternatively, does it reflect the internationalising of the exterior landscape to a degree where it ceases to exist? The contrast is all the more acute when one considers the vast literature left by visitors and travellers from other countries and cultures who spent time in India. There was a multiplicity of visitors with an equal multiplicity of purposes.

Some visitors were part of the entourage of successful invaders. Thus, Nearchus who came with Alexander of Macedon in 326 B.C. was placed in charge of the Greek fleet which sailed down the Indus and up the Gulf in the following year when Alexander returned to Babylon. Much later, the central Asian scholar, Alberuni, was brought to India by Mahmud of Ghazni in the eleventh century A.D. Alberuni came from Khavarazm and was among the finest intellects of his time. His ten-year stay in India was forced on him by Mahmud as indeed was his work on India, the *Kitab-ul-Hind*.

Among ambassadors, the most renowned was Megasthenes, the Seleucid ambassador at the court of Chandragupta Maurya, who was in India at the end of the fourth century A.D. and whose account, the *Indika*, has had to be pieced together from quotations in later Greek texts, the original having been lost; equally distinguished was the ambassador from the court of St. James, Sir Thomas Roe, accredited to the Mughal court of Jehangir.

Some never actually visited India but put together the information from those who had. This was incorporated into geographical texts and navigational guides. These included the geography of Strabo and that of Ptolemy and the famous *Periplus* of the Erythreaen Sea. The latter was a guide to navigation in the Indian Ocean and composed in about the first century A.D. It claims to be based on some personal information and on eye-witness accounts of sailors and travellers. Both Ptolemy's *Geography* and the *Periplus* were widely used by sailors navigating in these areas despite certain errors such as the joining of Asia to Africa in the south. The *Periplus* lists the ports all along the coastline from the Red Sea via Arabia, the Gulf, the west coast of India and up as far as the Ganges delta with some description of the products and the hinterland of each. Maps based on Ptolemy's *Geography* were current until the fifteenth century when new information came into Europe and the cartography of India underwent rapid changes becoming increasingly more accurate as is evident from the planisphere of Giacomo Castaldi in the fifteenth century, which became the basis for the projections of G. Mercator and G. Blaeu.

The biggest and most consistent category of visitors were of course merchants and traders who came as a constant stream from the west. Very few of their names have, however, survived until the arrival of the Arabs. Earlier accounts seem to give greater emphasis to the commodities of trade. Thus, Pliny refers to pepper: "The pepper tree resembles the juniper and is abundant as is also the use of pepper. It has neither sweetness nor appearance to make it attractive. The only thing to commend it is its pungency, and for this we go all the way to India to obtain it." The pepper trade was so lucrative for the Indians that pepper was called black gold.

From the ninth century onwards, Arab traders, mainly visiting western India, began to write accounts of their visits. Abu Zaid al Hassan has left an account as readable as that of the merchant Suleiman.

Among Europeans, the Polo family set the pace, as it were, with Marco Polo's description of a journey across Asia in the thirteenth century. The return journey overland from China took three years. The economy of the Italian city-states then required in part their capturing of the Asian trade with Europe. It was an era of Italian merchants travelling to distant parts of Asia in search of commercial contacts. The Mongol empire had stabilised and by now straddled a large part of the continent. Italian merchants were seeking to by-pass the Arabs and establish direct links with Asian merchants. Lurking in the background was also the desire to see unfamiliar lands, especially those such as India which from earlier accounts seemed to combine the fabulous with the fantastic. Nicolo dei Conti in the fifteenth century travelled extensively into the Indian hinter-land which he described at length in his memoirs. Filippo Sassetti came in the sixteenth century as a pepper merchant. Among his many lengthy letters home there is one which made him famous where he speaks of a link between Sanskrit and Italian, thus becoming almost the progenitor of the linguistic theory which was to result in the concept of the Indo-European languages.

All their sciences are written in a language that they call Sanikuta which means well-articulated and which they do not remember as a spoken language. . . . It takes six or seven years to learn and their present language has much in common with it. There is also much in common between our language and this one, especially the words for certain numbers such as 6, 7, 8 and 9 and words for god, snake and such like.

The Italians did not have a monopoly on the search for trade al-though they were the first in the field. The search for new merchan-dise, new markets, and new routes linking east and west took the Spanish and the Portuguese all round the world. Those who came to Goa naturally saw more of the peninsula, such as Duarte Barbosa, Domingo Paes and Fernao Nuniz, active in the sixteenth century. In the following century, French merchants such as Francois Bernier and Jean-Baptise Tavernier were travelling through the Mughal domains on a similar enterprise. From Russia came A. Nikitin who spent most of his time in the Deccan. The eighteenth century was to see a number of Greek and Armenian merchants as well, some going as far afield as Tibet.

Scattered amidst the traders from Asia and Europe were the free-booters, the adventurers in search of jobs and the soldiers of fortune. The establishment of Turkish, Afghan and, later, Mughal rule brought in the individuals seeking favours and jobs in India from

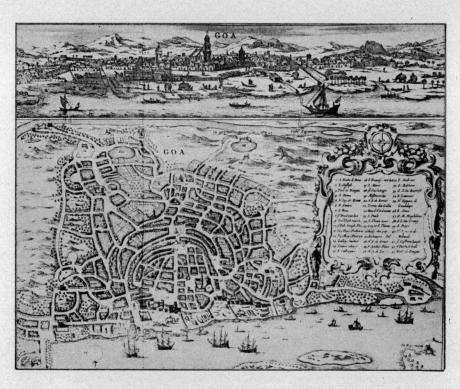

3. An old map of Goa.

various parts of the Islamic world—not least the irrepressible Ibn Battuta from Tangiers in north Africa who served in India in various capacities and has left one of the most lively documents on life in the fourteenth century. In later life he was to explore the source of the river Niger mistaking it for the Nile.

European free-booters often took service to train local armies, some as small as that of the Begum of Samru and others as effective as the forces of Ranjit Singh. They brought expertise in the most recent military technology, much of it new to the sub-continent. Undoubtedly, the most fascinating of such people was Nicolo Manucci, a seventeenth century stowaway from Venice who served as an officer in various Indian armies and as a diplomat between courts, finally settling down to a very successful medical profession which gave him access to the most important families of the land. His *Storio do Mogor* purporting to be a history of Mughal India in the latter half of the seventeenth century is a highly personalised and most informative narrative on what he saw and did.

Of an overtly less aggressive category were the pilgrims and missionaries. India produced only one religion for export—Buddhism—with a mechanism for proselytising, and this proved very successful. From the fourth century A.D. onwards, various Buddhist pilgrims visited India and among these the most prominent were the Chinese in search of the "western heaven", the holy land of the true doctrine and where the Buddha had lived. The accounts of their travels describe in detail the horrors which they had to overcome, fighting with demons and hostile supernatural forces, to reach India. They provide meticulous itineraries of places visited, Buddhist monasteries at which they stayed, and the general condition of Buddhism in India. The earliest of these pilgrims was Fa Hien who left China in A.D. 399 and travelled by slow stages stopping at various central Asian monasteries. He was followed in the seventh century by Hsuan Tsang and later by I Tsing. Fa Hien is fulsome in his praise for the homeland of the Buddha whereas the later pilgrims are more sober in their views. The perspective, however, remains strongly religious.

Another religious perspective, but from a generally antagonistic angle, was that of Christian missionaries. Unlike the Buddhists, they were not on pilgrimage to India but on a mission to convert. By far the most original minds were those of the early Jesuits, who argued that if the brahmans could be converted, the rest of society would follow suit; and in order to convert the brahmans it was necessary to meet them on their own terms. Thus, Roberto de Nobili in the seventeenth century took up *sanyasa,* studied the philosophy of India and entered into debate with the brahmans, but was accused of heresy by his fellow Catholics which thus virtually closed the future possibility of this approach. Christian missionary views on India tend to be harassed by the problem of the pagan and the destiny of the pagan in after-life. With the increasing entanglement of Anglican missionary activity with colonial administration, the urgency to bring light to the lot of the pagan became more acute. Among the more enlightened in terms of a healthy curiosity towards the people and culture of India was Reginald Heber, Lord Bishop of Calcutta.

Such a range of people left an equally varied range of descriptions. Some are valuable for the sheer information which they contain. Others are significant because they represent the perspective of the cultures from which the travellers came. Inevitably, there is a bias in each case which has to be kept in mind when reading the account. Thus, for Fa Hien, India was the Holy Land and he could see little that did not conform to the ideal conditions as described in the Buddhist scriptures. Alberuni, on the other hand, resented his enforced stay of ten years in India and this resentment can be seen in his frequent satirical comments on Indian ways.

Some of the initial reactions of these visitors are strikingly similar. India is the land of the fantastic and this enters into many descriptions, not least of the physician Ktesias at the Persian court in the fifth century B.C. who, writing on hearsay, describes an animal in almost mythical terms (J.W. McCrindle, *Ancient India*, P. 40):

In India is found a wild animal called in the native tongue the Martikhora. It is of great strength and ferocity, being about as big as a lion, of a red colour like cinnabar, and covered with shaggy hair like a dog. Its face, however, is not bestial, but resembles that of a human being. It has both in the upper and the lower jaw a double row of teeth which are extremely sharp at the points and larger than the canine. Its ears in their conformation are like the human, but they are larger and covered with shaggy hair. Its eyes also are like the human, and of a blue colour. It has the feet and the claws of a lion, but its tail, which may be more than a cubit long, is not only furnished at the tip with a scorpion's sting with which it smites any one who comes near it, and kills him therewith instantaneously, but if it is pursued it uses the side stings, discharging them like arrows against the pursuer, whom it can hit even though he be at a good distance off. When it fights, having the enemy in front, it bends the tail upward, but when, like the

4. A palanquin.

Sakians, it fights while retreating, it straightens it out to the fullest length. The stings, which are a foot long and as slender as a rush (or a fine thread), kill every animal they hit, with the exception of the elephant only.

Ktesias says that he had been assured by the Indians that those stings that are expended in fighting are replaced by a growth of new ones as if to perpetuate this accursed plague. Its favourite food, according to the same author, is human flesh, and to satisfy this lust, it kills a great many men, caring not to spring from its ambush upon a solitary traveller, but rather upon a band of two or three for which it is singly more than a match. All the beasts of the forest yield to its prowess, save only the lion, which it is impotent to subdue. That it loves above all things to gorge itself with flesh, is clearly shown by its name—for the Indian word Marti-khora means man-eater—and it has its name from this particular habit. It runs with all the nimbleness of a deer. The Indians hunt the young ones before the stings appear on their tails, and break the tails themselves in pieces on the rocks to prevent stings growing upon them. Its voice has a most striking resemblance to the sound of a trumpet.

Ktesias says that he had seen in Persia one of these animals, which had been sent from India as a gift to the Persian king. Such are the peculiarities of the Martikhora as described by Ktesias, and if any one thinks this Knidian writer a competent authority on such subjects, he must be content with the account which he has given.

The fantastic reappears even in otherwise sober accounts such as the *Indika* of Megasthenes:

Some accounts go beyond all bounds to the realm of myth when they speak of people ten feet long and six feet long, some without nostrils having instead merely two breathing holes above their mouths. There are stories of the people who sleep in their ears. . . . The wild people in the kingdom of Sandracotts (Chandragupta, the Mauryan emperor), who have their heels in front with toes and the flat of the foot behind. There are also certain mouthless people who are gentle by nature and live round the sources of the Ganges; they sustain themselves by means of vapours from roasted meats and odours from fruits and flowers, since instead of mouths they have only breathing holes, and they suffer pain when they breathe bad odours. There are some people who can run faster than horses, some whose ears extend to their feet so that they can sleep in them and they are strong enough to pluck up trees and to break bow-strings: and another people with dog's ears, with the eye in the middle of the forehead, with hair standing erect and with shaggy breasts. The Hypermoreans live for a thousand years. There are places where brass rains from the sky in brazen drops....

Some travelled to India in discomfort and suffered great hardships, such as the Chinese Buddhist pilgrims, but they were determined to reach it. The piety of the pilgrims was constantly rewarded by the wicked being converted to virtue. The brigands (in the account below) who try to sacrifice Hsuan Tsang see the light and become Buddhists (*The Life of Hiuen-Tsang* by Samuel Beal, p. 86 ff).

The Master of the Law left the kingdom of Ayodhya, having paid reverence to the sacred traces, and following the course of the river Ganges, proceeded eastward, being on board a vessel with about eighty other fellow-passengers. He wished to reach the kingdom of 'O-ye-mu-khi' (Hayamukha). After going about a hundred *li*, both banks of the river were shrouded by the thick foliage of an Asoka forest, and amid these trees on either bank were concealed some ten pirate boats. Then these boats, propelled by oars, all at once burst forth into the midstream. Some of those in the ship, terrified at the sight, cast themselves into the river, whilst the pirates, taking the ship in tow, brought it to the bank. They then ordered the men to take off their clothes, and searched them in quest of jewels and precious stones.

Now these pirates pay worship to Durga, a spirit of heaven, and every year during the autumn, they look out for a man of good form and comely features, whom they kill, and offer his flesh and blood in sacrifice to their divinity, to procure good fortune. Seeing that the Master of the Law was suitable for their purpose, both in respect of his distinguished bearing and his bodily strength and appearance, they exchanged joyful glances and said, 'We were letting the season for sacrificing to our god pass by, because we could not find a suitable person for it, but now this *sraman* is of noble form and pleasing features—let us kill him as a sacrifice, and we shall gain certain good fortune.'

The Master of the Law replied, 'If this poor defiled body of mine is indeed suitable for the purpose of the sacrifice you propose, I, in truth, dare not grudge (the offering), but as my intention in coming from a distance was to pay reverence to the image of Bodhi and the Grindhrakuta Mountain, and to inquire as to the character of the

Sacred Books and the Law (or, the Law of the Sacred Books), and as this purpose has not yet been accomplished, if you, my noble benefactors (*danapatis*) kill this body of mine, I fear it will bring you misfortune instead of good fortune.'

Moreover, his fellow-passengers all, with one voice, asked them to spare him, and some even prayed to be allowed to die in his stead, but the pirates would not consent.

Then the captain of the gang despatched some men with water to arrange the ground, and to erect in the midst of the flowering grove an altar besmeared with mud. He then commanded two of the company to take their drawn knives and to bind the Master of the Law upon the altar. And now, when they were about to use their knives for the purpose of sacrificing him, the Master of the Law showed no sign of fear in his face, insomuch that all the pirates were moved to astonishment.

When he saw there was no escape, however, he spoke to the pirates and begged them to allow him a little time and not to crowd round him painfully, but 'let me', he said, 'with a joyous mind, take my departure'.

Then the Master of the Law, with an undivided mind bent on the courts of Tusita heaven, thought on the Bodhisattva Maitreya, and earnestly prayed to be born in that place, that he might pay reverence and his religious offerings (to the Bodhisattva), and receive from him the *Yogachariya-bhumi-sastra,* and listen to the sound of the excellent Law. Then having perfected himself throughout in wisdom, 'let me return (he prayed) and be born here below, that I may instruct and convert these men, and cause them to practise themselves in doing good and to give up their evil deeds, and thus by diffusing, far and wide, the benefits of religion, to give rest to all the world'.

5. *The Chinese pilgrim, Hsuan Tsang.*

Then the Master of the Law, paying worship to the Buddhas of the ten regions, collected his mind into perfect composure, and sitting still, fixed his thoughts on Maitreya without any interruption. Thus he seemed in his innermost thoughts as if he rose up above Mount Sumeru and successively ascending one, two, three heavens, he gazed upon the courts of Tusita, the place of Maitreya, with its excellently precious adornments (galleries) and the multitude of *devas* surrounding him on every side. At this time his body and soul were ravished with joy, he knew nothing of the altar on which he was, he had no recollection of the robbers. And now, whilst his fellow passengers gave way to cries and tears, suddenly a black tempest (typhoon) arose from the four quarters of heaven,

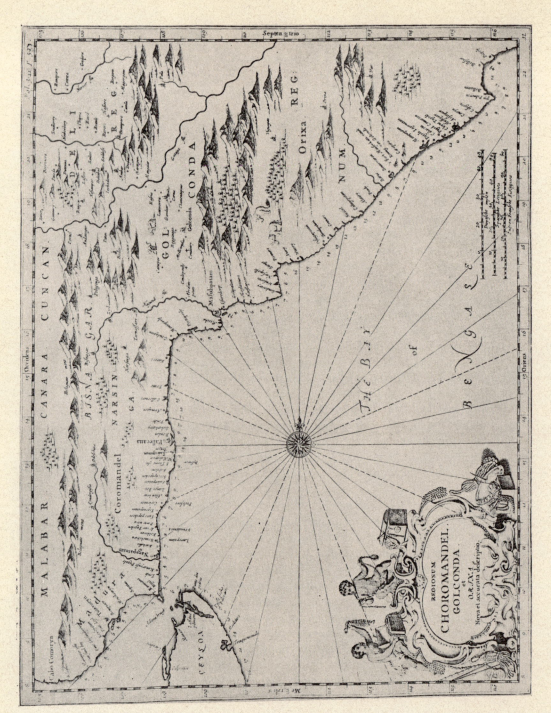

smiting down the trees; clouds of sand flew on every side; and the lashing waves of the river tossed the boats to and fro. The robbers and their company, greatly terrified, asked the companions of the Master, 'Whence comes this *sraman?*—what is his name and title?' and so on. They, answering, said, 'He comes from the country of China—he is the renowned person who is in search of the Law; if you, my masters kill him, your guilt will be immeasurable; look now and see the winds and waves—these are but indications of the anger of the spirit of heaven: haste then to repent!'

The pirates then, filled with fear, urged each other to repentance and confession of their fault; then with bowed heads they made profound obeisance (or, they embraced the religion of Buddha). And now one of the robbers accidentally touching the Master of the Law with his hand (or, touching the hand of the Master of the Law), he opened his eyes and said to the robber, 'Has the hour come?' The robber answered, 'We dare not hurt the Master! We pray you accept our repentance!' The Master then accepted their reverence and confession of faults, and then preached to them about the future punishment in Avichi of those who gave themselves up to murder, robbery, and impious sacrifices, and other evil deeds. 'How would you then risk the woes of the long-enduring *asankheya* of ages for the sake of this body of yours, which is but in point of time as the lightning flash or the dew of the morning?'

The robbers then bowed their heads and confessed their faults, saying: 'We indeed, individually, were perverted by a foolish turn of mind, and led to do what we ought not to do, and to sacrifice (pay religious rites) to what we ought not to sacrifice. If we had not met with the Master—whose religious merit has moved even the mysterious powers of heaven, how should we ever have been led to repentance? And now we ask to give up from the present day these evil ways of ours, and we pray the Master to be witness to our sincerity!'

On this they each encouraged one another to deeds of amendment, and collecting their various instruments of robbery together, they cast them into the river, and whatever clothes or private property they had taken, they restored these to their rightful owners, and then they took on themselves the five obligations of a lay-believer.

Then the winds and the floods subsided, and the pirates were all overcome with joy, and bowed their heads in adoration. His fellow voyagers, moreover, were filled with surprise and admiration more than ever, whilst those present and absent who heard of the event

6. *Facing page.*
An old map of the
east coast of India.

could not help exclaiming with wonder at the occurrence: 'If it were not for the power of his high resolve in seeking for the Law, this could not have come to pass!'

The descriptions range over every aspect of Indian life. Attempts were made to give geographical indications which however were often not accurate. Thus, a first century Roman writer, Quintus Curtius, quoting from a Greek source states: "India lies almost entirely towards the east and is smaller in breadth than in length. In the south are hills of considerable height...many famous rivers which rise in Mount Caucausus traverse the plains with languid currents. The Indus is colder than other rivers....The Ganges, which is the greatest of all rivers in the east, flows down to the south country—both rivers enter the Red Sea." Sir Thomas Roe is equally confused in the seventeenth century when speaking of the Jhelum river in Kashmir: "The river of Bhat (Jhelum) passeth through it (the city of Sirinakur) and findeth the sea by Ganges, or, some say, of itself in the north part of the Bay of Bengala."
Megasthenes attempts a reconstruction of early Indian history:

The Indian tribes number in all 118. The Indians were in old times nomadic. They did not till the soil but roamed about as the seasons varied; they had neither towns nor temples of the gods, but were so barbarous that they wore the skins of such wild animals as they could kill, and subsisted on the bark of trees and wild animals. Then the god Dionysus came and when he had conquered the people, founded cities and gave laws to these cities and introduced the use of wine amongst the Indians...and taught them to sow the land, himself supplying seeds for the purpose. The Indians worship various gods and Dionysus with cymbals and drums because he taught them so; and he instructed the Indians to let their hair grow long in honour of the god and to wear the turban; and he taught them to anoint themselves with unguents...the Indians were marshalled for battle to the sound of cymbals and drums.

Some faltering attempts are also made at ethnography. Strabo, writing in the first century A.D., explains: "As for the people of India, those in the south are like the Ethiopians in colour, although they are like the rest in respect of countenance and hair (for on account of the humidity of the air their hair does not curl), whereas those in the north are like the Egyptians."
A later author, Arrian, comments on youth and age: "...those

who live longest die at forty; for men who come so much sooner to old age, and with old age to death, must of course flower into manhood as much earlier as their life ends earlier. It follows hence that men of thirty would there (i.e., in India) be in their green old age, and young men would at twenty be past puberty, since the age of adulthood would be fifteen. And, quite compatibly with this, the women might be marriageable at the age of seven."

Of the flora and fauna of India, the elephant raised much curiosity even as late as the seventeenth century. Nicholos Downtown's description reads: "(He) hath a body like a house, but a tayle like a ratte, erecting it like a cedar; little eyes but great sight; very melancholly, but wise (they say) and full of understanding (or subtlety rather) for a beast. Some times they become mad (of what I know not) and breaking loose endanger multitudes. (He) is fed somewhat costly, as with good bread, musk millions (melons), sugarcanes, sweet stalks and sower grasse or sedge of the worst. (He) steers like a hulk, stiff-necked, almost all of one piece; feeds himselfe with his trunck or snoute, (that deadly instrument for his rage) being of a just length to the ground; taking his meat with the end thereof and winding it up (or under rather) to his mouth, so eates it, but drinkes there with a length."

Clothes and the eating habits particularly of the rich are the cause

7. Englishmen on a shikar.

of frequent comment. Arrian quotes Nearchus, Alexander's admiral: "The dress worn by the Indians is made of cotton produced on trees. But this cotton is either of a brighter white colour than any cotton found elsewhere, or the darkness of the Indian complexion makes their apparel look so much the whiter. They wear an undergarment of cotton which reaches below the knee halfway down to the ankles and also an upper garment which they throw partly over their shoulders and partly twist in folds around their head. The Indians also wear earrings of ivory, but only the very wealthy do this. Their beards they dye of various hues according to taste. Some dye their white beards to make them look as white as possible but others dye them blue; while some again prefer a red tint, some a purple and others a rank green. They use parasols as a screen from the heat. They wear shoes made of white leather, and these are elaborately trimmed, while the soles are variegated and made of great thickness to make the wearer seem so much taller."

The opulence of the wealthy is again commented upon in the ninth century A.D. by Abu Zaid al Hassan: "The kings of the Indies wear earrings of precious stones set in gold. They wear also collars of great price, adorned with precious stones of diverse colours, but especially green and red; yet pearls are what they most esteem and their value surpasses that of all other jewels; they at present hoard them up in their treasure with their most precious things. The grandees of the court, the great officers and captains, wear the like jewels on their collars; they dress in a half-vest, and carry a parasol of peacock feathers to shade them from the sun, and are surrounded by those of their train."

Alberuni is much more satirical:

They let the nails grow long, glorying on their idleness; since they do not use them for any business or work, they scratch their heads with them and examine their hair for lice. They have red teeth in consequence of chewing areca nuts with betel-leaves and chalk. They drink wine before having eaten anything and then they take their meal. They sip the stall of cows, but do not eat the meat. In washing they begin with the feet and then wash the face. The men wear articles of female dress: they use cosmetics, wear earrings, arm-rings, golden seal-rings on the ring finger as well as on the toes of the feet. They use turbans for trousers. Those who like to dress, wear trousers lined with so much cotton as would suffice to make a number of counter-panes and saddle-rugs.

Ibn Battuta describes a meal at the court:

Their dinners consist of bread, roasted meat, rice, chicken and samosa. The judges, orators, jurists, and holy men sit at the top end of the carpet on which the dinner is served. Then come the relatives of the Sultan, the great noblemen and the high officers. Each one has his appointed place and cannot sit where he pleases. When all the guests have taken their seats, the cup-bearers appear with goblets of gold, silver, copper and glass in which is served a sweet drink of sugar dissolved in water. As they drink this, the court officials call out Bismillah, and then the dinner begins. Before each guest is placed a set of all the various dishes served and he can eat whatever pleases him. At the conclusion of the dinner another drink is served and again there is the call of Bismillah. Each guest is then presented with fifteen betel-leaves tied together with a red silk thread and some spices. Once again the officer calls out Bismillah, and the guests bowing to each other depart. These meals are held twice a day, in the forenoon and in the afternoon.

In contrast to this, Francisco Palsaert describes the artisans' meals in Gujarat:

For their monotonous daily food, they have nothing but a little Khichri, made of green pulse mixed with rice, which is cooked with water over a little fire until the moisture has evaporated, and eaten hot with butter in the evening; in the daytime they munch a little parched pulse or other grain, which they say suffices for their lean stomachs.

Eating habits also attracted attention. Abu Zaid al Hassan writes in the ninth century:

There are certain Indians who never eat two out of the same dish or upon the same table and would deem it a very great sin if they should. Were they a hundred in number they must each have a separate dish without the least communication with the rest. Their kings and persons of high quality have fresh tables made for them everyday together with little dishes and plates wove of the coconut leaf in which they eat what is prepared for their subsistence; and their meal over, they throw the table, the dishes and plates into the water together with the fragments they have left. Thus at every meal they have a new service.

Ibn Battuta was intrigued as were many others by the eating of betel-leaves and their presentation on formal occasions. Regarding betel he says (*Rehala of Ibn Battuta*, M. Hussain, P. 36):

The betel is a plant which is grown like the grape-vine. They make for it a cane trellis as they make for grape-vine; else, they plant it in the neighbourhood of a coconut tree so that the betel should climb over it as is done in the case of the grape-vine and pepper. Betel bears no fruit but produces instead leaves which resemble those of the blackberry, the yellow ones being the best quality. These leaves are plucked every day and are highly appreciated by the Indians. If on visiting his friends a person is presented five betel-leaves he feels as if he is given the whole world and its wealth specially if the presenter be an amir or an important personality. And presenting a betel they consider as sublime and as signifying greater nobility than giving gold and silver.

The way to use the betel-leaf is this: in the first place they take a little betel-nut which is something like the nutmeg and crush it, tapering the sides into small pieces which are put into the mouth and chewed. In the second place they take the betel-leaf and pasting a little lime chew it together with the betel-nut. As a result, the breath is made aromatic and bad smell disappears from the mouth and it helps the digestion of the food and avoids harmfulness of water drunk against an empty stomach. Its chewing makes one cheerful and strengthens the powers of copulation. The Indian is accustomed to keep the betel by his bedside in the night so that whenever he is awakened of his own accord or by his wife or by the slave girl he takes some of these betel-leaves, which would remove whatever bad smell be in his mouth. I was told that the slave girls of the emperor and of the amirs in India did not eat anything beyond betel-leaves for this purpose.

8. The goddess Kali

But each one saw more of the food which appealed most to him. Fa Hien writes: "Throughout the whole country the people do not kill any living creature, nor drink intoxicating liquor, nor eat onions or garlic. The only exception is that of the Chandalas. In that country they do not keep pigs and fowls and do not sell live cattle; in the market there are no butchers' shops and no dealers in intoxicating drinks." And this at a time when Fa Hien's near contemporary, the poet Kalidasa, refers to the regular eating of meat and fish and the existence of slaughter-houses.

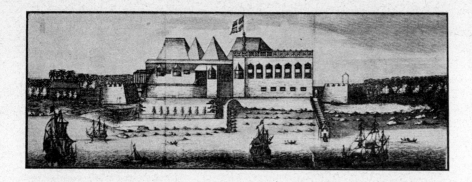

One of the customs which invariably drew agonised reactions from travellers, especially after the first millennium A.D., was that of the immolation of widows, their becoming *satis*. Ibn Battuta was among the earliest travellers to describe it at length. The social institution of caste was yet another item of curiosity. The earliest reference in any detail is that of Megasthenes:

9. Two views of the fort at Bombay.

> The population of India is divided into seven castes; the one first in honour but the fewest in numbers consists of the philosophers. The second caste is that of the farmers who are not only the most numerous, but also the most highly respected, because of their exemption from military service and right of freedom in their farming. . . . The third caste is that of the shepherds and hunters, who alone are permitted to hunt, to breed cattle and to sell or hire out beasts of burden. . . . After these follows the fourth caste—the artisans, the tradesmen and the day-labourers; of these some pay tribute to the state and render services prescribed by the state, whereas some, such as the armour-makers, work for the king alone. The fifth caste is that of the warriors, who when they are not in

service, spend their lives in idleness and in drinking bouts, being maintained at the expense of the royal treasury. The sixth is that of the inspectors, to whom it is given to inspect what is being done and report secretly to the king. These inspectors use the courtesans as colleagues. The seventh is that of the advisers and councillors of the king who hold the chief offices of state, the judgeships and the administration of everything. It is not legal for a man either to marry a wife from another caste or to change his pursuit or work from one to another.

From the Mauryan period to the Mughal there are some similarities and some changes in caste society as understood by our travellers. The condition of the people and of the state are variously referred to. Fa Hien describes it in glowing terms:

All south of this (Mathura) is named the Middle Kingdom. In it the cold and heat are finely tempered and there is neither hoarfrost nor snow. The people are numerous and happy: they have not to register their households, or attend to any magistrates and their rules; only those who cultivate the royal land have to pay (a portion of) the gain from it. If they want to go they go; if they want to stay on they stay. The king governs without decapitation or (other) corporal punishments. Criminals are simply fined, lightly or heavily, according to the circumstances (of each case). Even in cases of repeated attempts at wicked rebellion, they only have their right hands cut off. The king's bodyguard and attendants all have salaries.

And of the Chandalas he says: "That is the name for those who are (held to be) wicked men, and live apart from others. When they enter the gate of a city or a market-place, they strike a piece of wood to make themselves known, so that men know and avoid them, and do not come into contact with them....Only the Chandalas are fishermen and hunters and sell flesh-meat." It is curious that even as a Buddhist he has a comment to make on the condition of the Chandalas. Alberuni writes more accurately at least on matters of tax:

It is obligatory with them everyday to give alms as much as possible. With regard to that which he earns from the crops or from the cattle, he is bound first to pay to the ruler of the country, the tax which attaches to the soil or to the pasture ground. Further, he pays him one-sixth of the income, in recognition of the protection which the king affords to his subjects, their property and their families. After the taxes have been paid, one-ninth of the remaining income is for alms. This is divided into three parts. One is kept in reserve to guarantee the heart against anxiety. The second is spent on trade to bring profit. Some divide their income into four. A quarter is destined for common expenses, the second for liberal works of a noble kind, the third for alms and the fourth for being kept in reserve. Usury is forbidden. Only the shudra is allowed to take percentages but it must not exceed two per cent.

The splendour of the royal court was regarded with some awe. Quintus Curtius, the Roman, basing himself again on existing accounts, provides us with an almost Cecil B. de Mille view of *ex oriente lux:*

When the king condescends to show himself in public his attendants carry in their hands silver censers, and perfume with incense all the road by which it is his pleasure to be conveyed. He lolls in a golden palanquin garnished with pearls, which dangle all round it and he is robed in fine muslin embroidered with purple and gold. The palace is adorned with gilded pillars and is open to all comers even when the king is having his hair combed and dressed. He rides on horseback when making short journeys, but when bound on a distant expedition he rides in a carriage mounted on an elephant, and, huge as these animals are, their bodies are covered completely over with trappings of gold. His food is prepared by women who also serve him with wine, which is much used by all the Indians. When the king falls into a drunken sleep his courtesans carry him away to his bedchamber, invoking the gods of the night in their native hymns.

The Portuguese stayed at the court of the king of Vijayanagara hoping to do a deal in horses and diamonds. Domingo Paes writes (*A Forgotten Empire,* R. Sewell, pp. 269-70):

Should anyone ask what revenues this king possesses, and what his treasure is that enables him to pay so many troops, since he has so many and such great lords in his kingdom, who, the greater part of them, have themselves revenues, I answer thus: These captains whom he has over these troops of his are the nobles of his kingdom; they are lords, and they hold the city, and the towns and

10. The Jantar Mantar at Delhi.

villages of the kingdom; there are captains amongst them who have a revenue of a million and a half pardaos, others a hundred thousand pardaos, others two hundred, three hundred or five hundred thousand pardaos, and as each one has revenue so the king fixes for him the number of troops he must maintain, in foot, horse, and elephants. These troops are always ready for duty, whenever they may be called out and wherever they may have to go; and in this way he has this million of fighting men always ready. Each of these captains labours to turn out the best troops he can get because he pays them their salaries; and in this review there were the finest young men possible to be seen or that ever could be seen, for in all this array I did not see a man that would act the coward.

Besides maintaining these troops, each captain has to make his annual payments to the king, and the king has his own salaried troops to whom he gives pay. He has eight hundred elephants attached to his person, and five hundred horses always in his stables, and for the expenses of these horses and elephants he has devoted the revenues that he receives from this city of Bisnaga. You may well imagine how great these expenses may be, and besides these those of the servants who have the care of the horses and elephants; and by this you will be able to judge what will be the revenue of this city.

This king of Bisnaga has five kings as his subjects and vassals, besides other captains and lords having large territories and great revenues; whenever a son happens to be born to this king, or a daughter, all the nobles of the kingdom offer him great presents of money and jewels of price, and so they do to him every year on the day of his birth.

Since the major interest was trade, there are, as is to be expected, detailed descriptions of trading towns and items of trade. The *Periplus* lists Ozene (Ujjaini) as a major trading centre in the hinterland, exporting its goods mainly from the port on the west coast, Barygaza (Broach):

Eastward of Barygaza is the city called Ozene, formerly the capital wherein the king resided. From it there is brought down to Barygaza every commodity for the supply of the country and for export to our own markets...onyx stones, porcelain, fine muslins, mallow-coloured muslins, and no small quantity of ordinary cottons....The imports of Barygaza are wine, mainly Italian and

Arabian, brass or copper, tin and lead, coral and gold, cloth plain and mixed of all sorts, storax, sweet clover; gold and silver specie, yielding a profit when exchanged for native money: perfumes of unguents. In those times moreover there were imported as presents to the king, costly silver vases, instruments of music, handsome young women as concubines, superior wine, apparel both plain and costly and the choicest unguents....

Horses and diamonds were what most merchants sought to trade in. The horse trade has of course been to the advantage of those bringing in the horses since early times. Ibn Battuta refers to the cost of horses in the fourteenth century. European merchants of the seventeenth century were more interested in the diamond trade. Tavernier (*Travels in India*, Vol. II, pp. 53-54) describes the sale of a packet of stones:

I have to record a rather singular and curious account of the manner in which the Indians, whether they are idolaters or Mussalmans, make their sales of all kinds of commodities. All passes in complete silence and without anyone speaking. The seller and the buyer sit facing one another, like two tailors, and one of the two opening his waistband, the seller takes the right hand of the buyer and covers his own with his waistband, under which in the presence of many other merchants, who occupy themselves sometimes in the same manner, the sale is completed secretly without anyone having cognizance of it. For the seller and buyer talk neither by means of their lips nor their eyes, but only by the hand, which they manage to do in the following manner: When the seller takes the whole hand of the buyer that means 1,000, and as many times as he presses it so many thousands of pagodas or rupees, according to the coin which may be in question. When he takes only five fingers that means 500, and when he takes only one it means 100. By taking only the half up to the middle joint, 50 is meant, and the end of the finger up to the first signifies 10. This is the whole mystery employed by the Indians in their sales, and it often happens that, in a place where there are many people, a single parcel will change hands five or six times without those present knowing for how much it has been sold on each occasion. As for the weight of the stones, one need not be deceived if he does not buy in secret. For when one buys them in public there is a man specially employed by the King to weigh diamonds, who receives no fees from private persons. When he names the weight, both buyer and seller accept his statement, since he has no interest in favouring either party.

Inevitably, religious practices combined the fabulous with the metaphysical and were always a source of credulous interest. Abu Zaid al Hassan describes the *faqirs*:

> In the Indies there are certain men called Bicar (Bhikari) who go all their lifetime naked and suffer their hair to grow till it hides their bodies. They suffer also their nails to grow so that they become pointed and sharp as swords, nor do they ever cut them, but leave them to break and fall off as it happens and this they observe as a religious duty. Each of them has a string about his neck whereto hangs an earthen porringer; and when they are pressed by hunger they stop at the door of some Indian house and those within immediately and joyfully bring out rice to them, believing there is great merit in so doing. . . .

The mystery of levitation enthralled Ibn Battuta as much as it did other travellers, and in medieval times held the same fascination for visitors as the rope trick in more recent centuries. Astrology was another hardy perennial. Francois Bernier writes of it somewhat condescendingly:

> The large majority of Asiatics are so infatuated in favour of judicial astrology, that, according to their phraseology, no circumstances can happen below which is not written above. In every enterprise they consult their astrologers; when two armies have completed every preparation for battle, no consideration can induce the generals to commence the engagement until the *sahet* be performed—that is until the propitious moment for attack be ascertained. In like manner no commanding officer is nominated, no marriage takes place, and no journey is undertaken without consulting these seers. Their advice is considered absolutely necessary even on the most trifling occasions as the proposed purchase of a slave or the first wearing of new clothes. This silly superstition is so general an annoyance and attended with such important and disagreeable consequences, that I am astonished that it has continued so long: the astrologer is necessarily made acquainted with every transaction public and private, with every project, common and extraordinary.

The theory of transmigration was linked with Pythagorus in the European mind. Therefore Sir Thomas Roe writes: "The severest sect of these are Pythagorians for the opinion of the soul's trans-

migration, and will not kyll any living creature, no, not the vermin
that bites them, for fear of displeasing the spirit of some friend
departed."

11. A view of Surat.

Alberuni is critical of such beliefs, not surprisingly, and argues that
there is an absence of an ordering of knowledge among Indians:
"They are in a state of utter confusion, devoid of any logical order,
and in the last instance always mixed up with the silly notions of the
crowd. I can only compare their mathematical and astronomical
knowledge to a mixture of pearl shells and sour dates, or of pearls
and dung, or of costly crystals and common pebbles. Both kinds of
things are equal in their eyes since they cannot raise themselves to
the methods of a strictly scientific deduction."

Ultimately, however, it was the fact of travelling through India
which linked these many characters and the seventeenth century
travellers provided detailed accounts of how they travelled. Tavernier
describes the transportation (*Travels in India*, Vol. 1, pp. 32-39):

Differing from the custom in Persia, you do not employ in India in
caravans or journeys either asses, mules, or horses, everything
being carried here on oxen or by waggon, as the country is sufficiently level. If any merchant takes a horse from Persia he does it

only for show, and to have him led by hand, or in order to sell him advantageously to some noble.

They give an ox a load weighing 300 or 350 livres, and it is an astonishing sight to behold caravans numbering 10,000 or 12,000 oxen together, for the transport of rice, corn, and salt—in the places where they exchange these commodities—carrying rice to where only corn grows, and corn to where only rice grows, and salt to the places where there is none. They use camels also for caravans, but rarely, and they are specially reserved to carry the baggage of the nobles.

When the season presses, and they wish to get the goods quickly to Surat, in order to ship them, they load them on oxen, and not on carts. As all the territories of the Great Mogul are well cultivated, the fields are enclosed by good ditches, and each has its tank or reservoir for irrigation. This makes it so inconvenient for travellers, because, when they meet caravans of this description in narrow roads, they are sometimes obliged to wait two or three days till all have passed. Those who drive these oxen follow no other trade all their lives; they never dwell in houses, and they take with them their women and children. Some of them possess 100 oxen, others have more or less, and they all have a chief who acts as a prince, and who always has a chain of pearls hanging from his neck.

When the caravan which carries corn and that which carries rice meet, rather than give way one to the other, they often engage in very sanguinary encounters. The Great Mogul, considering that these quarrels were prejudicial to commerce and to the transport of food in his kingdom, arranged that the Chiefs of the two caravans should come to see him. When they arrived, the King, after he had advised them for their mutual benefit to live for the future in harmony with each other, and not to fight again when they met, presented each of them with a lakh, or 100,000 rupees, and a chain of pearls.

In order to enable the reader to understand this manner of carrying in India, it should be remarked that among the idolaters of this country there are four tribes, whom they call Manaris, of which each numbers about one hundred thousand souls. These people dwell in tents, as I have said, and have no other trade but to transport provisions from one country to another. The first of these tribes has to do with corn only, the second with rice, the third with pulse, and the fourth with salt, which it obtains from Surat, and even from as far as Cape Comorin. You can also distinguish these tribes in this manner—their priests, of whom I shall elsewhere speak, mark those of the first with a red gum, of the size of a crown, on the middle of the forehead, and make a streak along the nose, attaching to it above some grains of corn, sometimes nine, sometimes twelve, in the form of a rose. Those of the second are marked with a yellow gum, in the same places, but with grains of rice; those of the third with a grey gum, with grains of millet, and also on the shoulders, but without placing grains there. As for those of the fourth, they carry a lump of salt, suspended from the neck in a bag, which weighs sometimes from 8 to 10 livres (for the heavier it is the more honour they have in carrying it), with which, by way of penance before praying, they beat their stomachs every morning. Generally all have a string, or beads, round the shoulders, from which hangs a small box of silver in the form of a reliquary, of the size of a good hazel nut, in which they keep a superstitious writing which their priests have enclosed in it. They place them also on their oxen, and on the other animals born in their herds, for which they entertain a special affection, loving them as dearly as they would do their children, especially when they happen to be childless.

The dress of the women is but a simple cloth white or coloured, which is bound five or six times like a petticoat from the waist downwards, as if they had three or four one above the other. From the waist upwards they tattoo their skin with flowers, as when one applies cupping glasses, and they paint these flowers diverse colours with the juice of roots, in such a manner that it seems as though their skin was a flowered fabric.

While the men load their animals in the morning and the women fold up their tents, the priests who follow them set up in the most beautiful parts of the plain where they are encamped, an idol in the form of a serpent, entwined about a staff of six or seven feet in height, and each one in order goes to make reverence to it, the girls turning round it three times. After all have passed, the priests take care to remove the idol and to load it on an ox assigned for that purpose.

The caravans of waggons do not ordinarily consist of more than one hundred or two hundred at the most. Each waggon is drawn by ten or twelve oxen, and accompanied by four soldiers, whom the owner of the merchandise is obliged to pay. Two of them walk on each side of the waggon, over which two ropes are passed, and the four ends are held by the soldiers, so that if the waggon threatens to upset in a place, the two soldiers who are on the opposite side hold the ropes tight, and prevent it turning over.

All the waggons which come to Surat from Agra or from other places in the empire, and return by Agra and Jahanabad, are compelled to carry lime, which comes from Broach, which, as soon as it is used, becomes as hard as marble. It is a great source of profit to the Emperor, who sends this lime where he pleases; but, on the other hand, he takes no dues from the waggons.

I come to the manner of travelling in India, where oxen take the place of horses, and there are some of them whose paces are as easy as those of our hacks. But you should take care when you buy or hire an ox for riding that he has not horns longer than a foot, because, if they are longer, when the flies sting him, he chafes and tosses back the head, and may plant a horn in your stomach, as has happened several times. These oxen allow themselves to be driven like our horses, and have for a bridle only a cord, which passes through the tendon of the muzzle or the nostrils. In level tracts, where there are no stones, they do not slow these oxen, but they always do so in rough places, both on account of the pebbles and because of the heat, which may injure the hoof. Whereas in Europe we attach our oxen by the horns, those of India have a large hump on the neck, which keeps in position a leather collar about four fingers wide, which they have only to throw over the head when they harness them.

They have also, for travelling, small, very light carriages, which can carry two persons; but usually you travel alone, in order to be more comfortable, being then able to have your clothes with you; the canteen of wine and some small requisites for the journey having their place under the carriage, to which they harness only a pair of oxen. These carriages, which are provided, like ours, with curtains and cushions, are not slung; but, on the occasion of my last journey, I had one made after our manner, and the two oxen by which it was drawn cost me very nearly 600 rupees. The reader need not be astonished at this price, for there are some of them which are strong, and make journeys lasting 60 days, at 12 or 15 leagues a day, and always at the trot. When they have accomplished half the journey, they give to each two or three balls of the size of our penny rolls, made of wheaten flour, kneaded with butter and black sugar, and in the evening they have a meal of chick-peas, crushed and steeped in water for half an hour. The hire of a carriage amounts to about a rupee a day. The journey from Surat to Agra occupies thirty-five or forty days' journey by road, and you pay for the whole journey from 40 to 45 rupees. From Surat to Golkonda it is nearly the same distance and the same price, and it is in the same proportion throughout the whole of India.

Those who can afford to take their ease make use of a palankeen, in which they travel very comfortably. It is a kind of bed, 6 or 7 feet long and 3 feet wide, with a small rail all round. A sort of cane, called bamboo, which they bend when young, in order to cause it to take the form of a bow in the middle, supports the cover of the palankeen, which is of satin or brocade; and when the sun shines on one side, an attendant, who walks near the palankeen, takes care to lower the covering. There is another, who carries at the end of a stick a kind of basket-work shield, covered with some kind of beautiful stuff, in order that he may be able promptly to shelter the occupant of the palankeen from the heat of the sun when it turns and strikes him on the face. The ends of the bamboo are attached on both sides to the body of the palankeen between two poles, joined together in a saltier, or St. Andrew's Cross, and each of these poles is 5 or 6 feet long. Some of these bamboos cost as much as 200 ecus, and I have paid 125 for one.

Three men at most place themselves at each of these ends, and carry the palankeen on their shoulders, one on the right and the other on the left, and they travel in this way faster than our chairmen in Paris, and with an easier pace, being trained to the trade from an early age. When you wish to make haste, and travel as much as 13 or 14 leagues a day, you take 12 men to carry the palankeen, so that they may relieve one another from time to time. You pay each of them only 4 rupees a month inclusive, but you pay up to 5 rupees when the journey is long, and when they are required to travel for more than sixty days.

He who desires to travel with honour in India, whether by carriage or palankeen, ought to take with him 20 or 30 armed men, some with bows and arrows and others with muskets, and you pay them as much per month as those who carry the palankeen. Sometimes, for greater show, you carry a flag. This is always done by the English and Dutch, for the honour of their Companies. These attendants not only conduce to you honour, but they watch also for your protection, and act as sentinels at night, relieving one another, and striving to give you no cause of complaint against them. For it should be mentioned that in the towns where you hire them they have a head man who answers for their honesty, and when you employ them, each one gives him a rupee.

In the large villages there is generally a Musalman governor, and there you find sheep, fowl, and pigeons for sale; but in the places where there are only Banians, you find only flour, rice, vegetables, and milk.

The great heat of India compels travellers who are not accustomed to it to travel by night, in order to rest by day. When they enter towns which are closed they must leave by sunset, if they wish to take the road. For when night comes, and the gates are closed, the Governor of the place, who has to answer for thefts which occur within his jurisdiction, does not allow any one to go out, and says that it is the Emperor's order, which he must obey. When I entered such places I took provisions, and left early, in order to camp outside under some tree in the shade, waiting till it was time to march. They measure the distances of places in India by gos and by coss. A gos is about four of our common leagues, and a coss about one league.

Caravanserais were the equivalent of inns and hotels. Bernier is not too complimentary: "The Eastern Karavans-Serrah resemble large barns, raised and paved all round, in the same manner as our Pont Neuf. Hundreds of human beings are seen in them mingled with their horses, mules and camels. In summer these buildings are hot and suffocating and in winter nothing but the breath of so many animals prevents the inmates of dying of cold."

Most travellers engaged guards to travel with them or else took the protection of a caravan and travelled with it. In Gujerat there seems to have been the ingenious system of using *charans*. These were traditionally bards and geneaologists who in early times had also acted as envoys. The latter function made them inviolable and even when they ceased to be envoys it was regarded as a heinous crime to kill a *charan*.

The image of India, blurred to begin with, gradually acquired a sharper focus over time. For early travellers, the journey to and through India was almost a life-time venture. Those who travelled by sea arrived relatively quickly, taking only a few months over the journey, but those travelling overland spent many years. Technological advance in shipping and transport changed this over the centuries. Nevertheless even though the journey became shorter the curiosity about India increased and many more travellers visited India with a view to experiencing personally all that they had gathered from hearsay.

At Delhi's Court

REGINALD HEBER

(1824–1825)

The 31st December was fixed for my presentation to the emperor, which was appointed for half past eight in the morning. Lushington and a Captain Wade also chose to take the same opportunity. At eight I went accompanied by Mr. Elliot with nearly the same formalities as at Lucknow, except that we were on elephants instead of in palanqueens, and that the procession was perhaps less splendid, and the beggars both less numerous and far less vociferous and unfortunate. We were received by presented arms of the troops of the palace drawn up within the barbican and proceeded still on our elephants, through the noblest gateway and vestibule which I ever saw. It consists not merely of a splendid gothic arck in the centre of the great gate-tower, but, after that, of a long vaulted aisle, like that of a court in its centre, all of granite, and all finely carved with inscriptions from the Koran, and with flowers. This ended in a ruinous and exceedingly dirty stable-yard where we were received by Captain Grant, as the Moghul's officer on guard, and by a number of elderly men with large gold headed canes, the usual ensign of office here and one of which Mr. Elliot also carried.

We were now told to dismount and proceed on foot, a task which the late rain made inconvenient to my gown and cassock, and thin shoes, and during which we were pestered by a fresh swarm of miserable beggars, the wives and children of the stable servants. After this we passed another richly carved, but ruinous and dirty gateway, where our guides, withdrawing a canvass screen, called out in a kind of a harsh chaunt, "Lo, the ornament of the world! Lo, the asylum of the nations! King of Kings! The emperor Akbar Shah! Just, fortunate, victorious!" We saw in fact a very handsome and striking court, about as big as that at All Souls, with low, but richly ornamented buildings. Opposite to us was a beautiful, open pavilion of white marble, richly carved, flanked by rose bushes and fountains, and some tapestry and striped curtains hanging in festoons about it, within which was a crowd of people, and the

12. *The King's palace at Delhi.*

poor old descendant of Tamerlane seated in the midst of them. Mr. Elliot here bowed three times very low in which we followed his example.

This ceremony was repeated twice as we advanced up the steps of the pavilion, the heralds each time repeating the same expressions about their master's greatness. We then stood in a row on the right hand side of the throne, which is a sort of marble bedstead richly ornamented with gilding, and raised on two or three steps. Mr. Elliot then stepped forwards, and with joined hands, in the usual eastern way, announced in a low voice to the emperor who I was. I then advanced, bowed three times again and offered a *nuzzur* of fifty-one gold *mohurs* in an embroidered purse, laid on my handkerchief, in the way practised by the baboos of Calcutta. This was received and laid on one side, and I remained standing for a few minutes, while the usual court questions about my health, my travels, when I left Calcutta etc. were asked. I had thus an opportunity of seeing the old gentleman more plainly.

He has a pale, thin but handsome face, with an aquiline nose, and a long white beard. His complexion is a little, if at all darker than that of a European. His hands are very fair and delicate, and he had some valuable looking rings on them. His hands and face were all I saw of him, for the morning being cold, he was so wrapped up in shawls, that he reminded me extremely of the Druid's head on a Welsh half penny. I then stepped back to my former place, and returned again with five *mohurs* to make my offering to the heir apparent, who stood at his father's left hand, the right being occupied by the resident. Next my two companions were introduced with nearly the same forms, except that their offerings were less, and that the emperor did not speak to them.

The emperor then beckoned me to come forwards, and Mr. Elliot told me to take off my hat, which had till now remained on my head, on which the emperor tied a flimsy turban of brocade round my head with his own hands, for which, however, I paid four gold *mohurs* more. We were then directed to retire to receive the *khelats* (honorary dresses) which the bounty of "the Asylum of the World" had provided for us. I was accordingly taken into a small private room, adjoining the *zennana*, where I found a handsome flowered caftan edged with fur, and a pair of common looking shawls, which my servants, who had the delight of witnessing all this show, put on instead of my gown, my cassock remaining as before.

In this strange dress I had to walk back again having my name announced by the criers (something in the same way as Lord Marmion's was) "as Bahadur, Boozoony, Dowhit-mund" etc. to the presence where I found my two companions who had not been honoured by a private dressing room, but had their *khelats* put on them in the gateway of the court. They were, I apprehend, still queerer figures than I was, having their hats wrapped with scarves of flowered gauze, and a strange garment of gauze, tinsel and faded ribbands, flung over their shoulders above their coats.

I now again came forward and offered my third present to the emperor, being a copy of the Arabic Bible and the Hindoostanee Common Prayer, handsomely bound in blue velvet laced with gold, and wrapped up in a piece of brocade. He then motioned me to stoop, and put a string of pearls round my neck, and two glittering but not costly ornaments in the front of my turban, for which I again offered five gold *mohurs*. It was lastly announced that a horse was waiting for my acceptance at which fresh instance of Imperial munificence, the heralds again made a proclamation of largesse, and I again paid five gold *mohurs*. It ended by my taking my leave with three times three salaams, making up, I think, the sum of about threescore, and I retired with Mr. Elliot to my dressing room, whence I sent to her majesty the Queen, as she is generally called, though Empress would be the ancient and more proper title, a present of five *mohurs* more, and the emperor's Chobdars came eagerly up to know when they should attend to receive their baksheesh.

It must not, however, be supposed that this inter-change of civilities was very expensive either to his majesty or to me. All the presents which he gave, the horse included, though really the handsomest which had been at the court of Delhi for many years, and though the old gentleman evidently intended to be extremely civil, were not worth much more than 300 rupees, so that he and his family gained 800 rupees by the morning's work, besides what he received from my two companions, which was all clear gain, since the *khelats* which they got in return were only fit for May-day, and made up, I fancy, from the cast off finery of the Begum. On the other hand, since the Company have wisely ordered that all the presents given by native princes to Europeans should be disposed of on the government account, they have liberally, at the same time, taken on themselves the expense of paying the usual money *nuzzars* made by public men on these occasions.

In consequence none of my offerings were at my own charge, except the professional and private one of the two books, with which, as they were unexpected, the emperor, as I was told, was very much pleased. I had, of course, several baksheeshes to give afterwards to his servants, but these fell considerably short of my expenses at Lucknow. To return to the hall of audience. While in the small apartment where I got rid of my shining garments, I was struck with its beautiful ornaments. It was entirely hued with white marble inlaid with flowers and leaves of green serpentine lapis lazuli and blue and red porphyry; the flowers were of the best Italian style of workmanship, and evidently the labour of an artist of that country. All, however, was dirty, desolate and forlorn. Half the flowers and leaves had been picked out or otherwise defaced.

Dilli Door Ast

AKHILESH MITHAL

Nostalgia—a form of melancholia caused by prolonged absence from one's country or home. The *Dilliwaalaa* is prone to attacks of nostalgia when exiled to Lutyen's pseudo imperial city or a "colony" of more noveau riche origin. The symptoms are a feeling of lethargy, of listlessness—a deadening of the senses and a loss of awareness, particularly of surroundings.

Suddenly, and without knowing where he is going, in the middle of the day and during working hours, the nostalgic *Dilliwaalaa* may find himself holding a leaf bowl in outstretched hands waiting patiently for his turn to be served *chaat* in Maaleewaaraa or *kabaabs* in Galee Kabaabiyaan. He is sleepwalking.

The first bite—a delicious sting on the tongue—sensation returns! Fluids startle out of the eyes, the nose, and the mouth. Perspiration breaks out on the scalp, the forehead, and the face. Eardrums become moist. The registration and transmission of messages to the brain begins again.

He notices the clank-clank of tin bowls struck together by *bahishtees* merchandising the water in their goatskin bags. He can either drink it or, as an act of piety, have the steps or courtyard of the mosque washed. He hears the singsong of vendors offering a whole panorama of temptations—*kaseyroo* and *singhaaraa* (water chestnuts); *kulfee* frozen in the fifty stick cigarette tins of a bygone age; *chaat* (relish) made of *shakarkandee* (sweet potato), *kakree* (cucumber) or *phoot* (squash); *chaat* made out of a myriad salt "snacks", *kachauree, samoasaa, papree, qualmi barey, mungauree* and *chanaa*; *chaat* redolent with the aroma of all the condiments and spices which occasioned the discovery of America, which caused the Crusades; *chaat* dappled by sauces based on yoghurt, tamarind and mint; *chaat* made out of boiled potatoes and steamed ripe peas; roasted peanuts, horsegram and corn—he is inside an Ali

(*Dilli Door Ast* means "It is a far cry to Delhi !")

13. *A Daniell etching of 1837 showing the deserted houses of Patan chiefs.*

Baba's cave of the enchanted superabundance of well cultivated tastes and smells. This treasure trove of delights is heart's ease and home for the refugee *Dilliwaalaa*—momentarily he has succeeded in identifying with the past—his own and that of the city.

This past goes back aeons. In it history ceases to count measly potsherds. The glory and fantasy of myth and legend come into their own. His river, the Jamnaa or Yamunaa, is twin sister to Yama, the Lord of Death and was created with Him when Time began. The Yamunaa at Dilli boasts the Nigamboadh Ghaat. *Nigam* refers to the *Vedas* and *ghaat* means bank or shore. At the beginning of the *Dwaapar Yuga*, the knowledge of the *Vedas* was lost to all Creation. Even Brahmaa, the author, had forgotten. Tormented by a sense of his great loss Brahmaa wandered everywhere observing fasts, undergoing penances and offering sacrifices without avail.

One day he came to the Yamunaa. He took his ritual purificatory bath in its sacred blue waters. In a flash the *Vedas*—all four of them—came back to him. The river bank where he recovered this lost knowledge of the *Vedas* is called Nigamboadh. Bathing at this spot represents great good fortune for the Hindu and cremation here is a guarantee of release from the ceaseless cycle of births and deaths. The river Yamunaa looks after her own.

In times since past, the Hindu population of *Dilli* could be found bathing in the river around dawn. The bathers and worshippers in knots and groups came from the city singing praises of the river and carrying gifts. The bath was preceded by ritual worship of the Yamunaa. A leaf bowlful of rose petals or marigold blossoms with a jasmine or two, a sliver of *paan*, a fragment of betel and a small *bataashaa* were offered to the river by the bather. The dark tresses of the river were thus decorated with flowers and flower petals by the *Dilliwaalaa* as part of a daily ritual. On certain nights lamps were fashioned out of kneaded flour filled with butter, put on leaf boats, lit and floated downstream.

The temples and *muths* (monastic establishments) on the river bank provided the *Dilliwaalaa* natural surroundings near flowing water and amongst trees for his devotions. There were *akhaaraas* (gymnasiums) where masters of skills such as wrestling and stick-fighting taught apprentices. For the Emperor, the princes and the gentry, moonlight boat rides, fishing and hawking with shikaar across the river provided hours, days and nights of excitement and adventure.

From Wazeeraabaad, where a bridge, a mosque and the tomb of a fourteenth century saint called Shah Aalam remain as a memory of the time of Firoaz Shah (1351-88) to Keelookheree (Humaayoon's tomb) the riverside was bustling with residences, gardens, mosques, palaces, colleges and seminaries. Shah Jahaan's city, like its predecessors, was walled only on three sides. The Yamunaa provided protection on the fourth. Daraa Shikoah, eldest son of Shah Jahaan, built a college on the river bank near Kashmeeree Darwaazaa, where Persian *maulvees* and Sanskrit pandits collaborated under his inspired guidance to translate the *Upanishad* and publish the result as "The Great Mystery or the Secret of Secrets".

Shah Jahaan used the river bank to build his *Urdooey Moalla* or the exalted camp now called the Red Fort. This was a translation into marble, gold, silver and jewels of the Paradise lost to the Semitic civilisation by Adam. It was here that light refracted through the perfumed flow of the *Nahr-i-Bahisht* to seemingly move the delicate tendrils of flowers and leaves wrought in marble and adorned with precious stone inlay.

Between the fort and the river was the *maidaan* or plain where the great spectacles of the time—elephant fights, the muster of troops for royal inspection, the exhibition of presents from foreign rulers, and the trophies of war could be seen and enjoyed. Beyond the Red Fort the river flowed past the citadel of Firoaz Shah, then called Kushk-i-Firoaz. Here stood the famous mosque where Taiymoor and his victorious army offered their thanksgiving after conquering the Sultanate in 1938. It was a *Dilli* of another time.

...with its thousand colleges, seventy hospitals, extensive bazaars, public baths and palaces (*Dilli*) was the noblest city in the world of Islam...Khusrau sings of beautiful palaces...of edifices gleaming like jewels in the bright sunshine of India, Ibn Battootaa records that the Tughlaqaabaad palace was covered by gilded tiles...when the sun rose they glittered brightly and flashed with such a dazzling light that the eye could not rest on them....On three sides of the city—the fourth was flanked by the river—extended gardens and orchards for twelve miles to supply fruit and take the sting out of the hot summer winds. The people, drawn by the cooler air, thronged them on summer afternoons when, in the words of the immortal Khusrau, the melodies of the *'ood* and the *rubaab* intoxicated the trees and made the fountains drowsy...' Within this emerald ring lay that jewel of glittering brilliance, the metropolis of a great empire, 'a twin sister of the blessed heaven, a very paradise on earth'.

Taiymoor sacked, plundered and burnt this city and massacred its inhabitants. Master craftsmen and builders were enslaved and taken as prisoners to build palaces, mosques and mausolea in Samarqand.

Beyond Kushk-i-Firoaz, on the river bank was the great Indarpat plain. This plain lay within the Dilli of the Sultans and without Shahjahaanaabad's Dillee Darwaazaa or Delhi Gate (so called because it leads out to the Old City). Dilli has undergone many changes of names—Indraprastha, Joaginipur, Dillee, Qilaa Rai Pithowaraa, Seeree, Tughlaqaabaad, Jahaanpanaah, Koatlaa Feroaz Shah, Jahaanpanaah again, Shahjahaanaabad and New Delhi, but the pundit invoking the gods at births, marriages, deaths and for anniversaries still calls it Indraprastha. Indraprastha—the city built by supernatural beings, like Muya Daanava, for the superhuman Paandavaas.

Muya wrought golden pillared halls scintillating with jewels. The mirror shining on polished stone floors, columns and ceilings helped create mirage after mind bending mirage. This was the Paandavaas' answer to their collaterals and rivals, the Kauravaas, for making of them hunted fugitives, exiled from the luxuries of ancestral Hastinaapur and for the deprivations suffered during

14. *The Purana Quila or Old Fort at Delhi.*

an adolescence and early youth spent in dark, danger filled jungles.

Naturally, the house-warming celebration included a conducted (and well observed from the balconies!) tour for the rivals. When the party reached what appeared to them to be the brink of a shallow pool, the Kauravaas raised their flowing robes knee-high to save them from getting wet. The pool turned out to be a mirage caused by the deep mirror-like gloss of the polished stone. Embarrassed by having fallen for this trick, the Kauravaas proceeded sheepishly until the phenomenon appeared to repeat itself a little further on. This time they did not hesitate and strode on. This was a shallow pool just deep enough to wet, mortify, embarrass and humiliate. The Kauravaas of Hastinaapur were now the country bumpkins!

Draupadee from behind her vantage observation point burst into peal after coruscating peal of laughter interspersed with sarcastic comments upon the effect the blindness of parents has upon the vision of the progeny. This humiliation and the desire for revenge led to the famous gambling match with loaded dice. The ultimate holocaust of the *Mahaabhaarat* occurred at nearby Kurukhshetra, where the massive legions of the rival factions were annihilated in just eighteen days of fighting.

Although the archaeologist's spade has taken the history of the site where Indraprastha (the Old Fort) stands on the Jamuna, right back to the second century B.C., the handiwork of Muya Daanava has still to be unearthed. The only evidence of demonaic presence is provided by the chimneys of the Indraprastha Power House which are reputed to belch nearly a ton per hour of soot, crude, grit, ash or whatever the pollutant is called. This foul exudate has begrimed and disfigured all buildings. To the injury of losing the waterfront suffered by these buildings is added this continuing insult. The deep glaze on the encaustic tiles of the gracious Neelee Chatree has gone forever. Even the colour of the tiles is no longer of the bright "Delhi" blue. Like *Dilli*, the blue is a wistful, faded, neglected and abandoned shade of its former radiant and glorious self.

Fortunately, marble can take a lot more beating. When it rains the pearly perfection of the dome of Humaayoon's Tomb is rinsed of its soot and grime to shine like a rival to the full moon. The marble of the dome of Shamsuddeen Atkah Khan has turned black, while that of Chaunsathkhambah (the tomb of Mirzaa Azeez Koakaltaash) has become a graceless yellow, but elbow grease and a little loving care could perhaps revive the former glory.

The *Dilliwaalaa* was in his element when Shah Jahaan built the Red Fort. He connected it with the already existing Saleemgarh fort in such a manner as to blend the two structures into a unit. The river was guided to flow between the two forts. Paris has also been remodelled by various rulers. The Ile de France is an example of how to treat a river in a city. But then Shah Jahaan was three quarters Rajpoot and wholly Indian while Baron Hausmann was a European. Our town planners are difficult to place.

Today, thirty years after independence, both the Red Fort and Saleemgarh are still occupied by the army. Ours must be the only modern army in the world still living in forts. The ugly barracks built by the British continue to disfigure the Red Fort. Recently a monstrous water tank has been added to enhance the hideousness of army occupation. This structure dominates the skyline above Deewaan-e-Khaas and the Pearl Mosque.

Our attitude towards the past—whether distant Mauryaa or near Rajghat—is to treat it as if it were an Egyptian mummy. Something curious and remarkable but unconnected with everyday life. The smoke belching powerhouse on the river bank, the ugly municipal school which looks like a slap across the face of the riverside mosque called Zeenut-ul-masaajid (the ornament of mosques), and the state of the river at Nigamboadh are evidence of the abject cultural poverty of westernised Indians.

The memorials to Mahatma Gandhi and to two prime ministers

of India have come up in the same area as the Red Fort, Saleemgarh and Zeenut-ul-Masaajid. Each structure is on its own. There is no attempt to blend the past with the new and make of the whole something which would figure in the everyday life of the citizen as a place where children can gambol and their laughter can echo.

The westernized oriental gentleman has achieved the status designed for him by the Hon'ble Thomas Babington Macaulay in his Minute on Education dated 2nd February 1835: "a class of persons Indian in blood and colour, but English in tastes, in opinions, in morals and in intellect". Their assessment of the relative importance of Indian and European tradition appears to approximate Macaulay's own:

> ...whether when we teach European science we shall teach systems which, by universal confession wherever they differ from Europe, differ for the worse, and whether when we can patronize sound philosophy and true history we shall countenance at public expense medical doctrines which would disgrace an English farrier, astronomy which would move laughter in girls at an English boarding school, history abounding with kings thirty feet high and reigns thirty thousand years long, and geography made of seas of treacle and seas of butter!

The alienation of the city from the river, of the citizens from their past and of new buildings like the Supreme Court from grace, elegance and beauty, all stem from this attitude.

Until 1857, the British lived and built their own houses alongside the river. The prime example of their domestic architectural style was Metcalfe House near Indraprastha College. The British also followed the Court to Mehrauli for the rainy season. In this area they took over the tombs of nobles and divines of earlier times and converted them into residences. Gateways of 18th century English fashion still stand at the buildings of the Mehrauli bypass in memory of those days. One tomb at least still has a porch which the intruders added for their carriages to drive into.

In this, the Qutub area, there is an object to confound both the wogs and their mentor, Macaulay. It provides evidence of the remarkable metallurgical skill the Indians had achieved in the 4th century A.D. This object is the column called the Iron Pillar.

Sixteen hundred years of exposure to the elements has caused little rusting and has no noticeable effect upon the seven metre high column. Its capital—wrought into an *amalaka* or a lotus shape—remains a standard of beauty unaffected by changing fashion. Countless generations have been awed, astonished and enthralled by the Iron Pillar. There is nothing like it in the whole world. Before the Bessemer process was evolved, this was the largest single iron object known to mankind.

This wondrous object has, deservedly, its own super myth. This myth links up with the basic myth of creation as evolved by the Hindus. In Hindu myth, the earth rests upon one of the thousand hoods of the king of the cobras, Naagaraaja Vaasukee. When the load bearing hood wearies of the strain, the Naagaraaja flips it off and moves it on to a fresh hood. This periodic toss causes a universal shake up. Earthquakes, floods, landslides and avalanches occur in all parts of the earth. Kings tumble off their thrones. Dynasties disappear. From the time of its founding by Yudhishtira (fifteenth century B.C. according to Sir Syed Ahmed's computation made in 1846) Indraprastha has had its share of dynastic changes at frequent intervals caused no doubt by the Naagaraaja. During the Rajput period there came to the throne a Raja Meydhaavee (meaning the brainy one) who was as clever as his name. He worked out a plan to foil Vaasukee and to perpetuate the rule of his dynasty.

The raja began by hiring the most puissant of the Brahmins. They collected all the necessary ingredients and commenced a mammoth sacrifice to propitiate all the gods, and in particular Agnee, the Lord of Fire. Scores of animals and tons of *ghee* were fed to the sacrificial fire. The gods thus appeased, the Brahmin next fashioned a miraculous metal stake. This done, they consulted the stars for the most auspicious time. At the precise moment determined, the stake was thrust right through the earth into the very hood of the sleeping Naagaraaja Vaasukee! The earth shuddered as the king cobra winced with the pain. He was, however, helpless and transfixed. Dynastic change had been banished for ever.

The clever Meydhaavee was succeeded by generation after generation of kings, confident of their continued lordship. Ease bred complacence and soon there was on the throne a curious fool who would not believe that the Iron Pillar went all the way through the earth and into the king serpent's head. He had to see the buried end for himself.

It is not easy to thwart a king's obstinacy. Reluctant Brahmins and frightened workmen commenced the task of unearthing this magic column which their clever ancestors had buried for all time. As the pillar was dislodged from its bed the earth shuddered. When the end came out, a sound of hissing, as if of an angry cobra, arose from the empty hole. The end itself was found with fresh steaming blood.

A frightened king made the attempt to undo the damage. The pillar was hurriedly reinstalled. Its end remained loose. This time Vaasukee was wary and would not be a cushion. This looseness (*dhillaa* for the masculine and *dhillee* for the feminine gender) of the column gave the city its name—*Dilli*. The end of Rajput rule was now inevitable. The dreaded retribution appeared soon enough. Wave after wave of fierce and blood-thirsty Turcoman tribes poured into India through the passes of the North West Frontier. Everyone who came in their way was killed and everything they could carry away was looted. What had to be left behind was burnt

Under the pressure the Chauhan Rajputs threw up their mightiest, doughtiest, most chivalrous hero, Rai Pithowraa. His manhood was quite unique as he alone of all the multitude of heroes that India has produced had no vestige at all of the female—not even rudimentary mammary glands.

In the first battle, Rai Pithowraa swept the invaders off the battlefield with the shock of his fierce cavalry charge. The sultan was captured. Pithowraa sent him back with a spinning wheel wearing a woman's veil, with henna on his palms, bangles on his wrists and bells on his toes. The second battle saw Rai Pithowraa defeated, the Laal Koat stormed, the palaces and the temples razed to the ground. The Rajputs were killed in their saffron robes and the beautiful Sanyoagitaa (who had chosen Rai Pithowraa from out of all the kings of Hind although she was 16 to his 60) became a heap of heroic *jauhar* ashes with her fair hand-maidens.

The Iron Pillar alone survived the devastation. The victors planted it as a trophy in the courtyard of the first mosque they assembled out of the rubble heap of the razed temples. The inscriptions on the pillar remained a mystery until the nineteenth century when Prinsep identified and deciphered the script. It records an elegy to a dead king called Chandra. The glory of this Chandra cascades out of the inscription in verse after incandescent verse from the inscription. Scholars are not yet sure whether this was the imperial Chandragupta (375-413 A.D.), or some other Chandra. Even the glory remained unknown until Prinsep came on the scene. Folklore would no doubt allege that it is quite common for people who come afterwards to write their names on what others created earlier.

They would point out to the Qutub as an example of how this is done. This tower is situated well outside the original courtyard of the mosque (called Quwwat'ul Islaam, or 'the power of the true

15. *The* baoli
(*step-well*)
*and remains of
Jehangir's palace,
Delhi, 1839.*

faith'), the first congregational or Jaamaa Masjid of *Dilli* which Qutubuddeen Aybek hastily threw up using the material of the temples demolished. This tower entrance faces north—it has no plinth and juts straight out of the earth like a Mauryan column or the Iron Pillar itself.

Contrariwise, the unfinished tower of Alaauddeen Khiljee has a plinth and the entrance faces west. Thus the Qutub is a Rajput structure. All Qutubuddeen did to the Rajput tower he found was to remove stones with graven images and turn them around. He had verses from the *Quraan* carved as decoration. He also inscribed his own name and title (*Sipah Saalaar, Ameer'ul Umreaa*), that of his Sultan, and of the priest who was going to run the place (Maulvee Fuzzeel, son of Abool Moaly Mutwallee) on the entrance to the first story of the Qutub. The inscription on the second story of the Qutub establishes the point further by recording the instructions given to Mohammed Ameercho, engineer, by Sultan Shamsuddeen Iltumish. The height of the tower was to be increased by adding new storeys.

Iltumish had extended the frontiers of the Sultanate. There was a larger army. More space was needed for the congregation. The Quwwat'ul Islaam mosque was enlarged and new screens thrown up

to the west of the extended courtyard. These scree   s er and
more formal than those executed under Qutubu(ubud-
deen's screens, with their blend of floral motifs and arabic letters,
produce an effect of elegance, richness and restraint found in the
poetry of *Dilli* and in its music.

From Iltumish's time (1211-36 A.D.) the Qutub has become a
symbol of Delhi. The tower was repeatedly broken by thunderbolts.
Repairs have been carried out by many hands. Inscriptions exist
of repairs by Sultan Firoaz Shah (1368) and Sultan Sikander Lodee
(1503 A.D.). The John Company Bahadur also repaired it in the
early nineteenth century. The engineer in charge, Major Smith,
crowned it with a cupola. This looked so incongruous that it was
removed in 1848. It now stands in the lawn to the north of the
mosque.

Although as a result of these repairs the first three storeys look
quite different from the top two, the height of the Qutub and the
beauty of the support of its balconies makes it one of the most
remarkable sights in the world. The south west of the mosque
is a building which started a new class of monument—the tomb
or mausoleum. This red sandstone building fully carved and with
marble inlay is the last resting place of Iltumish. There is a false
marble cenotaph in the centre of the chamber. The actual tomb
of the Sultan is located in a crypt approachable by a flight of steps
starting outside the tomb.

In semitic belief, the dead will be resurrected when the trump of
doom is sounded to announce the dawn of the Day of Judgment.
Each person will arise and be judged for the deeds of his life.
Each ruler thought his tomb inviolate, its endowments perpetual,
and the building everlasting. He himself would lie under a marble
tombstone which extolled his name and fame in exquisite calli-
graphy and was covered with samet silk, velvet or gold brocade.
Around him would be arranged his personal regalia, arms, armour,
books and other favourite objects.

His endowments would continue to succour widows and orphans.
Priests would recite the holy scriptures for the benefit of his soul.
The whispered recitation would merge with the perfumed smoke
of the incense burning in scalloped niches. The dappled light from
the chandeliers swaying from incandescent ceilings would reveal
a scene of splendid glorious piety. Thus splendidly served, the Sultan
had nothing to fear on the Day of Judgment. He would arise, don
his regalia and present himself before the Supreme Ruler with the
confidence of one who has good deeds to his credit.

An example of this attitude is provided by Sultan Firoaz Shah. This Sultan succeeded his cousin Fakhruddeen Mohammed Jaunaa known to history as Muhammad bin Tughlaq and to contemporaries as Jaunaa Shah. Jaunaa was a most remarkable person. His experiments include the idea of two capitals, one for the North and the other at Daulataabaad Deogeer in the South, token currency, and land revenue reform. The complexity of contemporary commercial transactions may be judged from the fact that a coin had no face value. It was worth only its own metal weight. The value of the metals in relation to each other fluctuated according to supply and demand. Thus a *tankah* (silver coin) could be exchanged one year for 40 *jitals* (copper coin) and in another for 60. Like many innovators and men of genius, Jaunaa Shah was a failure. He strove to succeed on the basis of terror. Firoaz was worried about what all the victims of Jaunaa Shah would depose on the Day of Judgment. He therefore patiently sought out the heirs of the deceased and bought pardons by paying blood money. All these documents were deposited in a sealed box in the burial chamber at Tughlaqaabaad where Jaunaa Shah lies alongside his father, Malik Ghaazee.

Alas for the hopes of the Sultans and all the provisions made for Doomsday. The carpets, curtains, books, arms, armour, have all been looted by the invaders of Dilli from Emir Taimoor in 1398 to the British in 1857. Even Firoaz Shah's boxful of quittances has disappeared. The very tombstones have been taken away as building material. No one today remembers that but for warriors like Malik Ghaazee, India would have been overrun by the Mongols, the male inhabitants slaughtered, the women and children carried away in slavery and the cities sacked and burnt.

The Mongols carried fire and death from Europe in the West to China in the East. The Baghdaad Caliphate was obliterated and Iran overrun. *Dilli* became the refuge of scholars, saints, doctors, craftsmen, cooks, calligraphists, soldiers—in short of all those with talent who could escape the Mongol holocaust. The Sultan who withstood the initial shock was Alaaudeen Khiljee. His price control system based on the collection of agricultural produce as revenue enabled him to raise, maintain, and equip an army which could take on the invader. His General, Malik Ghaazee, fought and defeated the Mongols in twenty-four pitched battles. Their severed heads were fashioned into pyramids—a practice started by the Mongols to strike terror in the hearts of their enemies. He added the classic Indian dimension to the Mongol knowledge

16. *A Daniell etching of Safdarjung's tomb, 1837.*

of terror—captive Mongols were crushed under the feet of huge elephants. A few were allowed to escape to carry the glad tidings back to the horde.

The victorious Alaauddeen became so rich and powerful that he styled himself the equal of or the second Alexander. His architectural plans were magnificent—quadrupling the Quwwat'ul Islaam Mosque, adding a tower twice the girth and twice the height of the Qutub, and building red sandstone and marble gateways at each entrance to the Quwwat'ul Islaam Mosque. Only half the first storey of the tower and the joyous Alasee Darwaazaa with its horseshoe marble arches and its deep and exquisitely carved doorways remain. The Sultan's tomb adjacent to the mosque, with a seminary and college complex attached (so that prayers for his soul could be offered for all time), is in desolate ruins.

By the time Tughlaqaabaad and the tomb of Malik Ghaazee were planned, the Sultans had become wholly Indian. The Hindus burn their dead alongside a river, stream or lake. A *chattree* (memorial) is raised to mark the spot at which a hero dies in battle or a heroine commits *suttee* or a king is cremated. The importance of water as a dimension of peace, of tranquillity, and of eternity was accepted by the Sultans. Malik Ghaazee's tomb therefore stands at an elevation and was originally surrounded by a large artificial lake. The causeway which connected the fort and the mausoleum still exists. The water has evaporated. Firoaz Shah repaired and extended the lake created by Alaaudeen Khiljee for the needs of his new and populous city of Siri. On the banks of this lake he built a college. His own tomb built during his life time was integrated with the campus. There is today no more water in Hauz Khas near Firoaz Shah's tomb than there is at Tughlaqaabaad.

The nostalgia of the *Dilliwaallaa* is for the gracious days when water was visible and added a dimension of joy and ease in every house, garden, palace and street. Then the Jamuna was an everyday experience, an integral part of the citizen's life involved in both joys as well as sorrows. Today the river is dead and used only for open air or electric cremation and for sewage disposal. There is no water in the lakes of Hauz Khas or Tughlaqaabaad. Humaayoon's Tomb, Roshanaara Bagh, the Red Fort, Safdarjung, are all dry. The canal no longer flows through the Urdoo Baazaar into Chandni Chowk, to Fatehpuri Masjid, or down Faiz Baazaar. Even Saawan and Bhadon, the Rang Mahal, and other Red Fort palaces are dry. School children in their thousands run up and down the cascades and the streams, wearing out the delicate traceries of the marble with their English style boots. Foreign tourists are provided thin cotton overshoes to cover thick boots and allowed to trample marble inlay in Moti Masjid where emperors walked barefoot.

Dilliwaalaas Meer Taquee Meer and Mirzaa Asadullaah Ghaalib have wept for a Dilli despoiled, ravished, plundered, and sacked by alien invaders. What can contemporary *Dilliwaalaas* say except to sigh and repeat: *"Dilli door ast: Hanoaz Dilli door ast."*

Agra and Fatehpur

EDWARD LEAR

(1873–1875)

Feb. 16. Came to the Taj Mahal; descriptions of this wonderfully lovely place are simply silly, as no words can describe it at all. What a garden! What flowers! What gorgeously dressed and be-ringed women; some of them very good-looking too, and all well clothed though apparently poor. Men, mostly in white, some with red shawls, some quite dressed in red, or red-brown; orange, yellow, scarlet, or purple shawls, or white; effects of colour absolutely astonishing, the great centre of the picture being ever the vast glittering ivory-white Taj Mahal, and the accompaniment and contrast of the dark green of cypresses, with the rich yellow green trees of all sorts!

And then the effect of the innumerable flights of bright green parrots flitting across like live emeralds; and of the scarlet poincian-nas and countless other flowers beaming bright off the dark green! The tinker or tinpot bird ever at work; pigeons, hoopoes and, I think, a new sort of mynah, pale dove colour and gray, also squir-rels, and all tame, and endlessly numerous. Poinsettias are in huge crimson masses, and the purple flowered bougainvillaea runs up the cypress trees. Aloes also, and some new sort of fern or palm, I don't know which. The garden is indescribable. Below the Taj Mahal is a scene of pilgrim-washing and shrines, altogether Indian and lovely. What can I describe here? Certainly not the architec-ture, which I naturally shall not attempt, except perhaps in a slight sketch of one or two direct garden views. Henceforth, let the inhabi-tants of the world be divided into two classes—them as has seen the Taj Mahal, and them as hasn't.

Feb. 26. Rose early and repacked every thing before *chota hazri.* Off 11.30 in a good *garry* and about 22nd or 23rd mile, we get inside the vast walled fortress of Fatehpur Sikri, but soon stick in the steep sandy ascent. All kinds of persuasions of no use. At length, by hard and perpetual persevering work, we got to the top of the road, and into a vast court of ruins, and so on to a fine old red sandstone building, now used as a dak bungalow, but formerly one of the swell

palaces of Akbar the Great. The great mosque cloisters, and the vast gate, the surprising white marble tomb of the Paternal Fakir, struck and impressed me greatly. Everything here is elaborated and worked out incredibly, but the architecture seems to me coarse and eccentric as to general effect, rather than beautiful.

17. The garry.

Feb. 27. Unable to sleep from violently chirping crickets, also from the incessant noise from the fiesta of the Mussulman village below—drums, etc. These tambouri are just like the noise made by a gigantic steam boiler in a steamer, and never, never cease. The general effect of this celebrated place of ruin has rather disappointed, though I cannot help thinking one would grow to like this very strange solitude of past grandeur, if one stayed on. There are some things, of which one sees almost nothing by glimpses, and long observation is often required to perceive well what is most worthy of being understood.

Went again to the big mosque, and in spite of extent and wonderful detail, I seem confirmed in my non-liking of it as a whole. The immense gate seems to me utterly out of proportion, and the mosque dome low and ugly. The cloisters and the two tombs are superb. The abundance of pigeons and Alexandrina parrots here is incredible, the whole air seems made of pigeons' voices. The fortress extends a long way west, but I don't find any bits to be very enthu-

18. *A view of the Taj Mahal, Agra.*

siastic about. Wandered about this maze of semi-Moslem ruins, but growing tired of looking at red stone pillars, came back to the bungalow and applied plaster to bad heel. Then a breakfast of cold beef and bread-cum-tea, of our own brewing. Now I repose and the Suliot sews and mends linen; but he won't undertake to cover my, or his, solar topee. Much of this squarey-holeful architecture seems to me clumsy and dwarfy, full of the defects of Egyptian buildings but wanting their grandeur.

Notwithstanding all this, I drew a little bit of moskyness and the plain, and after revisiting all the very queer places of the Emperor's and Empress's habitat, went down to the Deer Minar and made one more drawing there.

Feb. 28 Went down to draw the porcupine pillar scene before *chota hazri*. A very beautiful scene too, the pure bright orange pillar and vast, smooth, green plain contrasting with the deep-shadowed trees, shaded pale sandy road, and dark, weedy, broken walls. On the whole this Fatehpur Sikri is not an advisable place to go to unless one has lots of time to spare. Now being slowly pulled along by two buffali on a sandy and stony ascent and at 10.45 reach good hard road and divest ourselves of buffali. Still the high, vast, gate of the Fatehpur Sikri mosque is seen on the ridge far behind. Now off with horses. High mud walls divide fields. Yellow-flowered plant, resembling thistle, grows along the road edge.

We get on fast over the last few remaining miles, and reach Bharatpur and a highly respectable looking dak bungalow at noon. Lots of horses visible near the place; endless wide roads, and the Residency a long way off. Presently we get some tea, cold beef, and bread, and thought nobody so happy as we. This dak bungalow is a stunner, having good rooms all round it, and it stands in a garden of Urbs! I went out, intending to call at the Residency, but some lovely elephantine pictures prevailed and I went not. The women here are all over the place quite surprisingly finely dressed, and in such orange, red, yellow, crimson, and red-brown dresses. Bharatpur is a most Indian town, but all things clean and cared for, and a people of intensely picturesque colour and dress. Finally, I drew in the street, but with bad eyes, and near a bad smell or drain.

After I had done my sketch, we walked for a long while through the bazaars, which I think, after Cairo, are the most picturesque I ever saw. The long streets, broad and well-paved, are flanked each side by shops, raised on a broad platform, each shop being an archway surrounded by stonework of the most elaborate workmanship. Above these arches is a cornice of stone, upholding galleries equally remarkable, and with here and there a covered verandah or gallery surpassingly pretty. The streets, red and blue; on camels, mounted police; women in every hue of the kaleidoscope; and with all this throng, not a word or look of incivility. The shawls; turbans; the bangles; the small children all naked; but gold caps and silver ornaments! The men too, are a finer and more manly-looking race than those of Bengal, and I fancy more intelligent. Have we had less to do with them, and are they less stupid or less feigning to be so in consequence?

Across the Desert on Camel-back

LOUIS ROUSSELET

(1865)

I had fixed the departure of our caravan for 19th December, and at the appointed hour the camels, grouped in the courtyard of the bungalow, were waiting to be laden. The two on which we were to ride were smartly caparisoned with housings of silk and a profusion of tassels; but all these ornaments were in honour of the ceremony of departure, and would disappear when we were once on the road. Our party consisted of our four servants, two *saniwallahs,* and seven camel-drivers. All were armed with sabres and guns, and each imagined it extremely probable that he would shortly be called upon to make use of them. I assembled them all before the steps of the bungalow and made them a brief speech, assuring them that the country we were about to traverse was perfectly safe, and that, moreover, being well armed, we should have nothing to fear from the Bheels. I appointed a leader of the caravan; and, having consulted the itinerary I had drawn up, I ordered him to encamp that same night at the village of Rajpoor fifteen miles to the north-east of Ahmedabad. As for our two selves, I had decided that we should pass one more night beneath the hospitable roof of the bungalow, and only join our camp next morning.

Our baggage was soon laden, amid the terrible cries of the camels, and I saw the little band set off, surrounded by friends and relatives who were going to escort them as far as the gates of the city. Some officers came to pass the evening with us, and kept us up till midnight. At four o'clock I was awoke by my *saniwallah,* who came to warn me that it was time to be starting. I, in turn, woke Schaumburg, and in a few minutes we were ready. The *sani,* or riding-camel, squatted at the door, waiting for me: I threw some coverings over the saddle to make it more comfortable, and took my place on the hind seat; my driver bestrode that in front, and the camel sprang to his feet.

The saddle used for camel-riding, as no doubt most of my readers are aware, is double, so that the two riders find themselves fitted

close to one another. The position of the one who is behind is not the most agreeable on account of this proximity; but I had chosen it to accustom myself a little to the motion of the camel before I attempted to guide it myself. I remained for half an hour without being able to find my equilibrium, violently jolted and clinging to the back of the camel; my companion, however, suffered equally with myself. At the end of this time I felt more at my ease, and was able to take some notice of the road we were travelling. Ahmedabad was already far off, and the daybreak lighted up an immense plain covered with bare fields and dotted with groups of trees, denoting the sites of the villages.

At Rajpoor, which we reached at six o'clock, I found our tent pitched under a large tree on the bank of a river. Our baggage was arranged round another tree, where our attendants had established the kitchen and their headquarters. Muskets and sabres, hanging from the boughs, gave the whole a somewhat warlike aspect. I cannot express how this scene, gilded by the splendour of the morning sun, transported me with joy. It was, indeed, the commencement of the serious part of my journey. Hitherto I had followed beaten paths in countries where the influence of civilization made itself felt, and where I had full directions how to proceed; here all was strange to me. What I should find in Rajpootana—a good or a bad reception, a paradise or a desert—I knew not. I spent that day in going about the village, and in shooting a few hares and peacocks, which latter were not held sacred here; and towards night I enjoyed the spectacle of the return of the cattle, four or five hundred oxen and buffaloes passing at full speed, rushing towards the river to quench their thirst after a long day of drought.

I here transcribe my diary, which will enable me to present to my readers a more succinct and accurate account of this journey than I otherwise could bring before them.

December 21. We leave Rajpoor at two o'clock in the morning. The night is very dark, but, the country being perfectly flat, our camels proceed without any difficulty. The villages are all at some distance from the road, for we do not come to one before reaching Deagaum, a town of considerable importance, where we arrived at four o'clock. We are stopped at the gate by some *sowars,* who inquire our destination, and procure us *bohmias,* or guides, to conduct us to the next village. This institution of *bohmias* is one of the most curious and most useful in this country. They are persons of low caste, appointed, by way of rent-service, to guide travellers from one village to another. Their service is obligatory, and the council of the village recompenses them by according to them the right of sojourning in the locality, and giving them certain portions of arable land. The country being wholly destitute of roads, the traveller would run great risk of going astray without the assistance of these guides. The poor fellows have a very troublesome vocation, being obliged to get up at all hours of the night to escort, for several leagues, parties of travellers, who pay them a halfpenny per coss, or two English miles. Indeed, they think themselves fortunate if they are not compelled to go at a double pace, and are not sent away without any remuneration at all.

The dawn finds us still in the midst of these interminable plains; meanwhile the trees become more numerous and form small forests, which proclaim that we are approaching a mountainous region. At six o'clock we reach the village of Resial, where we encamp for the day. Here we essay in vain to procure provisions, and are obliged to

20. *The departure.*

content ourselves with our chickens and the produce of our sport. The chief of the village comes to pay me a visit, and asks me to make him a present of one of the peacocks I have killed. I give him one, and distribute the rest amongst our escort.

December 22. On setting out from Resial, which we leave at two o'clock in the morning, we enter upon extensive sandy wastes, where the cold makes itself keenly felt. Our attendants, enveloped in their wrappings, appear to suffer very greatly from it. At day-break we penetrate into deep ravines, hollowed out by the rains. The steep banks assume most fantastic shapes, and the villages perched on their summits appear to be situated on the heights of inaccessible hills, whereas in reality they are on a level with the plain. Near the village of Hursole we pass a beautiful river, flowing between precipitous cliffs some fifty feet high. The great width of its bed, the height of these earthen walls, and the total absence of vegetation gives an aspect of wild grandeur to this nearly dry nullah. On the other side we ascend on to the plane, where we find the ruins of Hursole, an old English cantonment which has been abandoned some years. The broken roofs of the barracks and bungalows are covered with creeping plants; and the gardens, whose walls are still standing and the gratings closed, are filled with an exuberant vegetation.

Some miles from this ruined encampment runs a chain of hills, bare and of low elevation, which may be considered as the base of the

Doungher Mountains, on the Goojerat side. Behind these hills, then, commences the Bagur, or country of the Bheels—that wild and mountainous region which separates the table-lands of Malwa from Goojerat, and which forms the south-eastern boundary of the vast country of the Rajpoots. The mountains that cover this district form the point of junction of the two great Indian chains of the Aravalis and the Vindhyas, and are generally known by the inhabitants of the country under the name of Doungher. On crossing these hills the heat becomes excessive, so we delay only a very few moments to pursue and kill an antelope.

An hour's journey across a sandy plain, with the sun darting his rays upon us, brings us to the village of Bar Daukrol. Through an error in my calculations, today's journey has been about twenty-two miles, and all my party arrive at their camping-ground worn out with fatigue; for this stage, which in Europe would be considered very moderate, is almost a forced march in a pathless country where you have continually to make a round in this or that direction. Bar Daukrol is a tolerably large village in the midst of a beautiful wood of mango-trees. Its inhabitants are still of the Goojerat type, and appear to have as much aversion for the Bheels as their fellow-countrymen of the plain. During the evening I make an important addition to our caravan—four soldiers from Puttiala, who are returning to their country, and ask leave to join us in order to cross the country of the Bheels. They are stout, lively fellows, armed with sabres and matchlocks, and I at once accept their proposal, promising that if they behave themselves well from this to that, I will recompense them generously when we reach Oudeypoor. The arrival of these auxiliaries is welcomed joyfully by my people, and the guard of the encampment is entrusted to them for that night.

December 23. Some few hours' night marching brings us to the far end of those monotonous plains over which we have been travelling since we left Baroda, and in the morning we reach a pretty village whose huts are ranged on a picturesque hill of milky quartz. We traverse a beautiful forest, on leaving which we reach the borders of a lake. The scene is one of the greatest possible beauty. This vast sheet of water, covered with lotuses in flower, amid which thousands of aquatic birds are sporting, is encompassed with a screen of banyans and other giants of the tropics, of sombre foliage. No human being appears on these shores, and the inhabitants of the lake enjoy the beautiful morning in perfect tranquillity. Long rows of flamingoes, with roseate wings, seem to be holding a grand review on one of the little islands almost on a level with the water; battalions of wild geese, and ducks of a hundred different species furrow these deep waters into regular waves; water-fowls of purple or indigo plumage hop over the large leaves of the lotus, while herons, adjutants, and *karkhoondj* perch on the submerged boughs of the trees along the bank. I forbid my folks to disturb this aquatic people, and we proceed along the beach without creating any great flutter. The country becomes more and more beautiful. How fortunate I am to have preferred these laughing mountain lands to the broiling plains of Deesa!

As we near Tintoui, where we are to encamp, the country is again traversed by rills and covered with fields of enchanting verdure. The roads go between flowery hedges which rise above our heads, and form a charming avenue which leads to the Mookam.

The Mookam, or "place of encampment", is in general a wood, situated near a village, and of which the soil is levelled. It is specially reserved for travellers, and always provided with a reservoir and sometimes with a small temple, so that the pilgrim finds there everything necessary for him—water, shade, and a sacred place wherein to perform his devotions. The Mookam of Tintoui is of the greatest beauty: great mango trees, *neems,* and banyans surround a glade clovered with green and smooth grass, where I had our tent pitched. At a little distance appeared the village, seated on a hill, at the entrance of sombre defiles, whose bluish peaks stand out on the horizon; a fort with crenellated ramparts commanding the country around.

Tintoui is of great importance from its position at the entrance of the defiles of the Dougher Mountains. This town is the residence of a Rajpoot baron, or *thakur,* who is a tributary of the Mahrattas, but is the real king of the country. These *thakurs* correspond in all respects with our barons of the feudal age; and it is very curious to find this system existing in our days, and especially to find it with all the particulars that belong to our institutions of the middle ages. Like our lords of the olden time, the *thakurs* have the right to administer justice throughout their territories, and only acknowledge their dependence on the sovereign by a tribute in men-at-arms or money and some rare visits to the capital. Haughty and turbulent, they are engaged in continual quarrels with their neighbours, and live largely on the pillage of the caravans that traverse their country. The English Government has, it is true, apparently put this system of brigandage into good order; but instead of making it disappear, it has merely moderated and regulated it. From being the robber of the caravans, the *thakur* has become their protector; instead of pillaging them, he taxes them, after the system of "black mail" practised formerly amongst the Highlanders. A caravan, on reaching the territory of a *thakur,* has to pay so much per cent on the value of its cargo, in consideration of which the *thakur* guarantees it a safe passage through the defiles. If, on the contrary, trusting in its own strength, it risks itself without this safe-conduct, it is sure to be attacked and pillaged by all the mountain bands put on the alert by their chief, who is no other than the *thakur.*

The latter, exercising the functions of a magistrate, receives the complaints of the unfortunate victims, records them with much ceremony, and sets his whole garrison on the move; but the searches are always in vain—the soldiers return without a prisoner; and, by way of solitary consolation, the *thakur* points out to the merchants what folly and rashness they have displayed in refusing the aid of his redoubtable arm.

On my arrival at Tintoui I am received by the *thakur's* guards, who present his respects to me, and announce his intention to call on me; but, being curious to see the castle, I beg them to conduct me to the presence of their chief. A very steep declivity, paved with large flags on which the horses slip at every step, leads us to the gate of the keep, which is defended by small towers and a circle of stakes bound with iron. The interior so greatly resembles our feudal fortresses of the twelfth and thirteenth centuries that the reader may picture to himself the earliest of the numerous castles that adorn the banks of the Rhine. An odd medley of towers, pinnacles, and terraces on one side overlooks the precipice, at the bottom of which are seen the peaceful mansions of Tintoui. The *thakur,* a white-bearded Rajpoot noble, receives me with much affability, and inquires the object of my visit. At the name of his suzerain, Khunderao, he bows profoundly, while he replies that, as I am the friend of the powerful Guicowar, he is but my humble slave, and that I may freely dispose of his person, his followers, and his country. I content myself with only demanding his protection in passing through the defiles, and a few horsemen, to add to the importance of my caravan. I next question him as to these famous Bheels, their habits and customs, and I obtain a mass of interesting details. He deplores, with real sorrow, the too considerable depredations carried on by his tribes, which have ruined the country by diverting the caravans into other tracks. The good man complains very naturally of the rapacity of his neighbours, which hinders him from indulging his own.

Some hours after my visit the chief comes to pay me his respects in my camp. He is accompanied by a troop of Rajpoot horsemen who caracole on their beautiful Kattywar horses, while the villagers from a respectful distance contemplate the interview. The movements of the old *thakur* are full of dignity, and his slightest words breathe the politeness, replete with etiquette, characteristic of a courtier of the court of Oudeypoor—the model of *bon ton* for the whole of India. On quitting me he clasps me in his arms, assuring me that if so many winters had not passed over his head, he would not have yielded to any one the honour of guiding my caravan as far as the outposts of Kairwara. His son and three horsemen, however, join us, and they come that same evening to pitch their tent beside ours.

The Mookam of Tintoui possesses one of those antique cisterns known by the name of *baolis,* and which one may class among the most interesting monuments of the country. It consists externally of a range of *chatris,* or kiosks, placed at an equal distance from one another. The entrance of the *baoli* is under the first kiosk, whence a staircase goes down to a landing-place, situated immediately beneath the second kiosk, which thus is supported by two storeys of columns. The staircase continually descends, the number of storeys of columns augmenting from one kiosk to another up to the last, which consequently has four or five storeys surrounded by galleries; at the extremity is a large circular well, the water of which, at its level, bathes the last steps of the staircase. These structures are sometimes upwards of three hundred feet long, and contain regular rooms with roofs, supported by elegant pillars and walls decorated with bas reliefs. When they are found, as at Tintoui, in a desert place, I know few monuments that strike the traveller more, when, entering them for the first time, he penetrates gradually into these mysterious galleries.

December 24. This morning, at the moment of departure, there is nearly a revolt amongst our troop, who refuse to march before sunrise. The cause of this strange conduct is the news that there is at this moment, lying in wait by the roadside, an *admikhanewalla,* that is to say, a tiger of the class called "man-eaters". The young *thakur* joins me in persuading them to start, and succeeds in this by pointing out to them that, as the tiger had recently killed a man (for this was the news that had so frightened them), he must be satiated, and that this is the most favourable moment for passing safe and sound. We leave the camp amid the murmurs of the camel-drivers, who find that it is already quite enough to expose their camels to be taken by the Bheels, without tigers joining the party. Our troop has, however, become sufficiently imposing to keep these enemies at a distance; it now amounts to twenty-three armed men wherewith to sustain a

21. *Paying homage to the local* thakur.

battle against the Bheels.

Buktawar Singh, the young *thakur*, rides by my side, and entertains me with anecdotes about the Bheels. He tells me also of the devastations committed in the country by this man-eater, that has so terrified our people, who passes very few days without finding a new victim, and is so crafty that the hunters have never yet been able to take him. The Hindoos pretend that a tiger which has once tasted human flesh will never more eat any other kind; on the other hand, European hunters, having frequently remarked that these man-eaters are always bare of parts of their coat, and sickly, have attributed this condition to the effect of human flesh.

The most simple explanation of these two hypotheses is this: when the tiger grows old, he loses, like all animals, a great part of his strength and all his agility. Should he then attack, as before, a strong bullock on the mountain, he is repulsed or only brings it down with difficulty; should he pursue a stag or an antelope, he finds it impossible to catch it. He therefore watches anxiously by the roadside and sees a man approaching; his hunger overcomes the fear he always has for this strange animal, and he finds him an ample and easy prey. This is why he abandons every other kind of chase, and lives on mankind only.

A short distance from Tintoui the defiles become narrower, and at daybreak we find ourselves at the bottom of a narrow gorge, over-hung everywhere by walls of nearly black rock, a thick forest, com-posed of the most magnificent odorous shrubs of India, covering the sides and the crest of the mountain. The landscape is of a wild and grand beauty, surpassing our most beautiful European scenes. Enor-mous blocks of white quartz, thrown here and there, sparkle in the sun. The *pals* of the Bheels, placed on the summit of the cliffs, with a scanty circle of fields at their feet, resemble, with their walls of backwood, gigantic eagles' nests. At various distances, the dark figure of a Bheel stands out on the summit of a rock. These are the sentinels who keep watch over the road; not one of our movements escapes their observation, but our number and the protection of the *thakur* guarantee us against any attack.

December 25. Having to cross some difficult passes, we did not raise our encampment till six o'clock in the morning. The country is of an aspect indescribably wild. The depths of the valleys are en-cumbered with piled-up fragments of rock, between which wind narrow paths; and it is marvellous to see with what patience and address our heavily laden camels overcome all these obstacles. The horsemen of Tintoui and the soldiers from Puttiala form with me the advanced guard. Our camels, with their drivers, and thirty Indian travellers who have joined us at different places on the route to cross the defiles under our protection, are together in the centre; and Schaumburg, with some horsemen, brings up the rear. This redoubl-ing of precautions has been recommended to us, for we have to cross one of the most redoubtable districts, the inhabitants of which do not respect any caravan. After several very narrow passes, we enter a fertile valley, shut in between superb mountains: the *coup d'oeil* is very imposing; these masses of rock, these forests covering the declivities, form a whole of much grandeur.

The *pals* are very numerous, and appear in ranges on both sides. Scarcely had we entered this place when an incident occurred that might have put a stop to our journey altogether. During the morning we passed some Bheels, who went by calm and silent, without res-ponding to the fraternal salutes which our *sowars* addressed to them. One of the latter, indignant at this incivility, took advantage of one of these men being alone to throw himself upon him, beat him, and snatch away his bow and arrows. This affair, which might have had such terrible consequences for us, took place unknown to me, occu-pied as I was in discussion with Buktawar; but I was soon informed of it, for the soldier, knowing that I had manifested a desire to possess some Bheel arrows, came in triumph to bring me his trophy.

I at once comprehended the danger we ran, and had scarcely had time to give some orders when the war-cry resounded in the valley, and was repeated by all the echoes. From every *pal* that we could see, men came running down towards us. To describe the confusion that then broke out in the centre of our caravan would be almost an impossibility. The women shrieked; the merchants behaved like madmen; even the camel-drivers joined in the uproar. As for our soldiers, their attitude was worthy of all praise. They proceeded to charge their pieces and light their matches, and awaited my orders. The Bheels, seeing us take up our position, advanced irresolutely; our fire-arms intimidated them somewhat. However, they were already in great force, and some ventured to shoot arrows at us, but out of range. A few of them managed to draw near us by creeping behind the bushes, and discharged a few shots, one of which hit a camel, which began bellowing and thereby added to the disorder.

I was about to give orders to respond by opening fire upon them when I saw an old Rajpoot horseman of our escort from Sameyra set off at a gallop towards some high tufts of grass near which were our camels. Buktawar and I followed him. At the moment we joined him, we saw him face about and fall, with raised sabre, upon a poor old Bheel, cowering in the grass, who was soon made prisoner, and in the twinkling of an eye had his hands bound. This action produced a magical effect. I heard terrible cries raised around; arrows fell thickly about us; and several shots were fired on the part of the caravan. We beat a retreat with our prisoner; and the old *sowar* having had time to explain that he knew the old fellow very well as the chief of one of the *pals,* I had it proclaimed to the Bheels that if they continued to assail us, our first act should be to kill the old chief, to which they replied with loud cries, but did not retire. When I had the old Bheel unbound, he explained to me, in bad Hindostani, how deeply the people of his tribe had been pained and shocked by the insult we had inflicted upon them in maltreating one of their number. They thought themselves, he said, under the protection of Europeans, and were not accustomed to such proceedings. He demanded the restoration of the bow and arrows lately despoiled. I assured him that I deplored the event, and offered to give up the bow and arrows, and to make the *sowar* apologize. The bow and arrows were then returned; but, as for himself, we detained him till we got out of the valley.

At the moment of restoring him to liberty, I had a large glass of brandy filled, which he drank off at a single draught, and which seemed to gain me his entire friendship. He quickly rejoined his own friends, who had followed us in silence; and thereupon he launched against our party all the imprecations imaginable, crying out that he did not recognise the obligation of salutation, except in the presence of sahibs, and that, if he ever again saw any of our followers in the valley, they should feel his vengeance. This last menace apparently did not in the least disturb our *sowars,* although they had to return home by the same road.

On the morning of the 28th of December our caravan started from Khairwara, escorted by five horsemen from the contingent of Oudey-poor, who, by the orders of Major Nixon, took the place of the *sowars* of Sameyra and Tintoui, whom I had dismissed.

At the distance of one or two miles from the station, we entered the defiles. The aspect of the mountains was completely changed; their lofty peaks, bare and rugged, differed very much from the steep hills of southern Bagur, while their chains being farther apart formed broad valleys furrowed by water-courses. We had left the Vindhyas and had now entered the Aravalis. This chain which, separating from the great network of mountains, runs in a northerly direction through the whole of Rajpootana as far as Delhi, is one of the richest and least known throughout India. The greater part of it is composed of granite, resting on massive and compact beds of dark blue slate; its valleys abound in coloured quartz, and in schistous, laminated slate, which present every possible tint from purple to gold. Its productions are inexhaustible, and here are often found black and coloured marble, gneiss, and syenite. Besides gold, silver, copper, lead, and tin, this chain contains rock crystal, amethysts, chrysoline, carbuncles, and garnets, as well as a few small emeralds, all which riches lie unused.

After a long march we reached Pursad, where we were to encamp. The valley surrounding the village had been cleared of wood to make r oom for fields, which enabled one to take in the whole view at a glance. The houses are prettily grouped on the ridge of a sterile hill, crowned with rose-coloured quartz; the gardens slope down gently to a nullah; and, rising above all, stand the sharp peak of a pagoda and the towers of the baronial castle. The higher parts of the mountain are inhabited by Pal Bheels. We hesitated for an instant between an ancient and picturesque caravansary and a venerable banyan tree o n the edge of the nullah; but the latter secured the choice, and we pitched our tents beneath its enormous branches. I received the visit of the *thakur,* and during the march two *sowars* from Khairwara joined us, having been sent as a reinforcement by Major Nixon. Our caravan, like a snowball, had so increased in size since we left

Ahmedabad that, in the evening, when all the camp-fires were lighted, a stranger might have taken us for the vanguard of an expedition, instead of peaceable travellers on the march.

Several times during the night I was awakened by the piercing cries of jackals prowling round the camp. Annoyed by their perseverance, I went out of my tent to tell one of the sentries to drive them off by firing. But the soldiers, tired out by their long day's march, were all fast asleep round the fires, having left the custody of the camp to the moon, which was shining with unusual brilliancy. I walked towards the lazy men to recall them to their duty, when I saw, at a short distance from me, an animal rise to its feet and move away slowly; it was a cheetah which had approached our fires in the hope of surprising one of our dogs. I allowed it to go off in peace, and awoke the guards with a sharp reprimand for their negligence.

On the morning of the 29th we entered a series of gorges, ravines, and defiles, of a character so wild and rugged that, for a moment, I feared the route would be impracticable for our beasts of burden. The ground was formed of dark slate, presenting its edges like knife-blades; and I am still at a loss to understand how our poor camels managed to get over it without wounds. To look at their long feet and huge humps, one can scarcely believe that these desert ships are so useful amongst the mountains, carrying heavy boxes simply balanced, and passing, with the confidence of mountain mules, over the most difficult places.

At eleven o'clock we descended into a beautiful valley, through which ran a deep *nullah*. A magnificent group of temples, built of white marble, stood in the centre of the plain, at a short distance from the village of Jowar. Major Mackenzie had recommended me to pay them a visit, and had even advised me to establish myself in one of them. I followed his advice, and, whilst our men were pitching their tents beneath the gigantic banyan trees which guarded the entrance, I took possession of a splendid hall in the largest pagoda. This was the first specimen of the famous Jain architecture of Rajasthan which I had had the opportunity of seeing and I examined it with the greatest interest.

One stage only separated us now from Oudeypoor, but, as a long march was before us, I announced to my men that we would take advantage of the full moon to strike the camp at one o'clock in the morning. Accordingly we only took a nap; and at the hour above mentioned, having provided ourselves with Bheel guides, supplied by the *thakur* of Jowar, we started on our march. The moon lighted up the country brilliantly, and we were advancing rapidly, when the guide suddenly declared that he had mistaken the way. This did not seem probable; nevertheless, we had to resign ourselves to our fate and follow him across the forest, our camels stumbling against the rocks and impeded by the prickly bushes. We dismounted, and, fires being lighted, watchfully and patiently awaited the dawn. At about five o'clock in the morning we started afresh on our journey, and had the satisfaction of finding a path which led to a village. Before reaching it a tiger caused us some alarm. It crossed our path, gazed at us for a few moments, and then buried itself in the jungle; but the camels were very much frightened at the sight of it, and gave us much trouble all the way to the village. On arriving, the Bheels answered our inquiries most courteously, and, offering themselves as guides, abused the man who had guided us from Jowar.

By sunrise we were crossing magnificent forests, where we saw numerous herds of wild boar. The forest then seemed to come to an abrupt termination; and at seven o'clock we found ourselves surrounded by numberless small mounds, which were covered with luxuriant crops of a herb called *kalam*. I have rarely seen such an original-looking country. Game was abundant among the grass and bushes, and I killed, even from our path, a great many partridges and jungle-fowl.

At length we passed round the last hill, and Oudeypoor, the capital of Meywar, was before us. My men shouted and danced for joy. As for myself, I stood in ecstasy gazing on the sublime panorama spread out at my feet. Never had I even hoped to see anything so beautiful: it resembled one of the fairy cities in the Arabian Nights. In the foreground a long line of forts, pagodas, and palaces stood out from a background of gardens, above which appeared the town, a fantastic assemblage of bell-turrets, towers, and kiosks, built up the side of a pyramidical hill; on the summit of which was an immense palace of white marble, which contrasted finely with the dark blue of the mountains behind it. This palace, with its splendid proportions, appeared to soar like the New Jerusalem above a terrestrial city. Neither pen nor pencil could give the marvellous effect of that town, which is well named Oudeypoor, the City of the Rising Sun. Soon, however, this beautiful sight disappeared as we descended with difficulty into the desolate ravines which guard this paradise.

The Governor of the Prisons, who came occasionally to see me, invited me to visit the principal prison. It is a little fort, pleasantly situated on the summit of one of the low hills which overlook the town ramparts. Above the principal entrance is the main building, with turrets, and balconies to the windows, having a heavy over-

22. *Resting under a banyan tree.*

hanging cornice of handsome appearance. The *thanadar* lives there. The prisoners are lodged under great sheds, where they sleep on the hardened earth, and long iron bars run the whole length of the halls, to which their chains are attached at night. They are treated humanely enough; their chains are light, and simply riveted to their ankles, and are long enough to allow them to run. Each prisoner keeps the costume in which he entered the prison, and everything which concerns his caste is scrupulously respected; each one daily receiving his food and preparing it himself; for which purpose he is allowed to light a fire and draw water in perfect liberty. These prisoners are employed in making roads and keeping them in repair; but their daily work of a few hours is not subject to strict supervision: in fact, they have very little to complain of, and the inhabitants of our European prisons would consider themselves well off under similar circumstances.

In the morning we found an elephant sent by the Rao, with a *jemadar* and four *sowars* as an escort. Bulwant Rao, the king's secretary, who filled the place of cicerone to us, led us through a suburb of the town, which contained the villas of the rich inhabitants of Oudeypoor. On all sides were little hills covered with shady gardens, in which we could see pretty kiosks, and pavilions built on the edge of ornamental pieces of water, together with numerous marble temples. We entered the town through a gate flanked by bastions, and passed along the side of a handsome bazaar. The shops are placed under arcades on each side of the road, and have an air of regularity and cleanliness which surprised us who had seen the buildings at Goojerat. The general appearance of the town is most striking. Every house possesses its balconies and its stone trellised windows relieving the monotony of the walls; terraces are seen in picturesque disorder, and sculptures, arabesques, and frescoes are met with here and there.

Some of the streets are long and straight, and great animation reigns in them. In one live all the shoemakers, in another the turban-weavers: here every shop is a regular arsenal of swords, guns, and shields; and there brocade robes and jewellery fill the stalls. Each business and each trade occupies a quarter by itself, and everyone seems to ignore the competition of his neighbour.

The quarter of the nobility contains some magnificent buildings, regular castles, fortresses with loopholed walls, towers, palace, and barracks; but their beauty is disfigured by the numerous ruins which surround the most splendid palaces. The presence of these ruins in one part of the town, where the land is proportionately of high value, is accounted for by the ill-conceived respect of the Rajpoots for the works of their fathers. They do not like either to repair or to destroy them, so they leave them where their fate made them fall. From every part of the town the palace is visible—a majestic assemblage of domes, turrets, and porticoes.

With difficulty we climbed the roads which conducted to the buildings belonging to the palace; they are so steep that carriages can scarcely ascend them. On the high road which leads from the Hahtipoh to the palace, and close to the grand entrance, stands the pagoda, dedicated to Juggernauth, and built by Pertab Sing towards the end of the sixteenth century. It is situated on a lofty terrace, composed entirely of white marble, to which access is had by a handsome flight of steps, guarded by marble elephants with raised trunks. The whole temple, in fact, is built of white marble, and is covered with sculptures. The great tower is very elegant, and rears its summit to a height of about seventy-five feet, where the standard of the god floats from a golden staff.

A graceful pavilion, with a pyramidical roof supported by pillars, stands in front of the building; bas-reliefs representing incidents in the life of Krishna adorn the walls, and statuettes of elephants and lions surround its base. This peristyle is one of the most beautiful specimens of Jain architecture in Oudeypoor. We then descended the slope of the hill facing the lake, and reached a gateway built on the water's edge. This arch is, like all the monuments of Oudeypoor, built of white marble. It consists of three indented arches, and supports an elegant cupola surrounded with a balcony. The Indians regard this gateway, which is called Tripolia, or "Triple Gate" with great veneration. It is never used but for processions which go to the lake during the numerous festivals that are held there. A boat awaited us at the jetty to convey us to the islands, and soon we were floating on the tranquil waters of lake Peshola, in the calm depths of which the houses and gardens of the town, stretching along its shores, were reflected. The extremity of the lake is confined in a narrow channel by numerous promontories which are covered with palaces. Further on it expands into an enormous ellipsis, in the centre of which are the two islands of Jugnavas and Jugmunder. On the one side there is a chain of angular mountains, at the foot of which stands the town; on the other are swamps, surrounded by jungle and overlooked by several isolated hills of considerable height.

The island of Jugnavas was the nearest, so we landed on it. It is literally covered by a series of palaces which were built by the Rana Juggut Sing, and extends over an area of a hundred and sixty acres. These palaces contain reception-halls and apartments, and baths and kiosks of most beautiful architecture, ornamented with a richness quite fabulous. Marble is the only stone employed in their construction; pillars, vaults, reservoirs, garden walks, all are of marble, either white or black. The walls are ornamented with glittering mosaics, and the principal chambers are decorated with historical frescoes. Each mass of buildings has a garden attached to it surrounded by galleries, where flowers and orange and lemon trees grow near a stream, the different channels of which form a curious pattern. Immense mango trees and tamarinds shade these beautiful palaces, while the coconut and the date-palm raise, above the very domes, their feathery heads, which are gently swayed to and fro by the breeze from the lake. The smallest details harmonize with the beauty of the whole scene. There is nothing grand, nothing which inspires the mind with awe. The palaces are small, elegant, and comfortable; they are the abodes of pleasure, where the Rana can divest himself of solemn pomp, of which there is always so much at the Court of the Sun of the Hindoos.

I would willingly have remained on this island for hours, but Bulwant Rao pressed me to visit the second, Jugmunder, where breakfast, sent by the Rao of Baidlah, awaited us. We landed at a flight of marble steps, at the side of which a row of elephants with uplifted trunks appeared to support the quay. A gigantic mango tree nearly filled the first court, which is surrounded by the buildings of the palace. On the other side is a garden, occupying that entire end of the island which is overlooked by large buildings, surmounted by a Mogul dome, called by my guide the Palace of Shah Jehan. This prince, son of the Emperor Jehangir, having revolted from his father, sought refuge at the court of the Rana Kouroun, son of Oumra, who received him in a magnificent manner. He had a splendid palace built for him on the island of Jugmunder, on the summit of which he placed the Mussulman crescent. The interior was decorated with mosaics in jasper, agate, and onyx, and hung with rich draperies, and in one of the halls a throne was placed carved out of a solid block of greenish serpentine, supported by four female caryatides; and in the court a chapel, also of serpentine, was consecrated to the Mussulman saint, Madar. Many of these souvenirs of the princely hospitality of Kouroun still exist.

The palace of Oudeypoor is one of the largest, most beautiful, and most magnificent in all India, entirely covering the crest of a hill of some elevation running parallel with the lake from east to west. The plateau on which it is built not being of sufficient extent, the architects enlarged it by the construction, on one of the slopes of the hill, of an immense terrace, supported by three tiers of arched vaults. This stupendous work is built with such wonderful solidity that part of the palace is entirely supported by this artificial basis, the rest forming a vast enclosure in which are situated the barracks and sheds for the elephants.

The interior of the palace is quite in keeping with the grand style of the exterior, and is well adapted to this tropical climate. Darkened passages, ascending by an inclined plane from storey to storey, take the place of stairs. The well-lighted apartments are fitted with polished marble, which tends to preserve the freshness of the atmosphere, and courtyards, fountains, and flowers meet one at every turn. The grand saloons are hung with drapery; luxurious cushions and carpets cover the floors, and the walls are ornamented with mirrors and frescoes. One of the rooms decorated in a grotesque and fanciful manner, would excite the amusement of a European stranger, yet it is scarcely more ridiculous than the China galleries at Fontainebleau and elsewhere. The walls of the room are ornamented with European plates, cups, and saucers, the commonest pottery side by side with the finest Dresden, Bohemian glass next to a trumpery salt-cellar. The comparative value of these different objects mattered little to the Hindoo artist, who, only considering the colours, succeeded, with the aid of

23. *Night scene.* his natural taste, in achieving an effect at once original and harmonious out of these heterogeneous materials. The frescoes which cover the walls and ceilings of some of these chambers are of great interest. They comprise the portraits of all the Ranas, from Oudey Sing, the founder of Oudeypoor, to Sambhoo Sing, our contemporary, and these are followed by the most remarkable scenes in each reign. Painted with extreme care and delicacy of colouring, these frescoes are valuable memorials of the history and manners of the tribe of the Sesoudias.

One of the most curious features of the palace of Oudeypoor is, undoubtedly, its extensive hanging garden. It seems astounding to find trees of a hundred years' growth and lovely flower-beds situated at so great a height, and covering so many roofs of different elevations. In the centre of the garden there is a fountain, from which avenues paved with white marble diverge in all directions, the water being carried off in narrow channels, and lost to sight amidst groves of pomegranate and orange trees. A marble gallery encircles this enchanting spot, where the grandees of the Court, reclining on velvet sofas, indulge in pleasant day-dreams whilst taking their siesta. The view embraces the whole valley, and while gazing on this scene they can call to mind the great feats of arms of their ancestors who defended this country for centuries against the Mussulman hordes and converted it into a paradise. When fatigued with the grandeur of this immense panorama, they can turn and contemplate the fairy scene presented by the garden.

An occasion was immediately found to detain us. It was nothing less than the grand *battue* which the Rana holds annually in the Aravalis, and Major Nixon gave me such a description of this hunt, and of the magnitude of the scale on which it was conducted, that my departure was at once deferred.

On the morning of the 18th, the vicinity of the Residency bore the animated appearance which invariably prefaces the departure of any potentate in the East. Major Nixon, who took with him his whole domestic establishment, several elephants, and a great number of camels, was there, making arrangements for tents, baggage, and provisions. An excursion of pleasure in this country is no trifling matter. Luxury is an indispensable accompaniment, and for a fortnight's hunting expedition the Resident required a complete establishment— tables, sofas, arm-chairs, beds, sideboards, and plate. It would have been derogatory to the dignity of his high position if he had had one arm-chair or carpet the less in his camp bedroom than at Oudey-poor. This maxim is carried so far that, on entering a tent, you see whatnots covered with ornaments, books lying on the tables, and the *khanats* hung with pictures, exactly as in permanent dwellings.

At midday on the 20th, the preliminaries of the great annual hunt began. The Rana, seated on his hunting-elephant, issued from his palace, surrounded by a cortege of minstrels reciting hymns appropriate to the occasion, and waving great palm-branches decorated with roses. The master of the hunt, Maharaj Singjee, mounted on a richly caparisoned camel, marched in the midst of his huntsmen. The guests and nobles followed, each mounted on an elephant, and a numerous escort of mounted Rajpoots brought up the rear. The procession advanced slowly across the plain, closely surrounded on all sides by crowds of country people come to witness the sport.

When we had left the village about a league behind us, the Rana selected those who were to have the honour of hunting with him. These were only Major Nixon, Dr. Cunningham, Schaumburg, myself, and the two Raos of Baidlah and Pursoli. The rest had to content themselves with looking on. The preparations thus ended, the hunt began. The beaters spread themselves over the plain, and headed and turned a herd of wild boars, which crossed the line of elephants. Four were left dead upon the field, when the sport was considered sufficient for the first day. The procession was reformed, and returned to the camp in the same order as it went out. At the gate of the palace the nautch girls, attired in their richest apparel, met us, like the daughters of Israel of old, and congratulated us upon our success.

The four following days were devoted to hunting in the plain, in order to drive the game towards the mountains. Nothing could look more picturesque than the long line of elephants stretching through the valley. These huge animals rise above the low jungle like towers, and with a firm and silent tread advance into the midst of the thorny underwood. The most interesting part of these expeditions, and that which most displays the extraordinary sagacity of the hunting-elephants, is the pursuit of the wounded animals. The wild boars cross the line of hunters in herds, and, when wounded, they immediately detach themselves from the rest of the herd and bury themselves in the brushwood. As a wounded animal always belongs by right to him by whose ball he was first struck, the hunter has to separate himself from the other sportsmen, and start in pursuit of his game. The elephant on which the hunter is mounted must now serve him instead of a hound. He follows indefatigably the track of the wild boar from point to point, and his unshod feet tread the earth so noiselessly that he passes close to the most timid animals without disturbing them. Following, on an elephant, the track of a wounded animal, I have often seen groups of deer a few paces off, which continued peacefully to browse in spite of our presence. When the trail ceases the elephant is stopped, and one often has to look about for some time before discovering the unfortunate boar, breathless and exhausted, crouching beneath a thicket. A rifle-ball puts an end to its suffering.

On the 21st the shikaris informed us that we could now commence the *hankwa,* a word which means a "drive" in the mountains. According to their report, the game, scared by our shooting of the last few days, had taken refuge in considerable numbers among the wooded gorges. The plan of the hunt was immediately drawn up. We were to commence at the southern end of the range, and proceed thus from ravine to ravine as far as the defile which overlooks the rendezvous of Nahrmugra, where the last and great battle was to take place.

On the morning of the 25th, the hunting-party returned as far as Dubok; whence we proceeded to the *houdi,* from which we were to take part in the hunt. The name *houdi* is applied to small embattled forts, built as hiding-places for the hunters. They are generally placed at the entrance to a ravine, in order that the guns of the sportsmen may command the entire gorge. One was comfortably installed there, sofas having been prepared for the Rana and his guests, and refreshments such as beer, champagne, iced lemonade,

etc. not forgotten. Shooting from a *houdi* therefore is the least
fatiguing way imaginable of enjoying sport. Behind each sportsman
are stationed two shikaris, who preside over a regular battery of
guns. One of them is occupied in loading, while the other passes the
guns to the hunter as fast as he requires them, relieving him of those
which he has already discharged.

The *houdi* of Dubok occupies a charming position. Shaded by a
group of trees on the edge of a deep ravine, it commands an extensive
view of the plain and the Aravalis. The beaters, who had preceded
us, had ranged themselves on the heights of the mountains in large
numbers, leaving to the denizens of the forest no other way of escape
than that commanded by our guns. A great hubbub was soon heard
in the distance; a clamorous sound of gongs, trumpets, and tom-toms
rose from the depths of the jungle. In a few moments a loud crashing
was heard among the brushwood, and the first herd of about twenty
wild hogs rushed bewildered into the ravine.

The effects of our fire were apparent directly they came within
range. A few fell dead on the spot; some regained the mountains,
while others, with more sense, continued their course, and were lost
to sight on the plain. At the end of a quarter of an hour the confusion had become indescribable. The wild boars were crowded by
hundreds in the ravine, and the fire from the *houdi* thundered un-
interruptedly. Jackals and hyaenas mingled promiscuously with the
boars, the shooters occasionally bringing down one of them, as they
rushed past, maddened by terror. One panther, with more caution,
attempted to scale the rocks, and thus avoid the *houdi,* but the

stratagem did not succeed, and it rolled, pierced with balls, to the bottom of the ravine amid the joyful acclamations of the Rajpoots.

At length the beaters returned, and the hunt was over. We descended into the *nullah* to count the killed and examine our game. The sight that met our eyes was indeed frightful; the animals lay one upon the other in hideous disorder. More than twenty wild boars, about fifteen jackals, hyaenas, and jungle-dogs, and one panther, were the result of an hour and a half of *hankwa*. Of all these victims, the wild dogs interested me the most, as I had often heard of them, but till then had never seen one. This animal is of the same size as the jackal, which it greatly resembles about the head; but its fur is shorter and of a pale-red colour, and the tail is smooth. They collect in large packs, and pursue antelopes and deer, which fall an easy prey to their cunning and agility; but they never attack a man. They are not known ever to have been tamed, not even when taken quite young.

The beaters constructed litters, on which the dead animals were piled up, and our party re-entered Nahrmugra in triumph. To celebrate this day, the Rana in the evening gave us a grand dinner at the palace. The entertainment was prolonged far into the night, and we failed not to do honour to the royal champagne. The nautch girls and minstrels wiled away the long hours with their songs and dances, and we afforded them, I think, equal amusement by singing "God save the Queen" and the "Marseillaise".

In my conversation with the Maharana I learnt several curious particulars concerning the fauna of the country. Being passionately fond of hunting, he had carefully studied the habits of the animals with which his forests abounded, and appeared to possess great knowledge of them. On my expressing my surprise at the absence of tigers in the recent hunt, he replied that this, far from being unusual, was generally the case in those districts which were much infested by wild boars, as these animals, collecting in great numbers, always attacked the tigers, when they trespassed on their domain, and succeeded in expelling and even in killing them. As I appeared to doubt the possibility of such a feat on the part of animals possessing such slender means of attack, he promised that I should myself witness one of these combats, and thus prove the truth of his statement.

Our camp life at Nahrmugra was one continued series of amusements, and to give you an idea of it, I will take one day, selected at random, and describe it to you.

Our sleeping-tents were placed in a circle round two pavilion-tents, surrounded by verandahs, and luxuriously furnished. Of these one was the dining-room, the other the sitting-room or reunion tent. At six o'clock in the morning I was roused by the servant bringing me a glass of sherry. Jumping out of my charpoy with silver feet, I pulled off my clothes, and donning a simple *janghir* or close-fitting drawers, issued from my tent. I then took my place on a little heap of straw, and on looking round saw each of my companions in front of his tent in the same position and costume as myself. The *bhistees* arrived with their *mussucks,* and doused us vigorously with cold water. In a few moments more we were all assembled, in a more suitable dress, round the table in the mess tent, busily employed in discussing a plentiful *chota hazri,* or early breakfast. After a pleasant chat, whilst smoking some excellent Manila cheroots, we mounted our horses and went to explore the surrounding country, shooting a few wild fowl on the neighbouring lake.

At eleven o'clock the process of dressing was again gone through and a second breakfast served, with regard to which the only thing worth mentioning was the arrival of the Rana's messengers who every morning brought us a repast. A long file of servants, bearing dishes laden with a variety of meats were preceded by two attendants with gilt canes. These dishes consisted of roasted meats, haunches of wild boar, breast of kid, and strongly flavoured regouts and curries. Some of them, however, would do credit to the tables of our European grandees. About a dozen plates were filled with pickles of all kinds, roasted berries, and sweetmeats. We merely went through the form of tasting this huge breakfast, which served to regale our attendants, as we preferred the excellent cuisine of the Burra Sahib and the Moselle from the royal cellars. The middle of the day was set apart for the *hankwa.* At four o'clock, after refreshing myself with a second bath which effectually dispelled the fatigue of the hunt, I received visits from the Hindoo nobles who chatted pleasantly on all kinds of subjects. The dinner, as is usual in India, lasted till late and we were entertained up to midnight by the nautch girls, jugglers, and fireworks.

March 5th. The preparations for our departure are at length completed, though not without some trouble. In spite of the Rana having placed his camels at our disposal, the *vakeel,* for some unaccountable reasons, has put endless difficulties in our way. The beasts that he first sent me were either lame, or unmanageable, or too weak, and had to be sent back. At length I threatened to report it to the Resident, or even to the Rana himself, and by this means I have succeeded in procuring fifteen strong camels to carry our men, baggage, and tents, and two express dromedaries for ourselves. Our escort consists of twelve *sowars,* who, with our servants and camel-drivers, raise the number of our company to more than forty persons.

After a pleasant ride of twelve miles along the excellent road made by Taylor, at the Rana's expense, we arrived at Mynar. My head servant certainly has the eye of an artist. Our camp is delightfully situated on the shores of a beautiful lake overshadowed by gigantic trees; the village, with its graceful temple, crowns a small hill, its houses extending to the water's edge. Opposite lies a great march, whereon flocks of wild ducks disport themselves among the huge lotus leaves. I at once set off in that direction with my gun, and my first shot produced a marvellous effect; I could have fancied myself in Robinson Crusoe's island. The birds rose in a dense cloud, almost obsuring the light of the sun, and were so easily brought down that I was soon tired of such tame sport, and the *sowars,* collecting the game, carried it to my tent, secretly laughing. This was soon explained, for I had scarcely finished my breakfast when a visitor was announced, and I found myself confronted by a fat Brahmin who gesticulated wildly, declaring that shooting on the lake was against the laws, and that the village was *sahsun,* and consequently sacred. I could not tell whether his statement was correct, but I assured him that I had erred entirely through ignorance, though in fact I had right on my side, as the Rana had given me permission to hunt in every part of his dominions without any restriction; and as my good Brahmin did not appear satisfied with this explanation, I ordered him to leave the camp.

The day passed without my hearing anything more of the Brahmins of Mynar, but in the evening the Rana's *hulkara* came and told me that they had refused to obey the *purwana,* and to furnish the necessary provisions. They thought by these means to punish my indiscretion, but I tried to make them understand, through the *hulkaras,* that resistance was useless, as there were fifty of us who had had no dinner, and who were by no means disposed to go to bed fasting. As negotiations carried on at so great a distance produced no effect whatever, I gave the order to mount and proceeded toward the village accompanied by Schaumburg and my *sowars.* I inquired for the house of the chief, and in a few minutes was ushered into the presence of a stout Brahmin, full of sanctity and insolence. In vain I tried to argue with him calmly; he would not listen to reason, and only answered that I must remove my camp three miles from the village, after which he would perhaps think about sending us a few provisions. Provoked by such impertinence, I complained of his

25. *A river-crossing.*

conduct in no very measured terms, and threatened to report it to the Rana of Oudeypoor. This made him furious, and blind with rage, he brandished over my head his sceptre, a bamboo mounted with iron. At this outrageous conduct I lost all self-control and dealt him a blow which sent him flying among his counsellors. I then turned to my *sowars* and gave them permission to procure the necessary provisions as best they could. The Brahmins remained mute with astonishment.

March 7th. A march of thirteen miles, still in an easterly direction across a flat, slightly undulating country, brought us to the town of Muggerwara. This portion of Meywar forms part of the high table-land which slopes gradually towards the branches of the Vindhya mountains. The soil is rich, but the villages are few and scattered, and it is only at intervals that the monotony of the low jungle is broken by a field or a small wood.

Muggerwara, which means "Land of Crocodiles," is a town of some importance, situated on a rocky eminence, and surrounded by picturesque *jhils* (marshy pools). Our camp was pitched between the town and one of these swamps; and here I received the visits of the principal inhabitants, who were extremely obliging. Among these visitors was a *bhat,* or distinguished bard, who, when all were assembled round the fire in the evening, related to us several heroic incidents in the history of the Sesoudias, which occurred during the long wars carried on against the Mohammedan invaders, and which portrayed in the most vivid colours the chivalrous character of this people.

The village near which we are encamped goes by the strange name of Choorpara, that is, "refuge of thieves". The inhabitants, however, appear to be the most honest people in the world. They show the utmost readiness to carry out the orders of the *firman,* and bring us sheep, kids, fowls, eggs, and milk, &c., most willingly. The houses, which are numerous and well built, are almost all surrounded by fruit-trees, and the country is covered with rich poppy-fields and rice plantations, the whole landscape presenting a charming picture of peace and prosperity, and forming a pleasing contrast to the sterile moorlands through which we travelled in the morning. The blooming faces of the villagers beam with pleasure. They are charmingly sociable, and often come to chat with me. The surrounding country is flat, and to the east the level range of the Pathar mountains forms a long blue boundary-line, while before us, at a distance of twelve miles, stands like a sentinel the rock of Chittore, or "Parasol of the world," the palladium of Hindooism.

March 17th. We left Chittore this morning at daybreak, and directed our course northward towards Ajmere, the great city of the Aravalis. At nine o'clock we reached the town of Gungahar, which is the property of our good friend, the Rao of Baidlah, which circumstance induced us to make a short stay here. A sacred wood of small extent, composed of enormous trees of venerable age, lies within musket-shot of the village, and it afforded us a charmingly shady retreat where our camp was soon pitched in an open glade carpeted with smooth green turf and watered by a murmuring brook. I wandered through the wood admiring the beauty of the trees which surrounded me, and enjoying the delicious freshness, so rare in this country, while thousands of birds of brilliant plumage flew within my reach, squirrels played around me, and the monkeys examined me with curiosity. These peaceable inhabitants of the wood were not alarmed by my gun, as I took care not to break in upon the sacred calmness of the place.

March 18th. A short march of twelve miles brought us this morning to Ameergurh. At this season of the year the lake of Ameergurh dries up to half its usual size, and its creeks are transformed into marshes where wild fowl and even crocodiles may be found among the tall dead stalks of the lotus. In the rainy season it sometimes overflows its banks and inundates the country as far as the mountain; but the town is protected from the floods by a stone quay planted with trees. The surrounding country appears fertile, although but little cultivated, and much of it is still covered with a low jungle.

March 23rd. The province of Ajmere, which we entered this morning, is almost the only portion of Rajpootana proper that the English possess. It has belonged to them simply since the year 1818. The first town we reached was Deorah, situated on the outskirts of immense fertile plains. Many herds of antelopes were visible on all sides, and we managed to kill several before we reached the bungalow of Bunai. This little town occupies the centre of a valley formed by hills comparatively small, but which, being formed of immense blocks of granite, and being isolated in their position, have a grand appearance. A narrow gorge leads into the valley, and the road is commanded by the ancient castle of the Rajah of Bunai, which is built on the summit of a crag. The Rajah of Bunai is a descendant of the ancient Purihara dynasty of Mundore. Around the shores of a picturesque lake are ranged the cenotaphs of the princes of this family. The town consists entirely of huts built of mud and wood, and surrounded by a high wall of clay mixed with straw. It has anything but the bright and pleasant appearance of the towns of Meywar, with their brick walls and tiled roofs. The perpendicular sides of the mountain rise beyond the walls, and enormous rocks seem to threaten the houses beneath them with utter destruction. A *pir,* or Mussalman saint, in the olden time, had taken up his abode on the summit of this precipice, and his shrine is to this day a great place of resort for pilgrims.

On the 30th March we started for Ajmere, distant from us about fifteen miles. Scarcely had we left Nusserabad when the road led us into the mountains, and we were soon in the midst of the Aravalis. The sun rose as we passed the first defiles, and added to the beauty of the country. Sharp peaks rose on all sides of us, torn into strange forms, between which the precipices, still plunged in obscurity, formed many an abyss, and the luminous rays of the sun intercepted by the points of the rocks formed rosy halos round the lofty summits. Enormous cacti, the only vegetation in these ravines, grew here and there in fantastic groups, and on the plateaux a few large shrubs, flaming with their bunches of scarlet flowers, rose above the low jungle. Partridges, hidden amongst the herbage, were saluting the rising sun with their sharp cries, and once or twice a peacock flew off at our approach and passed before us like a sheaf of glittering emeralds.

The freshness of the morning, the songs of the birds, and the splendid view made us forget all our past fatigues. Everyone was gay, and my men chatted and laughed, for we were approaching the end of our journey and they would soon be able to return to their homes. On rounding a point we caught a glimpse of Ajmere and its celebrated fortress of Teraghur. It was a splendid view. The white houses of the town appeared framed in a thick belt of verdure, like an oasis in the midst of a desert of piled-up rocks and mountains. On approaching the town, one might have fancied one's self on the outskirts of Grasse or Nice. The country was covered with flowers, and there were fields of roses which produce the famous *attar*.

Ajmere ranks next after Jeypore for possessing the most beautiful bazaars of any town in Rajpootana.

No town in the East, not even Cairo itself, can offer such a picturesque and original sight. All the races of India elbow each other in these streets, which are narrow, and which form the principal market-place of a large tract of country, and the most various manufactures are spread out beneath the sombre stone arches of the stalls. You cannot think how amusing it is to walk through these bazaars. During my stay, I employed my mornings in wandering about, alone and on foot, through the midst of this good-natured crowd, and every day showed me something new, curious. I used to stop in front of the stalls and chat with the men who were always polite and civil. The jeweller, perched on his bench, on to which he has to climb by means of a ladder is invariably a man of high caste, with naked body bound with the sacred cord, and occupies himself in chiselling the most beautiful jewels, which would delight the hearts of the Parisian ladies, his nose supporting an enormous pair of spectacles which are indispensable to the dignity of a master goldsmith. Around him his workmen, probably his sons, mould or forge the precious metals. If I happened to speak a word to him, the good fellow, proud of my visit, would take off his spectacles, salute me, and spread before me his riches, taken from an iron box, explaining the smallest details of their manufacture with great complacency, and allowing me to choose some small trinket without annoying me by over-pressing offers.

Next him is the bracelet-maker, sitting before a fire, at which he melts his lacker, red or green, as the case may be, which he spreads over a conical mould. Dividing this with a sharp knife into narrow circles, it cools suddenly, and thus produces about twenty light rings. The bracelet-makers' wives assist them in the manufacture, and try the rings on the purchasers. There are no girls or married women of any rank or caste who do not wear several of these rings, sometimes the whole forearm is covered with them, and being as fragile as they are cheap there is a good trade in them. A little farther on I came to the musical-instrument makers, who manufacture great guitars, viols, and tom-toms. Then there are the coppersmiths, seated amidst piles of copper vessels of all shapes and sizes, from the *lota* to the amphora one yard in diameter.

Sometimes a whole street is inhabited solely by shoe-makers, dyers, or potters, who, without appearing to mind this competition, exhibit their goods side by side. The bazaars of the cloth trade and manu-factured stuffs of all kinds are the most aristocratic. These shops are clean and well lighted, and the merchants, seated on cushions of dazzling whiteness, gravely await customers, while their clerks scrib-ble figures from morning to night on interminable rolls of paper. In the midst of the gay crowd which fills these streets, there are a great many pedlars, whose cries reminded me of those of the Parisian cheap-jacks. They offer you balls of milk and sugar, besides vege-tables, knives, and betel leaves, and do all they can to impede your progress and to increase the hubbub.

On the 11th of April we marched towards Poshkur, a sacred oasis situated on the edge of the desert, nine miles to the west of Ajmere. We made the circuit of the lake, passing through the pleasant-looking suburbs formed by the villas which cover the banks of the Ana Sagur, on the other side of which rises a wall of rock, 500 feet high, which is crossed by a *ghat* impracticable for carriages. Blocks of black marble and enormous roots of fig-trees obstructed the road, along which our camels advanced with difficulty, and trees of great age, and gigantic cacti which have grown up in the midst of this chaos gave an appearance of wild grandeur to the place. The crest of the mountain consists of a perpendicular wall, sixty feet in breadth, through which runs the road, originally a natural fissure in the rock, enlarged for this purpose.

Before entering this narrow passage, we took a farewell look at Ajmere, whose houses and gardens covered the opposite banks of the lake, rising one above the other like an amphitheatre on the slopes of the beautiful Teraghur. It is impossible to imagine a more striking contrast than that which existed between this panorama and the country which met our view on the other side of the defile. Hills of sand rise on all sides up to the very summit of the Aravalis, and seem as though endeavouring to cross this barrier, which alone prevents them from overrunning the valley of Ajmere. The desert stretches to the horizon; and here and there jagged peaks, blackened as if by fire, break the monotony of its undulating surface.

We left Poshkur on the 16th, before daybreak. A short distance from the town there is a narrow valley, formed by two high mountain ranges running parallel to each other; in which the wind has driven the sand with so much violence that it is heaped up on either side to the very summit of the mountains. This unstable ground seemed to suit our camels, who advanced swiftly with their short elastic steps. The desert of Sahara does not present a more desolate appearance than did the scene before us. A few stunted bushes and here and there a blackened rock appeared above the waves of shifting sand which was ploughed into long furrows by the wind, and this dismal landscape was enlivened by a herd of gazelles drinking at a clear pool of water, which, taking to flight at our approach, disappeared among the sandy ravines.

April 28th. We left Doudon at four o'clock in the morning when the cold was intense. Thick vapours hung over the horizon, and shortly before sunrise we saw a most beautiful mirage. The picture was so perfect that both Schaumburg and I thought it was Jeypore, and it was with difficulty that our attendants could persuade us that what we saw was only an effect of the atmosphere. From the remotest antiquity, the inhabitants of plains and deserts have noticed the remarkable phenomenon of the mirage, and all in describing it have compared the effect to a sheet of water surrounded by fertile shores and fantastic buildings.

In India, where it frequently occurs, the mirage seldom resembles the effect described, and as a rule it is seen only on cold, misty mornings. At first a high band of vapour, resembling a chain of mountains, appears on the horizon, and gradually becomes more and more transparent as the first rays of the sun rest upon it, acquiring at the same time a wonderful power of refraction. It has the effect of a powerful lens, magnifying neighbouring objects, and thus transforming bushes into gigantic trees, and rocks into Cyclopean monuments. Suddenly, the top of the cloud is brilliantly tinted with the colours of the rainbow, and the lower part, becoming less transparent, has the appearance of a real mountain covered with trees and crowned with palaces, minarets, and palm-trees. This phenomenon lasts for about a minute, during which time every object is so clearly defined that, without immense experience, it is impossible to determine whether the town you see is a reality or not, and as the sun rises the vision gradually fades away. Sometimes the mirage is only a transformation of some very distant object.

The Indians have various appellations for this phenomenon. The shepherds of the great desert of Thoul call it *chittram,* or picture; the inhabitants of the steppes of Marwar and Jeypore, *seekote,* or castles in the air, and those of the fertile plains of the Chumbul and the Jumna, *depasur,* or illusion.

The difference between the *schral* of Arabia and the *seekote* of India comes from the fact that the stratification of the clouds in the first is horizontal, and in the second vertical. Whatever may be the causes of this marvellous natural phenomenon, it is certainly one of the most beautiful sights imaginable.

A Rajasthan Diary

KRISHEN KHANNA

16th Nov. Like all forts, the one in Jodhpur stands on a hill. The drive to it is pleasant enough now though it couldn't have been so for invading armies. At the entrance is the tragic emblem of young hands placed in a series of squares. Sati had been committed here too. The inner courtyards are spacious and the architecture is gracious without being ostentatious. Quite unlike other establishments of warfare, this one has rooms which open up like jewel boxes where every inch of wall and roof space is covered by large sized miniatures. These are not great paintings, but their profusion creates an atmosphere of gaiety and happiness. We are in an art gallery and not in a fortress. But the illusion disappears as we stride into a museum of arms and armaments. These are spectacular. Swords, guns, daggers of all kinds made with loving care and precision. Though their business is death, they are very beautiful.

The city sprawls lazily below with its noise of cars and loudspeakers happily dimmed by distance and height.

17th Nov. "And now," said our Rajasthani host, "I would like to show you some villages, because you'll never get the full flavour of Rajasthan until you make contact with the soil." I wondered what he knew of the soil being a senior member of the nobility. As it turned out he knew a great deal, of both the land and the people he identified himself with.

We launched across barren sandy tracts in our mechanised camel— the jeep. I won't say that the going wasn't rough. My city bred bones and muscles groaned each time the jeep descended and sharply ascended. There weren't any roads, of course, not even pathways; there were neither any tracks or marked physical features which could guide us—at least some that I could have recognised, but our friend confidently pointed out directions and navigated the vehicle with such precision as if he had a built-in compass. "Keep going straight" he would say—"A bit to the left now ... a little bit more ... and now straight ahead" and all this over flat arid land with not a soul in sight.

Land and stone for miles on end under a vast clear sky.

Eventually we came to a settlement called Khaldhar. It was in ruins. In its hey day it must have been a small township. The temple was more or less intact, but every other building was a ruin. There was a strange air of the place having been suddenly abandoned. As if there had been some terrible visitation, a plague, a drought, an earthquake, some fulfilment of an ancient curse.

I asked my friend what had happened and he confirmed my first impression. The place had been abandoned suddenly—as if fate had decreed one day that everyone must quit—pronto. This judgment wasn't limited to this township alone but to eighty-seven similar settlements which were inhabited by the Paliwal community. I was reminded of the partition of the Punjab when many of us lost our homes and many their lives. The Paliwals didn't lose any lives, and this was nice to know, especially in Rajasthan with its blood stained history where human lives were readily sacrificed on the high altar of honour and chivalry. The Paliwals left, according to one account, when the Dewan of Jaisalmer (the Chancellor of the Exchequer or the Finance Minister would be the present day counterpart) imposed very heavy taxes, and the entire Paliwal community decided to quit all at once. A clear case of brain drain even in those days, for it was the Paliwals who had traditionally provided the administrative brains for the State. The Paliwals were luckier than us in a way. They could move to other parts of the country and establish themselves without having to contend with such theories as "Sons of the Soil" and other obstructions which impede movement today.

Another account of the exodus of the Paliwals has it that the Dewan's son transgressed his status and position and made a pass at the daughter of the Ruling House, and since the Dewans of Jaisalmer were always Paliwals, the entire community decided to move. Such infringements of caste and class would not be tolerated, just as they are not tolerated today. Strange, but there seems to be some mysterious correlation between sand, honour and blood. In defence against frugal and unyielding nature and avaricious and ambitious neighbours, human societies built rigid and clear-cut systems to ensure their own survival. Transgressions of the order were threats to the community and the balance between man and nature—so the Paliwals had to go on account of the misplaced amorous inclinations of one of its junior members. I don't suppose this was the first or the last time that a privileged but indiscreet son brought ruin to a whole community.

What the son left unfinished, the newly rich in the towns comple-

ted. They tore down whole walls to obtain delicately carved windows and sculptures to adorn their own garish homes or to sell them in the antique markets. We visited two other such townships, Bhaonagar and Khuri, which had been equally devastated. I was left feeling sad and reduced.

18th Nov. Drove to Mandore which is about an hour's ride by car from Jodhpur. The countryside was beautiful. Spring was in the air and the constellations had decreed the marriage season open. Gaily attired marriage parties were a frequent sight and nowhere else on this earth is there such uninhibited use of colour in clothes as in Rajasthan. Reds, oranges, yellows of every hue and intensity were worn with such taste and carried with such dignity and poise that they made our urban fashion salons look tame. Taste is ingrained in these people. It is not individual or idiosyncratic. It is collective and has the maturity of centuries. One notices too that the more rustic the people the better the taste.

This is evident in architecture no less than in the choice of apparel. The earthen houses in and around Jaisalmer are entirely in keeping with the environment. The exteriors are primed with yellow ochre with a judicious use of black and white in sophisticated proportions —architect or artist, both the result of the collective aesthetic wisdom which has become second nature. All the same, there is the lure of the cities, the thoughts of economic betterment and the fantasies of urban delights which make young rural folk move away from their traditional surroundings.

Row upon row of uniform boxes like anthills bedeck the urban landscape. It isn't difficult to imagine that in due course these anthills will breed the same monotonous quality of life. Plastic mugs, buckets and sandals are ready replacements for the traditional, wrought-by-hand articles. After all, New York was bought for a string of beads. Civilisations get weary and tired. Anything new is preferable.

Logically enough the traditional articles of daily use are becoming collectors' items and museum pieces. Interior decorators have established supply lines to provide a "flavour of genuine tradition" to those urbanites who have never known any. So there is the frequent sad spectacle of what was once some rustic's *hooka* turned into a lamp stand. Instead of the *hooka* there could be a water jug or a piece of stone or wood carving filched from a deserted temple. To the filcher it's not filching. Since the object has no further use, it is an "antique" to be sold for a profit. This bastardised object, this combo of antiquity and futility becomes "the marriage of the old and the new".

We came to Mandore, the ancient capital of Marwar, and were taken to a gallery carved out of rock in which the gods of the Hindu pantheon are assembled. Each one with his or her attendants occupy separate spaces. Naturally they are larger than life size; they are God size, but humans have had the last say. They are all plastered white, the limbs and features being painted in garish colours. There is something humorous and jovial about them. Maybe, by endowing them with our own vulgar taste, they come closer to us and are more approachable. In an adjoining gallery are larger than life heroes of Rajasthan on their chargers. Many have been hallowed in song but more of that later.

There are strong looking *chhatris* at the entrance of the gardens commemorating the former rulers. The setting is idyllic with flowering trees and shrubs. Peacocks flash and glisten as they move. Long tailed grey langurs flit from tree to tree in graceful swinging movements. Their chatter is less disturbing than their visiting cousins down below.

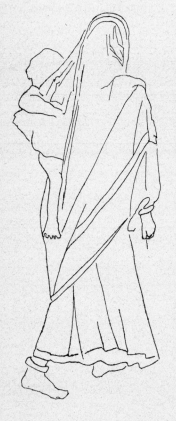

19th Nov. My friend and I were taken to Osian, some sixty odd kilometres away from Jodhpur. It must have been a large temple city once. I was reminded of Pagan in Burma, but that was in the Age of Faith. Ruins are scattered over a large area pervaded by a strange silence and a sense of infinity. The city, or what is left of it, is on its way out. Our host, a senior member of the royal household, took us to his palace. We entered a large disused courtyard. The caretaker, a man in his sixties, came to greet us. He lived there alone with his buffalo. A large Rajasthani lock was opened by turning a huge threaded key (the interior decorators of Delhi and Bombay would give their eyes for this piece of antiquity which still performed a function) and we were ushered into a spacious but empty interior. The lock seems to have been a formality.

Next to this gracious building was a Surya temple built with the most noble proportions, with two elegant pillars at the entrance and some superb bas reliefs. How naturally does art play its role. It functions in the service of the sublime, retaining its identity all the same. Nor is it important to know the names of the sculptors who fashioned it. It is there for such time as time will allow without the egocentric and pathological desire for perpetuity. Salutary thoughts for modern artists whose only venue of exposure seems to be a One Man Show and a commission agent.

The Sachiya Mata Temple is on a hill with flights of steps leading to it. We are received by the high priest and our royal hosts were led to the sanctum to have *darshan*. We followed suit. There is a profusion of sculptured pillars and the perambulatory passage is adorned by the most beautiful bas reliefs. We were given lunch which was rustic and delicious and very sustaining. We tired by now and my aesthetic appetite was on the wane, so while my friends went and inspected the 8th century Mahavira temple I spent the half hour with some gorgeous nymphs (in stone) who inhabit the walls of one of the smaller shrines in the courtyard. I cannot reconcile the voluptuous and sensual sculpture which abounds (and which I love) with the frugal and puritanical asceticism of Jainism.

My friends returned and told me that I had missed something marvellous. Apparently there are some beautiful dancing damsels in stone on the roof of a large hall next to the shrine and I was told that it was a "must" so I bestirred myself and took a look at them. They are nice—elongated and stylised and defying all sense of gravity—some of them have been abducted rather rudely no doubt by some curio dealer to make an expensive lamp stand.

On our way back we stopped at a village. Our party with our royal host was met by the village elders and behind them the men, women, children, oxen and dogs. We were taken to the headman's dwelling and formally welcomed. After being seated, tea and biscuits went round and a while later our local host offered each one of us a small black pill. It was bitter and, pretending to wipe my nose, I slipped the pill into my handkerchief. A Rajasthani friend of mine sitting next to me saw me and grinned. I raised an eyebrow and he whispered the magic word "opium". Apparently this is customary hospitality. In fact, all deals and contracts are sealed by an exchange of this pill. It is the final sealing of a pledge.

I thought it strange, and no one could give me the origin of this custom. I suppose when customs and rituals are actively practised the participants don't have to bother about origins—that's left for anthropologists to ponder over. I suppose the pill must have been quite important for those who were about to launch suicidal attacks, for no normal mind could cold-bloodedly commit the womenfolk to mass burnings—a wee dram of opium must have helped to attain the necessary degree of insensitivity to death.

By and by the musicians came in. Superb looking men with string and wind instruments. An old man with a lush white beard parted at the centre began to sing. His voice was gusty and his gestures matched. I couldn't follow the words but gathered that chivalry was his theme of "some battle long ago" very romantic, very Wordsworthian.

What an anachronism—a civilisation trying desperately to preserve itself and its antiquated values in the face of modern democratic forces. While the folk singer sings of ancient chivalry and his accompanist furiously plies the bow, a jeep rushes past on the main road with a crackling loudspeaker urging all to vote for Shri So-and-so in the coming by-election.

There are such parallel realities which don't seem to focus into a single image. On the one hand our royal host is treated with the respect and honour accorded to his position through the centuries. When they hear that he is coming or see his car parked near a rest house, entire villages will assemble to pay homage and seek his blessings. Yet the political process deprives him of his right to be their spokesman and their leader.

20th Nov. We went to see a village on the way to Sardar Samand. The inhabitants were almost without exception extremely handsome and good looking. I remarked on this and was told that this community was also well regarded for its intelligence and industry. So much so that young men from the community were eagerly sought and were even welcomed to improve the stock without binding them by marital ties.

24th Nov. We were taken to see the fort of Jaisalmer. It is about 290 kilometres from Jodhpur. I had been told that we would have to wade through sand dunes which appear and disappear as commanded by the winds. Indeed the shifting desert is on either side of the new road on which we drove and which makes Jaisalmer accessible. Tales of whole expeditions getting lost in the desert seem utterly believable. The fort is huge and crowns the top of a vast hill which rises dramatically out of the desert, its mellow gold luminous in the sun. The sort of monument which gives credence to all the legends which have grown around it, including the one about Lord Krishna's prophesying its subsequent history. After the initial vision the fort takes on the semblance of a freshly made sand castle.

There are houses and shops and bazaars, narrow cobbled lanes, which wind like a maze. A small Jain temple contains very beautiful old manuscripts, and in its courtyard kings gave audience and ladies were set ablaze. It would take days to see the entire fort—its Havelis, the gates, the temples, the houses of artisans and soldiers, the intricately carved pillars and screened windows. Every epoch made its contribution including our own practical and mundane age. The modern Indian contribution is in the shape of a large ugly water tank, higher than any of the ancient structures, and a blot on the view.

26th Nov. There is just too much to see and I'm beginning to show

signs of aesthetic indigestion. Our party is joined by two 'famous' people—Mulk Raj Anand, the writer, and Philip Johnson, the architect. We are being guided around the Sas-Bahu temples. Philip Johnson remarks on the similarity of style between these and Khajuraho and after examining the plinths declares that these are precursors. Mulk Raj Anand points to the upper structures and the abundant sculpture, and through wordy alchemy tries to dissolve all that solid stone into metaphysics. The stream of words ends, the sculpture remains.

As often happens, some local villagers have joined us. An old man carries a beautiful carved staff. Philip Johnson tries to acquire it. He is willing to pay a hundred (rupees or dollars not specified). The old man smiles. He is amused at the offer and Philip's desire to own it. Philip thinks the man is shrewd and is jacking up the rate. Finally he says he will pay whatever the old man wants.

The old man continues to pleasantly refuse and asks someone to explain to the sahib that this staff is a family heirloom and therefore cannot ever be sold. To think that Philip Johnson, an avid collector of art, was refused a sale by a Rajasthani peasant!

27th Nov. Chittorgarh. Another citadel crammed-jammed with history. Endless sequence of tales of heroism and valour, of treachery, tragedy, of sacrifice and passions. The walls still bear the evidence of young female hands on their last journey to the sacrificial flames. What, one wonders, was the point of it all. These stones stained by the blood of centuries, only to end up as grist for Colonel Todd's mill and as a tourist attraction. As we climbed the ramparts, our well versed and rehearsed guide pointed to a place where Jaimal made an heroic stand, and as he was about to continue his ballad of bravery, Philip Johnson intervened and said, "Yeah, but he lost eh?" So we climbed on till he pointed to a place where Patta was shot. Once again the paean of praise was cut short by Philip. "That's fine," he said. "But they lost out." This American insistence on the value of results seemed to dampen our guide. What did it matter (in terms of eternity) as to who won or lost. It was the quality of action that was indelible.

Sketches by Krishen Khanna

Over the Mountains on Horseback

H. TORRENS

(1862)

We were six white men in all. Our intention was to march from Simla due north to Le, the capital of Ladak; thence westward to Sreenuggur, the capital of Kashmir; thence in a south-easterly direction via Chumba and Kangra back to Simla—in all, a circuit considerably over one thousand miles.

Our servants were mostly Hill-men, the exceptions being our Chef de Cuisine, Ali Bux, and our *khitmutgars* or table servants—all swarthy Mussaulmen of the plains; also Mr. Terrear, or Terrear 'sahib', as he was called by his fellow-domestics.

A Madrassee by birth, a Christian in creed, and colloquially a fair English scholar, Terrear was invaluable. He was an old campaigner, too, having been servant to an English officer in the Crimea, and therefore no stranger to the hardships of cold and wet, or the mysteries of life in tents. On this expedition he was Captain Clarke's factotum, valet-de-chambre, keeper of the privy purse, nay, cook too, on sundry and not infrequent occasions when his master's appetite could not brook the long intervals in our (in his opinion) slowly recurring meals; and last, not least, packer of chemicals, and photographic assistant in general.

Our baggage was for the most part packed in *khiltas,* and the whole of it carried on men's backs, so that we had daily to hire from the villages on our route some fifty or sixty men to serve as beasts of burden for the day's march.

Our tents were of the ridge-pole pattern, or, as they are called in India, *pauls.* They were six in number. One served as mess tent, another housed the elite of the servants. Captain Clarke and myself had a tent a-piece, and our four companions doubled up in the two others. They were each of them, when dry, sufficiently light to be carried by one man, that is, the canvas part of them. The bamboo poles were tied in bundles and formed two or three extra loads. We carried with us a supply of iron tent-pegs—a most necessary precaution, for wooden pegs soon split and become useless after a little fair wear and tear; and in treeless countries such as Ladak there are no means of replacing them.

On a rainy morning in the middle of July, the 'official friend' and I turned our backs on Simla, and trotting briskly along the New Road, reached Mahasseo in time for breakfast. We were in saddle again at two p.m., and leisurely proceeded on our way towards Mattianah, a distance of some five-and-twenty miles from Simla.

The rainy season was at its height; dense clouds of mist clung to the hillsides, and clothed their summits with clouds of sodden grey, effectually concealing the beauties which on brighter days would have tempted us to linger on our road; and after some five hours' alternate riding and walking, we were not sorry to reach the Mattianah dak bungalow, or post-house, as evening was closing in.

Here we halted for the night, and renewed our march towards Narkundah at daybreak. Narkundah is justly celebrated for the magnificent view of the snowy range which the elevated ridge (nine thousand feet) on which the dak bungalow stands, commands. But on this tearful 18th day of July we were fated to see no such view.

The bridge over the Sutlej at this point is a noble one of its kind, formed of lengthy deodar beams, supported at either end by piers formed of mighty timbers wedged for half their length in the solid rock; the other half stretches out over the gulf below, and is surmounted by other timbers, which overlap those on which they rest by some two or three feet. These in turn are overlapped by others, and so gradually and cautiously the opposite buttresses yearn towards each other, and seem to strive to meet. Then come the lengthy deodar beams aforementioned, and span the length between.

26. Bridge over the Sutlej.

We had some misgivings as to whether our ponies would cross this somewhat perilous arch, for though the footing was of a good breadth, the low wooden parapet had on one side been stolen— for firewood, I presume. At any rate, there it was not, and the loose timbers creaked and trembled, and the entire structure heaved with our weight.

The contrast between the climate of the valley and that we had just left was most striking. Fever-impregnated and pestilential, with an atmosphere oppressively close, the short time we took in crossing it was long enough to give more than one of the party a headache. This, however, rapidly left us as the healthful breezes of the green hill-side, purer, cooler, and more bracing at every successive zig-zag of the precipitous ascent, fanned our cheeks.

What a road it was! We reached our tents about two hours before nightfall; they were pitched close to a large and tolerably well-built village called Dilass. Our photographer, who, for artistic purposes, had preceded us by some hours, was there to receive us, and had caused, so he said, a fatted lamb to be killed for our evening meal. The flesh was lean, indisputably, and the flavour somewhat rank—suggestive of kid of goat (if kid it was), or rather of a patriarch of that hirsute flock. We were too hungry for severe criticism, but one and all arrived tacitly at the determination that not again should our artist order dinner. No!—*ne sutor ultra crepidam*—let him stick to his chemicals.

Our route now descended rapidly for a couple of miles, and then proceeded along the side of a well-cultivated valley, dotted thick with villages. One of these was the point fixed on as our halting ground, and towards it we hurried, for again was the sky overcast and rain-clouds imminent.

Our tents were hardly pitched ere down came the storm, and from about four o'clock of this day, the 20th, to the morning of the 23rd, it rained with hardly an interval of sunshine worth the name. This we were, however, prepared for—it was only what we had a right to expect in the rainy season; and on the 21st and 22nd we trudged along wearily but hopefully through the wet, knowing that in a few marches we should be out of its influence.

Our halting-place on the 21st was Kot, a village beautifully situated on a rising ground which would anywhere else be called a mountain, but compared with its surrounding alp, appeared to our rapidly enlarging intellects but a molehill—a conclusion to which we arrived after reaching its summit, *bien entendu*.

Meanwhile, the coolies have been arriving one by one, slowly but surely toiling up the hill, and as the tents came up, dank and sodden with the constant wet, Chumpa, stripped to his shirt, which clings to his rounded limbs like an upper skin, seizes them, and rapidly spreads them out. "*Puthar, burra, burra puthar,*" is his cry as he inserts one end of the stout bamboo pole into their languid folds. A heave, and up it rises; but Chumpa has over-calculated his powers. Heavy with wet, the canvas droops and threatens again to collapse, when Nurput, that useful vagabond to the rescue with a rush and a shout and some very bad language, catches the tottering canopy! Two minutes more, and the close-packed mass of helpless canvas is a tent. A tent? A home for a king.

It was just the very day for Indian servants to outdo themselves. Surround them with luxuries, give them fireplaces, grates, ovens, and a park of batteries de cuisine, with meat the tenderest, and vegetables the most rare, and you will more than probably starve for want of a wholesome dish. But put them in camp in rainy weather, with no such appliances—say you want dinner, and you will get a feast!

Our road led us over the mighty shoulder of the Jilauri Mountain. At this it goes straight, without a swerve, without an apology for the extra exertion to which it is about to put you. No cunningly-devised zigzag is here to mask the difficulties of the way, and half-persuade you to lay the flattering unction to your soul that, after all, it is only a very gradual slope—long, perhaps, but very gradual. The stern reality stares you in the face without disguise; there is not the slightest attempt made to mitigate the incontrovertible fact that up that infernal hill you must go, and what is more, you must go straight.

The path down Jilauri towards the north-west is, in comparison with its ascent from the south-east, quite a gentlemanlike means of communication, though strongly marked by the characteristic straightforward obstinacy of all the Kulu roads, which, as a rule, ignore the proverb, "The longest way round is the shortest way there." Eschewing all divergence, they make straight for their destination, and great indeed must be the obstacle that turns them aside.

It was no use going on; we had outstripped the coolies, and tents and baggage were all behind, so there we sat and watched the long line of 'weight carriers' as they struggled down the mountainside, with cautious step and slow. But who is this coming along at a steady run, with bent back, but active feet? The coolies one and all make way for him as he rapidly passes them. As he draws near we perceive that he, too, has his burden—a small and light one, but carefully packed, and as carefully carried. He comes straight towards us, redoubling his pace, and makes obeisance. But his panting *salaam* is rudely interrupted by the "official friend", who, snatching the man's bundle, tears savagely at its wax-cloth covering. To our questions he makes no audible reply, but shies at our heads *pour toute reponse, Punches, Evening Mails, Saturday Reviews*, and, most welcome of all (with a mental reservation in regard to duns), letters from England!

It was the post! At the next two halts, Platch and Largi, are houses for the accommodation of travellers. This is a great advantage, enabling one to send on the tents independently to Bujoura, a distance of about five-and-forty miles. Two deep and rapid unbridged rivers have to be crossed between Largi and Bujoura, rendering the absence of tents and all such impedimenta highly desirable. It is a weary walk to Largi—a weary sixteen miles along a narrow gorge shut in on either side by high rocky cliffs, whose base stood in the mountain stream which foamed along beneath us.

We had a long day's work before us. Early to bed and early to rise was the order, and at five o'clock next morning we were at the river's bank, superintending the passage of the baggage by a *jhula,* or rope bridge. A sketch gives a better idea of the reality of a rope bridge than any word-painting can. Every item of our property had to be slung over separately, in the manner depicted, and everything reached the opposite bank in safety. In fact, there is no danger so long as the ropes hold; you are tied firmly into your seat and remain passive and powerless during the operation. The sensation is not a pleasant one, especially when you are kept pendant in the middle to be photographed, as befell me. Barring the sense of choking and the wrench to your neck, it must be very like hanging. My Jack Ketch left me dangling in mid-air for something like two minutes to give, forsooth, an air of interest to a photograph. I have sat for my portrait, but never sat I so still. Remonstrance I knew was in vain, for the roar of the torrent beneath would have drowned the cries of a Boanerges. My poor goats! They struggled vehemently for the first few seconds, but a glance below convinced them of the futility of resistance. Realizing at once the horrors of their helpless position, they stoically resigned themselves to their fate.

Another minute, and we were reclining in a state of indescribable beatitude, tended on by willing slaves, who proffered first, a light for our cigars, next, a hot, fragrant cup of tea! It was, barring the ladies, a pagan's paradise.

The scene before us was a most lovely one: we looked straight up a green valley some two or three miles broad, which stretched away till the eye could no longer distinguish where its fertile slopes ended, or where the mountains which bounded it began; above these again rose peaks so unearthly in their purity, that but that they moved not, we should have called them clouds.

Glittering down the centre of the valley rolled towards us the Beas river—now broad, still, and placid as a lake—now confined in a narrower channel, racing on with rush and roar till it entered a deep gorge on our left. Here it seemed so to curtain its fair proportions that it was difficult to persuade oneself that this narrow,

27. *A khilta* carrier.

dark, smooth stream was the same as that which just now seemed to fill the valley with its broad bosom.

About thirty natives stripped to the skin, each provided with a *deri* or inflated buffalo hide, were busily paddling our servants and baggage across the stream, here of great breadth, and running with a current so rapid as to carry the paddlers some distance down ere they reached the opposite bank. Then, shouldering their hides, they marched up the side to a point a good way above, and entering the water again, paddled back for a fresh load.

When heavy and bulky articles are to be transported, two skins are brought together, the ferryman of each laying hold of one of the projecting legs of the other skin, and a frame or raft supporting the burden lies across the backs of both. A *charpai*, or Hindustani bedstead, forms the most convenient raft. Horses and mules are led over, the waterman holding them by a string in one hand, whilst he paddles himself and his human load across in the manner above described.

When not inflated, the skin is slung over the back, and carried about without any inconvenience. It seems equally well adapted for the transport of large bodies of men and baggage over the most rapid rivers, or so likely to be serviceable as a wreck-buoy or float, to be carried on board ship. The cost of a *deri* is usually a rupee and a half (three shillings), and its weight not above sixteen pounds. A couple of *deri*-men usually accompany persons of rank hunting in the hills, in order to carry them across the mountain streams, the rapidity and fury, if not the depth of which, render it impossible to ford them without such assistance.

The Major and myself stripped and bathed a little higher up. We told each other that it was very jolly, and that we enjoyed it immensely, but our shivering limbs and chattering teeth gave the lie direct to our protestations. It was snowwater, not long emancipated from its parent glacier. I shudder as I write!

A few miles more and we reached our tents, pitched close to Bujoura, a small village commanded by a fort now in ruins; but it must formerly have been a place of some consequence. Moorcroft, who saw it some forty years before, calls it "a large square fort belonging to Kulu. It consists of square towers connected by a low curtain, the whole built of hewn stone, strengthened with beams of fir". Bujoura is situated on one of the main roads to Le. From Bujoura a march of about nine or ten miles took us to Sultanpore, otherwise called Kulu, and the capital of the province of that name.

The road is a good one, and appears to be kept in good repair. It passes between a youthful avenue of trees, which already afford a grateful shade, and is crossed in two places by branches of the Serbari river, a considerable feeder of the Beas. At the confluence of these two streams, a little higher up the valley, Sultanpore is built, in the angle formed by their uniting water.

28. Deris out of water.

Next morning brought us tidings of our ponies. They had arrived in Sultanpore, but in so sorry a plight, so battered, bruised, and footsore, that we did not order them to follow us; but, sending back for our saddles and bridles, directed the grooms to remain at Sultanpore till their poor charges had recovered from the effects of their mountain travel, and then to proceed by easy marches to Belaspore, on the Sutlej, where we hoped to meet them on our homewards in October.

After a short march of about eight miles we halted at Jug-et-sook, a small village, where is a good-sized bungalow for the accommodation of travellers. Soon after leaving Jug-et-sook the valley narrows rapidly. The road, such as it is, ascends at a more perceptible incline, cultivation grows less and less, and the 'forest primeval' encroaches more and more. On an eminence to the right were some hot springs, of the existence of which our Hindoo servants were eager to tell us, and also to ask leave to make a pilgrimage to them.

After leaving the hot spring, we scrambled on by an unfrequented bye-path to the banks of the Beas again, here so dwindled that we forded it without difficulty. Two or three miles more of a gradual ascent brought us to the village of Bourwa, a little beyond which we camped. We had now reached an elevation of fully seven thousand feet. All cultivation had ceased; the pine, the cypress, and the cedar took the place of peach, apricot, and walnut tree; and rugged cliffs and rocky mountain sides met the eye that so lately had rested on the trim enclosures and carefully irrigated fields of the valley.

To our right was the Rotang-ki-joth, or Rotang Pass, which we were to scale on the morrow. We could see but little of it for thick rain-clouds draped it almost to its feet, and what little we did see looked cold, wet, dreary, and inhospitable. The villagers, on learning our intentions, recommended us to send on as much of our baggage as we could spare at once, and in reply to our somewhat anxious inquiries as to the sort of weather we were likely to find up there, said, "It always rains on the Rotang-ki-joth!"

These birds of ill omen croaked falsely. The morrow broke bright and clear, and we reached the banks of the Chandra river without a drop of rain. It was a stiff walk—a good seventeen miles— in the course of which we ascended six, and descended three thousand feet.

Such the order of our march at starting: our path is a rough and slippery one; to our right roars unseen, at the bottom of a narrow gorge, the Beas, now reduced to the limits of a mere mountain stream, but pent in that confined channel, a formidable torrent still. To our left rises an overhanging cliff, dripping with constant moisture: now up, now down, now turning to the right and now to the left, there is no end to our path's vagaries. At last it debouches on a valley in miniature, not a quarter of a mile broad, and in length but little more. High cliffs crowned with pines shut it in on the right hand and on the left, and from their summits fall frequent cascades, which form into rivulets at the bottom, and intersect the valley. I counted nine of these cascades, and never remember to have seen a more picturesque spot. After crossing the little valley we arrived at the foot of the pass proper.

The pass itself is of a good breadth, and almost level, the ascent on either side becoming less and less steep as it approaches the summit. The surface is wet and spongy from the number of small springs which ooze from the ground in all directions. The top is marked by a cairn of stones surmounted by a few sticks, from which rags of cloth flutter. This is erected for the purpose of propitiating the spirit of the mountain, who, to judge from the terrors of his favourite haunt, must be an awful bogie indeed.

A piercingly cold wind blew through this broad gap in the mighty ridge, and clouds obscured the mountains on either side. Moorcroft computes the height of the Rotang Pass as above thirteen thousand three hundred feet. Other writers make it a little lower, and call it thirteen thousand.

The descent, at first very gradual, soon becomes steep, and in some places almost precipitous. It leads down to the left bank of the Chandra river, which foams along at the bottom with great rapidity. We crossed by a suspension bridge, formed of ropes of birch twigs, about one hundred feet in length; this was the third different description of bridge which had occurred in the few last marches. We had walked across the wooden (*sango* or *shingzam*) bridge, we had been slung over by the rope-bridge (or *jhula*), we had sat astride on inflated skins (*deris*), and so been ferried across; but now had come the most ticklish operation of all.

Pendant between two ropes of birch twigs, which stretched across the stream from rude piers erected on either bank, hung, cradle-like, a continuous hurdle of the same frail material, attached to the ropes above by a sort of open basket-work; this was the footway, and the ropes above served as balustrades on either side. This footway was further supported by two or three smaller birchen ropes laid side by side beneath it and stretching across the stream in the same manner as the two upper ropes. This rude suspension bridge is called *chuq-*

29. Paddling on deris.

zam by the natives, and is common in many parts of Ladak.

We left the province of Kulu on the other side of the river, and were now in that of Lahoul. With a new country shall begin a fresh chapter, but first you shall read, if you have a mind, something staid and statistical, touching trade.

The Chandra river, at Koksar, is the principal obstacle to this line of traffic between the wool producing countries of the north and the plains, and is so serious a one that it threatens to close it entirely against beasts of burden, for the current is too rapid for them to be swum across in any safety.

We marched for about ten miles along the Chandra river to a village called Sisoo. Here we breakfasted under the shade of a little plantation of willows, the only trees we had seen since leaving Koksar. This province of Lahoul was a strange contrast to that of Kulu. Save where the hand of man had been at work, all was bare and barren. We passed several villages en route—the houses of stone, plastered with mud, flat-roofed, and two and three stories in height. As in Kulu, the cattle were lodged in the lower story. To those above, the notched stem of a pine-tree formed the only means of access.

Near each village was a carefully-cultivated willow orchard—all pollard trees—and patches of carefully-irrigated barley and buck-wheat. In the fields women were working; from the house-tops women stared at us; and women carried our baggage. Where, then, were the men? We found, on inquiry, that all the able-bodied males pass the summer in transporting merchandise between Ladak, Chumba, and Kulu, and sometimes further, on strong, well-shaped, surefooted ponies; and not a few, no doubt, spend the summer months in contraband traffic on their own account.

From Gundla we marched to Guruguntal, which is a small village situated near the confluence of the Chandra and the Bhaga rivers; two other villages were in sight at this point—Tandi and Gosha.

The missionaries of Lahoul are well acquainted with the Tibetan language, which they speak, read, and write with facility; they have translated into the dialect of the people around them a portion of the New Testament, the "Harmony of the Four Gospels," and some other works of a religious character; these have been printed with the aid of a lithographic press, which they work themselves and a number of copies have been distributed.

Our path on leaving the mission house passed through a good deal of cultivation, carefully fenced in small enclosures, and abundantly irrigated. It then entered an extensive grove of the pencil-

30. Facing page.
A jhula *or rope*
bridge.

cedar, after which it led through a barren country, pleasantly interrupted now and then by the patch of green which invariably surrounded every village or small cluster of houses. After about twelve miles it debouched on a little plain; here, close to a little village, was the paternal mansion of Tara Chund, differing in nothing save in size from the houses of the village; but a few ruined towers showed that once upon a time a small fort had stood there.

We came across a manufactory of grass shoes today. Some half-dozen women seated by the way-side, each with a bundle of grass beside her, were diligently plaiting the frail material into long strips of different degrees of thickness, while others rapidly made it up into sandals.

We sought the shade of a few pollared willow trees till our tents should arrive. Tara Chund and his sons came and squatted there as well, and a circle of villagers and retainers of the Lahoulee grandee stood at a respectful distance, and looked on at our proceedings with deep interest.

Soon the circle opens out and admits the passage of a grave procession, headed by an aged Tartar, bearing on high a mighty brass teapot, and followed by others with trays of sweetmeats and spices. These are placed in the midst of us, and Tara Chund proceeds to do the honours. The beverage flowed from the twisted spout in a thick, deep red stream; it tasted like rich chocolate, and but for a certain greasiness of flavour, this tea a la Tartare was very palatable. The teapot is soon empty, and returns for a fresh supply; but the second brew is hardly drinkable, for this time the tea has been seasoned with salt, not sweetened with sugar. . . .

We here first met the yak (bos grunniens). The yak is short, but of immense frame and strength, with a small head, short horns, and long black hair reaching to the ground, beneath which is a sort of undergrowth of short soft wool. The oxen mostly used in Ladak are hybrids between the yak and the common cow. The progeny, *dso* or *zho*, inherits much of the strength and power of endurance of the sire with the docility of the dam, and is used for ploughing, as well as carrying burdens. The milk of the hybrid cow, *dsomo* or *zhomo*, is much esteemed.

We made a short march next day to Dartcha, a hamlet of one or two houses, built in the angle formed by the confluence of the Dartcha and Bagha rivers.

We pressed on merrily next day to a camping ground called Patseo, to reach which we had to cross a rude bridge of felled trees and slabs of stone. But it was still early, and though already had

31. Facing page.
A twig bridge.

Chumpa pitched a tent or two, the "official friend" gave the order to strike and pack them, and we were soon en route again for Zing-Zing-beer, where, said Tara Chand, was a good piece of level ground for camping.

The scenery now became wilder at every step, and we soon entered a rocky valley, which towards its upper end divided into two deep gullies. It was up the right-hand one that we toiled. Mother earth had here clothed herself in armour of proof. Rock, bare rock, rose on either side; rocks, sharp rocks, lay under our feet, and above was a clear blue sky, from which poured fiercely down the rays of the mid-day sun, melting the snow which yet lingered in the clefts of the lofty crags into tiny cascades and rivulets, which came dancing, leaping, sparkling down, delighting in their escape from their icy prison above, while down the gorge, keen and cutting as a knife, drifted a wintry blast fresh from the eternal snows.

A mile or two more and the gorge widened. Our path now wound up the left bank of a rapid torrent. It was all "against the collar" and grew steeper and steeper as we advanced. We had commenced the ascent of the Bara Lacha.

On a sudden, turning in the pathway we come upon a young travelling merchant who had passed us in the morning, gazing attentively at some object on the mountain to our left. As we come up, he announces that some ibex are feeding up there, and that if the sahibs like, they can go and shoot them. We stare, and gaze, and look through fieldglasses, but no living thing can we see. He shows us the place, though, where the ibex had been feeding when he saw them and proves their late presence on the spot by indisputable facts, so we cannot be angry with him.

A dak arrives next morning before we are out of bed. There is a letter from Buckley, who is only three marches behind us, and begs us to wait for him. A halt is ordered in consequence, and scouts are sent in all directions to look out for ibex.

A bleak spot is the Zing-Zing-beer, well worthy of its barbarous appellation. It is situated about half-way up the Bara Lacha Pass, and must be at least fourteen thousand feet above the level of the sea. Our onward path led across a snow-bridge to our left, and so up the pass.

"Master! See! Big pheasant near to tent. Lord Sahib have gone to shoot." It was Terrear's voice which roused me, and I tumbled out of bed. In another moment two reports, rapidly following each other, told me that the "official friend" had fired "right and left". A minute after he passed by my tent-door, triumphant, but very cold and sleepy. He had shot a couple of snow-pheasants, and was going to bed again.

The snow-pheasant is an enormous bird, only found in or near the snow. Its colour, a dubious sort of neutral tint, is hardly distinguishable from the rocks on which it loves to dwell. It rarely flies, trusting to its sturdy legs rather than its pinions for safety when threatened with danger.

Excelsior! Higher and still higher we climb, till filling up a round basin in the solid rock, a clear, deep lake, of about a mile in circumference, meets our view. This is considered to be the source of the Surag-bhaga portion of the Chenab.

We rest awhile on its bank, and talk very pluckily about bathing, but without the slightest intention of committing any such imprudence. Another half-hour's walk brought us to the summit of the pass, sixteen thousand five hundred feet.

After crossing the plain we commenced a gradual descent along the left bank of a rivulet which took its rise on the summit of the pass. Frequent torrents now crossed our path, all flowing into the rivulet on our right, which increased rapidly in volume, till after a mile or two it flowed into a lake of singular stillness, about three miles round.

This lake is called the Yunam lake, and the rivulet which flows out again on the other side is, after its baptism in the lake's yellow waters, called the Yunam river. We skirted the left bank of this little lake, and then, following the course of the Yunam river, commenced a rapid descent through a very chaos of mighty fragments of red rock, which lay grouped about in grotesque attitudes, and pitched our tents on a small grassy plain which stretched below.

It was on this little plain that we first saw the marmot (Arctomys Thibetensis). It was quite a marmot warren. Their call is a peculiar shrill whistle, and they have immense confidence in the fancied celerity with which they can betake themselves to their holes on the approach of danger. They will sit on the mound of earth above their burrow, and let you approach, gun in hand, within ten paces, before they take refuge in it, and even then they pause to utter a warning note—a delay which is fatal to them. We shot two or three. Their fur is soft and thick, and of a rich brown, much esteemed by the natives.

We delayed starting next day for some hours, in the hope that the baggage of our new comrade would come up. This delay was nearly fatal to the precious boxes containing the camera and other paraphernalia appertaining to photography. Many of these mountain streams, fed as they are almost entirely by the melting of the snow, are easily fordable in the early morning, but later in the day become impassable; and again at night, when the frost checks the thaw caused by the mid-day sun, dwindle back into fordable insignificance.

So it was with the Lingtee river, which we did not cross till nearly eleven o'clock. It was as much as the ponies could do to stem the current; and the coolies were obliged to join hands, and, thus linked together, struggle across in a long chain. The men carrying the photographic boxes were about the centre of the line, and when in midstream they stumbled and fell prone in the rushing water, the whole line wavered for a moment, then with an effort joining again, minus the two broken links, reeled on to the opposite bank, regardless of the fate of their two fallen comrades, and mindful only of their own safety.

The feelings of our artist at this mishap can be more easily imagined than described. His impassioned gestures—for we could not hear what he said, the roaring of the torrent drowned every other voice (and perhaps this was as well)—attracted the notice of Nurput, Noura, and a few others. The chosen band of Ladakhis, seeing Noura, good at need, about to rush in to the rescue, dropped their loads and ran to the assistance of their leader. Joining hands, the stalwart party reach the fallen wretches, and drag them and their loads by main force to shore. They were only just in time—another minute of immersion and the men would have been drowned, and (which, between you and I, the artist thought of much more consequence) the boxes lost for ever!

Strange to say, nothing was broken, thanks to Terrear's good packing, and thanks to the well-fitting lids of the stout brass-bound boxes, only a few plates got wet. But it was long ere the photographer recovered his wonted equanimity. Next day we completed the ascent of the Lung Lacha (seventeen thousand feet), and descending gradually for some miles along a narrow and in many places very steep defile, we at last crossed and camped on the right bank of a little stream called the Leimgal.

This was a long and weary march, the general character of the scenery being the same as before—rocky valleys overhung by snow-clad crags, and at intervals small plains covered with a scanty vegetation. At starting, the heights on our left took most fantastic forms; they appeared to be composed of sandstone, deeply caverned in all directions, and their summits, broken into castellated shapes, gave the appearance of a long line of lofty battlements.

32. The black tents
of Rukchin.

We were now at the foot of the great plain of Kyang, one of the
loftiest in the world. It stretches for five-and-thirty miles from the
base of the Tung Lung Pass to the heights above the river on whose
bank we halted, its breadth varying from two to five miles. In the
summer months it is inhabited by a few shepherds, whose flocks
delight to browse on its scanty but nutritious herbage; but ere the
approach of winter they leave the wild expanse to its native
rulers—the wild horse, the monstrous wild sheep, the hare, and the
marmot.

Our camp was a most picturesque one; the tents, pitched on a
narrow slip of ground between the stream and the steep mountainside, gleamed white in the light of the fires which blazed at intervals
up the slope, lighting up with their flickering flame the wild faces
and forms grouped around them. "Just like a scene at the Princes-
ses," said the Major, and so it was.

The hunters of horses pursue their sport later in the day, but
when we meet that evening, at the black tents of Rukchin, nothing
has been bagged but a few hares, which fell to my gun. Rukchin is
an encampment of Tartar shepherds, whose low tents of black goat's-
hair cloth nestle in a little valley which debouches on the plain. A
little brook flows down it, and around it the grass grows thick and
green amid large clumps of furze. Thousands of sheep and goats and
a few yaks cover the low hills which bound it, dappled though
they are by frequent broad patches of snow. The flocks are driven
down into the valley at night, and a cordon of vigilant sheep-dogs,

whose baying makes the night hideous, prevents them from straying.

On the 13th August we bade adieu to the gentle shepherds and shepherdesses of the Alpine Arcadia of Rukchin, and slowly wended our way over the plain to the foot of the Tung Lung Pass. I more than once, when riding over this plain of Kyang, experienced the delusion of the mirage. I had ridden far and fast, enticed on and on by the distant gambols of a wild horse, who every now and then would stop, and paw the earth, and gaze wonderingly on the strange creature approaching him. Then, tossing his head and neighing shrilly, would vanish in a streak of dust, so rapid was his flight; and when this dust had cleared away, would be seen grazing peaceably half-a-mile off.

I give up the vain pursuit, and turn to retrace my steps. It is noon; the sun's rays beat down fiercer and fiercer. My eye-balls ache with the glare and the whole expanse around me seems to dance and quiver in the fervent heat. Then on the horizon would appear a cool sheet of water. I reason with myself about it, and wrestle and fight against the strange belief in what I know to be a cheat, which still gains ground despite my calmer judgment. I cry aloud that it is a delusion and a snare. But I lie. My heart believes it to be water; and my senses are now revelling in the anticipation of a cool delight which my intellect tells me is unreal; and when the distance that had lent its enchantment to the view was passed, and the cheat was palpable and evident, though mockery was on my tongue, and a sneer on my lips, as I said to them, "Lo! did I not tell ye so?" yet on my too credulous senses disappointment weighed bitterly.

Next morning we mount the Tung Lung Pass, seventeen thousand five hundred feet. It is not a long climb, for we camped at an elevation of at least sixteen thousand feet, but it is very steep, and the snow which fell in the night, and now covers the path to the depth of three or four inches, retards our progress a great deal. But the summit once reached we descend rapidly for some miles, and as evening comes on enter the picturesque town of Ghya.

We observed a change in the dress of the men here; instead of a close-fitting skull-cap, a slouching cap of rough woollen cloth, generally black, was worn. Grass shoes, too, had disappeared, and thick soled, square-toed boots, of which, to use an Irishism, "the upper leathers were of felt", had taken their place, much apparently to the comfort of the wearer. Above these, greaves of felt, reaching from the knee downwards, and confined by long garters of black coarse braid, neatly wound round them, helped still further to protect their nether man.

We had, for the last two marches, been rapidly descending, and were now at an elevation of about twelve thousand feet. The change of climate consequent on this difference of altitude had most beneficial effects on our invalids, who vowed that nothing should ever induce them to visit the elevated plains of Rukchin again.

Next day we journeyed for about nine miles along the left bank of the Indus. The first part of our march was over a bare, stony plain, utterly destitute of green, and surrounded by bleak, snow-tipped mountains. It widened out as we advanced, and in the distance began to appear belts of trees, promising from afar off shade and relief from glare and heat.

It was two marches to Le, a little over twenty miles, but the Khlon promised us as many coolies and ponies as we could possibly want, and we determined to make the double march. We left Marchalang early, and followed the left bank of the Indus for about ten miles to a village called Chachot, through a valley that increased in width and fertility at every step.

Our path led us now over broad grazing meadows, intersected with wet ditches, which supplied the smaller watercourse used for irrigation. Opposite us, on the other side of the river, built on a rocky eminence, was a castle, flanked by towers and surrounded by a battlemented wall, and at its foot a straggling village reached close up to the walls that protected it; while on the left bank, villages, farm-houses, and cultivation grew more and more frequent.

The entrance to the capital is very striking. We crossed the Indus by a wooden bridge, then, leaving the river, and turning off towards the mountains, which still hemmed in the valley on either side, passed over the stoniest road in the world to where, in a low-lying range of rocky hills about two miles from the river, a sudden dip appeared; through this, we were told, we could see Le.

After passing this range of hills we came on two manis, nearly half a mile in length, and flanked by lofty *tchoktens;* then came another narrow, steep, and rocky defile, up which the path wound. It was now quite dark, but the frequent lights, the hum of voices, and the barking of dogs told us we were in Le at last.

The tents were pitched in a grove of poplar trees on the other side of the city, and here we found our comrades wondering at our non-appearance, and clamorous for dinner.

It was the 17th August, exactly one month since the "official friend" and I rode out of Simla, during which we had crossed the Himalayas and marched at least four hundred miles.

Our camp at Le was pleasantly situated; a thick grove of poplars shaded us from the sun, and while we were not sufficiently far from the city to make a shopping expedition a weary walk, we were not near enough to run the risk of being mobbed by inquisitive towns-folk. We spent three days at Le, more for the sake of our servants, who were weary and footsore, and our invalids, who sorely wanted rest, than for sight-seeing purposes.

There is but little to interest the traveller in the capital of Ladak. From a distance, the city has an imposing appearance, which it owes entirely to the palace, which, built on a slight eminence, possesses a front of two hundred and fifty feet and is seven stories in height. It towers "like a tally bully" over the cluster of squalid houses and dirty lanes at its foot, an apt symbol of the Dogra rule. Its white walls, too, have a slight slant inwards from base to summit, as if they shrank back with aristocratic disdain from contact with the plebeian huts below.

Proud though it be, it however submits to the supremacy of the church; for high above it, on the summit of a rocky mountain, is a monastery, or lamasery, as Huc more correctly terms them, with its painted battlements and flags. In the centre of the city is a large open market-place; this on the arrival of a *khafila,* i.e., caravan from Yarkund and Persia, must be a busy scene. The city of Le itself is enclosed by a low wall, with square towers at intervals, which stretch-es up the slope of the hills. This appears in Moorcroft's time to have been in good order, but it is now in many places demolished and ruinous, and houses have been built outside it. Plantations of poplar surround the city on all sides.

The streets and lanes open out from either side of the market-place, and are narrow and tortuous, forming a most intricate laby-rinth. The houses are built generally of bricks burnt in the sun, and are sometimes three stories in height. The roofs are flat, formed of poles of poplar laid across, resting on the outer wall. Above these, a sort of hurdle of osiers gives support to a layer of straw and earth, a species of covering but badly calculated to keep out rain.

At Le we were joined by a sleek, well-dressed native, who brought to the "official friend" a letter of greeting from Rumbeer Singh, the Maharajah of Jumoo, in whose territories we now were, and inform-ing him that the sleek, well-whiskered *munshi*, the bearer of the flow-ery epistle, written on vellum, stamped with sprigs of gold, and encased in a kincob cover, would attend him throughout his journey-ings, and that a small guard of soldiers would also accompany us.

33. Facing page. A view of Leh from the market place.

We left Le on the morning of August 21st. Our road led us along

the little Le rivulet, past the fort, down to the Indus, and for some little distance followed the windings of its right bank. Then climbing a sandy hill up to the right, it traversed a weary plain of rock and sand for a few miles, when bethinking it of the green margin of the river it had so foolishly deserted, it turned suddenly to the left, down a steep ravine, which, after turnings and twistings without number, each of which it led us to believe was the last, finally debouched on a narrow plain skirting the river bank.

I was more than once vividly reminded of the scenery of the south of the Crimea as we marched through the Indus valley. There was the same abrupt contrast between luxuriant vegetation and bare rock constantly recurring. The villages were similarly situated, and even the inhabitants resembled greatly in dress and appearance their Crim Tartar brethren. From Nikra to Hemis was a short march of about ten miles. We finally pitched our tents about three miles from the great river, under a grove of the sacred *Shukpa*, or pencil cedar. We were stretched on the grass beneath the shade of these venerable trees, listlessly dreaming away the hours, when a sudden commotion in camp roused us from our reverie.

The Kahlone called for his pony, clambered up into the high-peaked saddle, and rode off at speed. Soon the stamp of advancing cavalry fell on our ears, and, winding down the steep defile in front of us, a brilliant cavalcade of about a hundred horsemen, armed with sword and spear, wretchedly mounted, but most gaily caparisoned, appeared in sight. In the midst of the troop, attended by a select staff of Sikh officers, rode the new governor.

I cannot say that any very great preparations were made on our part for the great man's reception. A rude *charpoi*, or native bedstead, was the "official friend's" throne of state; the cedar-grove his hall of audience; a faded dressing-gown, thrown over a flannel shirt of dubious hue, his robe of ceremony; his crown, the grey foragecap of the Simla Volunteers; and his courtiers some three or four sunburnt Englishmen in their shirt sleeves, with beards of a month's growth, and the appearance generally of Californian gold-diggers, while all were remarkable for that winning and conciliating demeanour towards foreigners that the Briton is so famous for, especially when those foreigners are, as we courteously term them—niggers!

From Nurla to Khallach the road followed the course of the Indus, which is here shut in on either side by lofty cliffs of red clay. Shortly after leaving Khallach we crossed the Indus by a good wooden bridge, which the Sikhs have fortified on the Le side of

the stream. A sudden and steep ascent up the cliff on the right, for about one thousand feet, brought us on to a large bed of yellow clay, after crossing which, the picturesque village and monastery of Lama Yurru came in sight.

34. Modern Ladakhi women, much as they would have looked like centuries ago.

Next day we crossed the Pass of Namikar, and halted at a place called Turgot, situated in a green valley shut in by lofty and barren mountains. Shortly before camping we had passed an enormous figure, sculptured in rude *alto relievo* on the face of an isolated rock that towered high above the pathway. The figure was that of Chamba, a Tibetan divinity, and its proportions were colossal. It seemed to mark the limit of the realms of Boodha—to say to Mahommedanism, "Thus far, and no farther"; and will, doubtless, stand sentry here long after the fierce tide of the religion of Islam has swept past it.

A march of about eleven miles through a long narrow valley brought us to Paskyun, which is a large but ill-built, and widely scattered hamlet, and its inhabitants are all Mahommedans. We remarked that Ali Bux here adopted a voluminous green turban, which he wore throughout the rest of the trip; and now that he had reached a country of true believers, of brother-followers of the Prophet, comported himself generally with a dignity and lofty arrogance of demeanour quite edifying to behold.

After breakfast we left the valley of Paskyun, and ascended the heights to the left. The summit reached, we found ourselves on a broad plateau, on whose stony surface not a blade of grass was visible. It sloped down gradually in front of us, narrowing as the slope became steeper, and finally came to an end where the waters of the Turu river, coming from the south-west, meet with those of stream, the Wakachu, we had followed as far as Paskyun.

The view from the crest of this plateau, looking to the left up the course of the Turu river, was one of the most striking I ever saw. I attempted to sketch it, but my brush has failed to give any idea of its grandeur. The Turu river, which at its confluence with the Wakachu spreads out to a great breadth, is crossed by a series of small wooden bridges and causeways, and on the tongue of land between the two rivers is a Sikh fort, built on the same principle as that of Le. After crossing the river, we encamped on its left bank opposite to the fort.

This was a long and trying march, especially for four-footed beasts and their riders; the path was in many places so narrow that ponies could with difficulty find a footing. Our poor little antelope, the gift of the Governor of Le, died today of fatigue, Noura said (to whose charge it had been confided), but over-eating was probably the real cause. We had killed it with kindness. Misfortunes never come singly. One of my milch goats, too, departed this life during the day's march, and with her, alas! her infant son, who had seen the light of day only a few hours.

We halted at Dras, and pushed on next day eagerly, for in front of us, behind the blue lines of mountains topped by snowy peaks, lay our Promised Land—the "terrestrial paradise," Kashmir.

After a walk of a few miles, the valley suddenly ceased, and our path dived headlong into a deep chasm, over which "*The crags closed round with black and jagged arms*". The descent was almost precipitous, but happily not a long one. At the bottom was a mass of ice and hardened snow, in which were embedded rocks, stones, and gravel. Through this a small stream with difficulty worked its way, and a few yards further on leaped into the black void of an abyss beyond. We could not see where it lighted after its springs but the sound of a continuous splash rose up from the depths below. A difficult zigzag cut in the face of the rock led us up the opposite side of the chasm. A forest of stunted birch trees clothed its summit, through which the path wound on, gradually ascending to where, about half a mile ahead, was the ridge of the pass. This ridge reached, Kashmir was before us!

It is a thing not easily to be forgotten, that first glimpse of Kashmir. The softer beauties of the vale proper, indeed, are hid from you. It is one of the many valleys whose sides, stretching from the snows of the Himalaya to the warmth and fertility at their base, seem to bind together summer and winter with one mighty wreath of green forest that lies before you. And it is in these valleys—which form as it were the "woods and forests" of the immense domain of which the vale, par excellence, is the flower garden—that, to my mind, Kashmir's richest and rarest gems, as far as inanimate beauty goes, are to be found.

The descent of the pass into the valley was very steep and rugged. Thick forest began as soon as the ridge was passed, and our path led through—"*One vast mass | Of mingling shade, whose brown magnificence | A narrow vale embosoms.*"

The name of this valley is Sindh, so called from the river which flows down it, and the pass we had just crossed was the Seogi-La, a continuation of the same range which we had before scaled by the Bara Lachi Pass. This chain of hills forms a natural boundary between India and Tibet.

Throughout the second day's march, our path led through a continuous orchard of walnut, apple, and pear trees growing wild, mingled with sycamore, horse-chestnut, and ash. After a while, houses built of logs appeared, and here and there land had been reclaimed from the forest and put under cultivation. Towards the close of day we crossed the Sindh river by a good wooden bridge, and ascending the left bank, which rose to a considerable height above the river, came in sight of the famous Vale of Kashmir, bathed in the warm rays of the setting sun. In the far distance rose the snowy peaks of the Pir Punjal, tinted with the rosy light of eve, and between stretched a vast expanse of undulating plain, which bore on its broad bosom cities, lakes, and gardens. But even as we looked the sun sank behind the western range of hills; and though the snow-crowned brows of the distant hills still sparkled in the gleam of his parting ray, over the valley shadows gathered fast, and veiled it from our sight.

We were now about twelve miles from Sreenuggur. The chunar tree (*Platanus orientalis*) is a very striking object in a Kashmir landscape. Notwithstanding their extreme luxuriance of foliage, and the stately height to which they attain, they are said not to be indigenous to the valley, but to have been introduced by a governor of the name of Ali Mirahan Khan, who held office from 1642 to

35. A Ladakhi chorten is seen at left.

1657 under the Mogul dynasty. Of the mosques and garden palaces, the marble founts, and sculptured pillars, with which a succession of Mogul emperors embellished the valley they loved so well, but few remain intact, and even these show marks of neglect, dilapidation, and rapid decay. But the chunars are in the lusty prime of life—more lasting memorials of the magnificence of the Delhi emperors than all the costlier monuments, the work of men's hand.

The suburbs of Sreenuggur call up reminiscences of those of Constantinople, with their turbaned tombs of departed Moslems—their green luxuriance of nature, and squalid penury of art—but the fancied resemblance grows less and less as you approach the city. To enter it you pass no imperial walls or massive gateways, but little by little the houses huddle themselves close together, and at last form a street, narrow and dirty and stony enough to induce a relapse into your dreamy memories of Stamboul, while here and there a high-featured face and stately form, in ample turban and flowing robe, stalks by and helps to keep up the delusion.

But now a gap in the wall of houses on your right lets in a stream of warm light on the dark, foul footway, and through it you see close by you, not the broad bosom of the breezy Bosphorus or the crowded waters of the Golden Horn, but a sluggish stream, glittering in the sunlight, and covered with boats of all sizes. Some heavily laden barges are being slowly punted upstream, while others of lighter build glide past merrily, propelled by the rapid strokes of half-a-dozen paddles—it is a busy scene. And on the opposite side of the river you see reproduced as in a mirror a facsimile of the bank you stand on—the same houses, the same landing-places, the same people—for it is the Jhelum that you look on, and on its right bank and on its left stand the crowded dwellings of the capital of Kashmir—Sreenuggur.

We fell quite naturally into "the even tenor" of the ways of the "do-nothings"; and as the shadows began to lengthen on the first day of our arrival, we found ourselves stepping into our canoes and preparing for our evening pull on the still waters of the Jhelum as if we had done so all our lives.

The delight of a plunge in the river is our first waking thought, and attired simply in dressing gown and slippers, we shuffle, half-awake, into our boat, which is paddled into mid-stream. Then, after pausing for one timorous instant on the gunwale, we throw ourselves overboard, and float lazily down stream, exulting in the refreshing chill of the water, as yet untouched by the sun. Then coffee or chocolate, a cigar, a stroll up the river-bank, a leisurely toilette, and so to breakfast about ten of the clock—such the daily programme of our early morning performances in Kashmir.

And now a crowd of Kashmiris, manufacturers of shawls, gun-makers, workers in leather, in papier maché, jewellers, tailors, shoemakers, watch-menders, etc. besiege us. They are remarkable for mechanical talent. Kashmir shawls have achieved a world-wide reputation; their gun, pistol, and matchlock barrels are much prized by natives, holding a second rank to those of Scinde only. Of their papier maché, all those who have the luck to see the Exhibition of 1862 will have an opportunity of judging. The jewellers, shoemakers, and tailors only want a pattern; they will imitate it with the minutest accuracy. And if your watch is out of order, you may entrust it without compunction to that ill-looking fellow in a greasy gaberdine, who will squat down in a corner of your room or tent, deliberately take it to pieces, and perform all necessary repairs there in your presence.

Let us, then, pass away from the crowded pathway of the Jhelum, leave behind us Sreenuggur and its busy traffic, and tell our boatmen to explore that canal to the left, the greensward and overhanging foliage of whose thickly-planted banks promise a pleasant change to the tumble-down houses and dark lanes that have so long hemmed us in.

A pair of massive wooden folding gates, through which your boat glides, is all that at first meets the eye; and they actually and prosaically form the entrance to the lake. But away to the right, a considerable eminence, known as the Tukht-i-Soliman, or Solomon's Seat, rises from a green bed of gardens and orchards, and may be said, poetically speaking, to form one side of a grand portal to the lake. But for the other side you have to look a long way—as far even as the height on which the fort is built, which from Solomon's Seat must be some three miles distant. So that this poetical portal is, to say the least, a tolerably wide one!

But we have still a long pull through a narrow channel ere the broad expanse of lake opens out in front of us, and then its surface is so thickly covered with the broad leaves and rosy flowers of the lotus, and the tangled green of the *sinhara,* or water-nut, its sides so concealed by floating gardens, that it is difficult to form any idea of its size. The first glimpse is, however, enough to convince you to its beauty. To the left, the eye wanders lingeringly over a fertile tract of lake and meadow, to where the Hurree-purwat Fort shows a castellated line against the blue sky.

I have purposely omitted to describe the Shahlimar Gardens whilst recounting the beauties of the lake in the sunshine. This queen of gardens does not look well by day light.

The proper thing to do is to give orders for a nautch at Shahlimar —to tell your Ali Bux that you will dine in the largest of the summer palaces—to read nothing but Lalla Rookh all day, and towards evening to step into your boat and glide over the still lake to the gardens, doing your best to feel "as felt the magnificent son of Ackbar".

We dine in a spacious hall, open on one side to a mimic lake, bristling with water-spouts, and fed by a prettily-managed waterfall, whose stream falls over niches in which little lamps are gleaming, now brightly, now dimly, as the watery veil that covers them varies in its volume. On the other side a handsome corridor leads out on to a stone platform of some extent, whence a long vista of lamps and sparkling jets d'eau stretches away down to the large lake. This path of light tapers away till the eye loses it in the distance. The black shadows of the trees and tangled thickets of the garden close it in on either side, and above, in a sea of fleecy vapour, floats serenely the lady moon. On this platform preparations are being made for the nautch. Already has a white floor-cloth been spread, the orchestra is beginning to tune up, and the merry prattle of women's voices tells us that the fair artistes are only awaiting our good pleasure to commence their performance.

Apart from the strange beauty of the scene around, the nautch itself was a vastly superior performance to any I had yet seen. The orchestra of pipes and tabors, guitars and drums, occupied the back of the stage. In front of them sat demurely about a dozen nautch girls, and between the ladies and our arm-chairs stretched the white floorcloth on which they were to dance, while on either side was a closely-packed row of turbaned heads, among which we easily recognise our friend Syf-oolah-Baba, and torch-bearers and boatmen, mingled with our own servants, are grouped at the back.

This over, we seriously think of going, but insist, before we actually depart, on one more song from Ghoolabie, the belle of the evening. But she is coy, and has got a cold, and is tired; in fact, she wants pressing, and it is some time ere she can be prevailed on to lay aside her Delhi looking-glass, the gift of some one of her many admirers, and yield to our entreaties. At last she comes forward and sings.

We now discarded the boats in which we had lounged about the environs of the city, and hired in their place large barges big enough to carry self, bed, baggage, and servants—of these we had one a-piece; the *munshi* and his men another; and Ali Bux, with his pots and pans, *khitmutghars,* and the rest of the servants, followed in two more. It was quite a little fleet, and our Ladakhi coolies, relieved of their loads, marched up the river bank besides us. Our progress was slow, for we were towed up the stream by drag ropes, harnessed to two or three men. But for people not in a hurry, and blessed with a climate such as that of Kashmir, it was the perfection of lazy travelling.

The valley of Kashmir is about 5,000 feet above the level of the sea, but the climate is not so cool as might be expected at such an altitude. In September the weather is what English people would call relaxing—like a Devonshire summer—and in June and July it is at times, I am told, very hot. But wood, and water, and the snowy peaks that gird the valley in, alike conspire to cheat the sojourner into the delusion that it is not so. There is a Persian proverb, a quaint paradox enough, but which expresses the same idea in terser language: *"Gurmush nah gurm ast / Surdush nah surd ast"* ("Heat there is, but hot 'tis not; cold there is, but cold 'tis not).

In the winter, the hills around are covered with snow, and it lies in the valley itself in January and February. The shooting at this season must be unrivalled—bears, leopards, deer, etc., all find their mountain haunts too cold, and seek the comparative warmth of the valley, and as native shikarees told us, actually mob the villagers. This somewhat startling statement, though doubtless a grossly exaggerated one, has yet a fair basis of truth to rest on. The magnificently antlered *bara-singa*, or 'stag of twelve tyne,' may be shot close to the habitations of men, and the smaller species—the antelope and musk-deer—are equally daring in their approach to the haunts of their natural enemy. As to bears—they must literally swarm, for during the fruit season the black bear abounds in the valley itself. And when food becomes scarce, the highlands too cold, and he is joined by his brown brother of the mountains, their number must be formidable indeed.

By all this time we have been progressing slowly but surely up the sluggish stream. The sun has set, and the little fleet comes to anchor. With the first glimmer of daylight we are in motion again, and when we awake, the place of our anchorage is far behind us. Early in the afternoon we reach a bridge similar to those of Sreenuggur. The sides of the river are thronged with boats, and the banks with people. We have reached Islamabad, and leaving our boats, walk to the town, situated about half a mile from the river. We pitch our tents in a small walled enclosure planted with giant plane-trees, and through which flows a clear stream full of fish. Over it are built summer-houses, humble imitations of those of Shahlimar—our "lines have fallen in pleasant places". We purchase a few of the

36. The ruins of Martundh.

patchwork carpets, for the manufacture of which the town is famous, dine in one of the cool summer-houses, and so to bed, full of virtuous resolutions to start on our march betimes on the morrow.

We breakfasted at Muttun, just outside the holy precincts of the shrine. Our Hindoo servants were at once pounced upon by a crowd of hungry Brahmins, summoning them to "wash and be clean"; it was some time, however, before a bargain was struck. Our people wanted to do their cleansing cheap, to pay in a lump, to take a family ticket, as it were, for the performance, but this very praiseworthy and economical desire on their part was fiercely combated by the priests, whose threats and exhortations eventually gained the day.

Our path led up a steep ascent for about three hundred yards on to a long, narrow plateau, which stretched out into the valley, and at the extremity of which were the ruins crowning the declivity which sloped in a graceful sweep down to the level of the vale below.

Though antiquaries assign to Martundh a date nearly as far back as the Christian era, its monolith pillars, massive walls, and imposing gateways still remain firm amongst the scattered debris that extend all along the plateau, showing that once upon a time a busy city stood there. Thanks to the enormous size and weight of the blocks and slabs of stone of which it is built, Martundh has resisted not only the slow march of time, the sudden shocks of earthquakes, but also the efforts made by man to sap its foundations; for so noble a monument of Hindoo greatness could not fail to be an eyesore to the modern conquerors, who plied the pickaxe in vain, and found fire of no avail against its solid strength.

The people of the country attribute these ruins to the Pandus, the favourite princes of the heroic age of Hindoo history, whose exploits and wars with the rival family of the Kurus constitute the main subject of the great Sanskrit epic, the *Mahabharata*.

We lingered here till the sun was high in the heavens, and then strode down the slope across the valley to Uchibal, where we found our camp ready pitched. Uchibal was the scene of many an imperial merry-making in the good old days of Mogul rule, of Shah Jehan and Jehanguire. Now the gardens are desolate and neglected, a tangled desert of weed and briar, but the stream, like a true philosopher, flows on calmly and contentedly as ever.

A Journey to Ladakh

PUPUL JAYAKAR

In the early 1950s no road connected the highlands of Sonemarg that lie at the base of the Zo-ji-la pass to the vast plateau of Ladakh, Tibet and, further still, to the main trade routes that cross Central Asia, routes that for centuries had travelled over mountains and deserts, to connect Western China to Eastern Europe. A tenuous air service had been established during the 1948 war with Pakistan, operated by the I.A.F., ferrying troops and vital supplies to military bases at strategic points on the route to Leh and the frontiers of Ladakh, Tibet, and Pakistan—forces guarding some of the highest passes in the world. Before Independence, a mule path to Leh, open for four months in the year, wandered through the Zo-ji-la pass, past Dras, with its thunderous winds blowing directly from the steppes of the distant North, on to the green oasis of Karghil.

In the hinterland of Karghil were the tiny village settlements of Garkund and Tarchik, inhabited by peoples claiming to be pure Aryan descendants of settlers who came into India with Alexander the Great. From there the path passed Maalbek, with its monumental free standing sculpture of the Bodhisatva Maitreya carved in the 7th/8th century by craftsmen from the Kashmir valley, a presence that spread abounding stillness and compassion to the weary traveller on the path, to the rocks and empty spaces. From here the way grew treacherous, narrowing, rising higher and higher till it traversed the terrifying rock held Fotela pass at a height of 13,397 ft., beyond which dramatically all snow, wind, clouds, trees and dust disappeared. The path continued over rocky, sun dried wastelands to the 12,000 ft. high plateau of Ladakh. The caravans that crossed this formidable route kept open a life line that brought to Ladakh cloth, salt, and other essential commodities in exchange for the precious raw wool clipped from the backs of the sheep that grazed on mountain sides 15,000 ft. high.

From my childhood I had dreamt of this land and, so, during the 1948 war with Pakistan, when a seemingly impossible air route

through the most dangerous air space in the world was established *37. Ruins of an* and army planes started flying between Srinagar and Leh, it was *old monastery in* inevitable that I should attempt to go there. Permission to fly was *Ladakh.* near impossible to obtain. I was informed that I needed clearance from the army chief, the Defence Minister, and ultimately the Prime Minister. However, in 1953 my connection with the handloom and craft industries and the anxiety of the government to stimulate the economy of Ladakh made it possible, after determined effort, for me to get permission. Ladakh was known for the spinning and weaving of wool, its silver and goldsmiths, its wood carvers and painters of *tankas*. It was early June when I undertook the journey. The snows lay blocking the Zo-ji-la and the Fotela passes. I was warned that it would be very cold and that a prolonged stay in the rarefied atmosphere of Leh could be dangerous unless one were acclimatized.

The army plane was a Dakota, it flew twice a week, landing at the Leh airport at a height of 12,000 ft. The journey was through precipitous gorges of the Indus Valley and other rivers that watered tiny tracts of this region. With a comparatively low flying height the Dakota could never fly above the clouds or mountains, and so the flight to Leh, at the time, was considered one of the most hazardous in the world. The early June morning of my flight was fortunately clear. At the airport I was asked to put on a parachute, was shown how to use it, the mechanism of which I promptly forgot, having a totally non-mechanical mind. I had gruesome visions of parachuting on to a steep mountain side or dropping into the depths of an inaccessible river gorge alone, forlorn and helpless. I questioned the pilot but he appeared embarrassed, and told me those were the rules, but assured me that nothing would happen.

A General, his staff, and another high ranking army officer were in the plane with me. The plane had no passenger seats and we sat on little wooden benches at the side. Later, I was invited to join the pilot and the General in the cockpit. We flew swiftly over Sonemarg and the Zo-ji-la. The snowfall had been heavy and a white landscape lay below us and above us and around us. In the distance we saw the giants of the ranges soaring into the piercing blue of the sky. The landscape was constantly changing and very soon we were approaching high rocky mountains, the dividing line that separated the snows, the dust and the winds from the desert tracts of Ladakh and Tibet. Precipitous gorges provided the route through these soaring mountains. Rapidly the plane entered the rock held route. Far below us was the fragile line of the Indus river with tender rice green borders outlining it. Then as the gorge narrowed it was as if we were entombed by savage cliffs, guarding the portals of this secret land. The sky was not visible nor was what lay below us. Beyond was endless rock.

At times the route was so narrow that it appeared possible to stretch one's arms out of the plane and touch the gnarled rock surfaces. The colours of the mineral and fossil held rock were constantly changing—dark rust reds, ochres, and umber browns predominated, with an occasional amethyst, lapiz lazuli, or the blue of a peacock's throat. As we came out of the gorge we found ourselves flying over a vast seascape of convoluting rock, hewn by millions of years into a sacred pattern, incomprehensible but narrating through its silent spaces and its sharp serrated pinnacles the story of this earth's struggles and its splendour. There was a total absence of wind, snow and sound. The alchemy of the early morning sun's rays was transforming the crevices and the jagged rock formations to a fantasy of cathedrals and temples. The colours of the rock were brilliant with the young tender sun, revealing the energy and primal life that lay awake within the seemingly dead stones.

Amidst this vast rock-held wasteland the monastery of Lamayuru, built in the 16th century, rose tier on tier against and part of the sheer cliff side. Its message of solitude and aloneness was devastating. The earthy colours, the buffs and deepening browns of the stone-

38. Facing page.
A dramatically
situated monastery.

built monastery, fused with the changing tones of the rocks. Beyond Lamayuru the mountains slowly receded and we were soon flying over the high plateau that lies close to Leh.

The air strip in Leh was primitive and dangerous as it directly faced a mountain at one end. We landed amidst crowds of Ladakhi men, women and children who had run on to the air field, making the landing even more prone to disaster. The flying machine was still an instrument of splendour, mystery, and delight to the Ladakhis, isolated from the rest of the world by impassable mountains. The Dakota's machine kept running while it was off-loading the General, his staff, and me along with the cargo. It would remain running till it flew back, as otherwise there was a danger of the machine freezing and the plane refusing to start.

An army jeep (there were only two in Leh, attached to the army base) met us and as soon as I was free of the parachute harness, I was driven to my residence, the house of the Collector of the district, a small adobe building with a flat stone roof and tiny holes for windows covered by thin rice paper instead of window panes through which the light filtered. There was a total absence of wood in the building, no window frames, no wooden rafters and of course no electricity. The toilet was a hole in the mud pressed floor.

In the afternoon, I visited a few craftsmen, and saw a famous painter of *tankas* finishing a painted cloth that had taken him three years to do. He was painting the cloth in an open courtyard. It was meant for the great festival at the monastery of Hemis that was due shortly. I saw a lone surviving silver smith, who was only prepared to produce against orders. The bazaar was a tiny street with shops selling cloth and utensils. In one of the shops I found a miniature horse with short legs, elongated body, and lean prehistoric jaws. A dark unburnished bronze, the animal had an archaic purity of line and a total absence of detail to distract from its proud desert head, lifted in an attitude of listening. Obviously cast in Central Asia, it suddenly became the focal point of this vast arid area of deserts and mountains and high solitudes.

The men and women of Ladakh wore brown woollen homespuns; the men had conical caps on their heads, while those worn by the wealthy were lined with fur and brocade. Round their necks, and on their head dresses most of the women had worn massive chunks of turquoise beads, pendants and intaglios, the chill blue of the stones sharply illuminating the dark tobacco toned garments. Seemingly, the turquoise, the sunsets and the sunrises were the only colours in the Ladakh landscape. The rest was an endless waste

of flat stretching dun coloured land with mud houses clustered around the main street. Overpowering the landscape, rose the palace of the kings of Leh, Le Chen Spal Khar, the building of which was started by Gyalpa Jam Yang Namgyal in 1570 and completed by his son Sen Go Namgyal in 1580. Rising tier upon tier into the stars it looked desolate and deserted, although the Raja and Rani still lived there.

39. Monks with traditional wind instruments, played usually at festivals.

It was evening, and the distant mountains turned to varied tones of ripe apricot, gold and smoky purple. In the dustless, windless spaces, colours assume an extra-sensory intensity. They pierce and probe, illuminate, flood and annihilate the viewer. Distances grow difficult to calculate. The mountains seemed within walking distance, though they were over seventy miles away. At night my host, knowing my interest in the esoteric, had invited some ancient Lamas noted for their wisdom and knowledge of the scriptures to meet me. It was difficult to converse as everything had to be translated. At first they were non-communicative and it was only when I asked them some questions in depth that their faces lighted up and they talked with some excitement. Speaking of the meditative states, one of the Lamas said, "We reveal to the mind of him who asks that which by him is understood"—a profound statement which to me had much meaning. We spoke of the Ka-grut-pa and other schools of Tibetan Buddhism, of Tantra and Yoga and of the unbroken line of the Gurus.

The next morning we started in an army jeep for the Hemis monastery. Built in the late 16th and 17th century, it was among the most sacred and important of the early *gumphas* of Ladakh. The road stretched for miles over a bleak, barren, flat landscape. After travelling some distance we came upon a lone horse and rider carrying a bundle on the back of the animal. We asked him his destination, and he said Lhasa, and that it would take him three months to reach. He was the only traveller we met on the thirty-odd miles to Hemis and he became a symbol of the lonely traveller, the cross fertilizer of the cultural streams of the world who through the centuries had journeyed along the ancient trade routes, undergoing formidable hardships to seek adventure, or wisdom at the feet of a Guru, carrying with him the culture and artifacts of his country and bringing back with him a fragrance of alien symbols, myths, religions, arts, sciences and technology. At various places along the road to Hemis were lime and mortar structures known as *chortens,* monuments built over the remains of *siddhas,* the enlightened ones, masters of Tantra and esoteric lore, practisers of magical ritual and secret doctrine. Around the *chortens* were piled river-smooth prayer pebbles, inscribed with the mantra *"Om Mani Padma Om"* deeply engraved in black, in Tibetan script.

The approach to Hemis was through hair splitting bends up a hillside. Distance in space and time distorts, but I have memories of a towering *gumpha* before the gates of which stood nearly a hundred monks—young boys and old men. With them, gnashing their teeth and growling, were numerous Lhasa terriers, tiny, long haired, fierce watch dogs of the *gumpha*. In front stood His Holiness, Stag-Tshang-Raspa, the boy head of the Hemis *gumpha*. Born in 1941, in Lhasa, the child had been revealed through the divinations of the oracles and the astrologers of the Durgpa School of Ka-Grut-Pa lineage of Tibetan Buddhism. No signs of the seeds of the sacred wisdom radiated through his fat laughing face or squat body. He had a child-like delight in the jeep, and before we could proceed into the *gumpha*, insisted on taking a joy ride on the precipitous approach road, much to the horror of the army personnel, afraid of an accident to the revered child.

At last Stag-Tshang-Raspa was ready to show us his treasures. We walked through a doorway into a square courtyard facing the main shrine. Memory over the years has dimmed, but there are lingering images of crumbling frescoes on the *gumpha* walls, images from the Tibetan pantheon, the Mahakala and the Dharmapals, guardians of the gateways, with masked ferocious faces, three eyed with blue-toned bodies and bare fangs and with skulls adorning their crowns, dancing with drawn swords their terrifying dance of death, terror, devastation and the futility of life. Of mysterious beings floating on green, red or golden clouds, and of naked *dakinis*. I particularly remember one wall where the compassionate face of the Buddha appeared in paintings unfolding the life of the enlightened one; mature, rich azures, rose madders and tender rice greens came through the centuries old grime. Memory evokes images of vast altars with numerous gilded icons of the Buddha, the Bodhisatva and Tara placed on the high places, that soared to the darkened roof; of incense and strong smelling musk diluting the smell of decay and mould.

The little boy-incarnation flitted from altar to altar, opening chests, bringing out armfuls of ancient brocaded fabrics, Chinese and Indian in origin, *tankas* which one had no time to examine, illuminated manuscripts, silver utensils and more gilded icons. At last he appeared satisfied and took us to his personal chapel, the shrine room where under the guidance of the wise men of the *gumpha*, he fasted and meditated through long stretches of the day and night. We

40. A monk.

41. The head lama conducts prayers. Notice the delicate frescoes in the background.

climbed endless steps to the roof till we came to a square room, every inch of the wall space either hung with *tankas* or gilded and lacquered with paintings of mythical animals and winding plants. A door from this room led to the meditation chamber. On the altar I saw two masterpieces of the bronze caster's skill, one of the Buddha and the other of Tara. Cast in the classical style, these gilded icons appeared very early specimens and possibly originated in India. Between them there was an exquisitely chased silver bowl, filled to the brim with water and shaped as a lotus flower; rose petals floated on the surface. We were told with pride that the petals were from the only rose bush in Ladakh. In the centre of the bowl floated majestically a celluloid duck. His Holiness, Stag-Tshang-Raspa, an incarnation of the divine essence of the Gurus, picked it up, crooned over it and said that it came from far away and was his most precious possession. We bowed low before the sacred shrine and returned to the courtyard, leaving the duck, made enchanted by the eyes and heart of a lonely child, to feast its celluloid eyes on sublime masterpieces of the metal-smith's art.

But great honours were still to be shown to us. Long horns were sounded by monks standing in a straight line, and to the sound of drum beats, masked dancers came into the square. The *papier-*

mâché masks worn by the dancers were of ferocious beings, the *mahakals* and *dakinis* or divine witches, and though the symbolic movements of the dance were difficult to interpret, they obviously centred around the exorcising of evil spirits. The movements of the dancers were slow, measured, each gesture highly meaningful. The costumes had colours and the dancers held handkerchiefs in their hands and waved them. The audience, which included the monks and the dogs, sat still and silent. After an hour it ended and we were offered refreshments of Ladakhi tea, the *chai,* boiled with yak fat and salt.

The time was nearing for our departure when the boy lama suddenly darted into the *gumpha*, tailed by his guardian monks. A short time later, he came out holding a medium size radio. He told us with pride that it was a gift from Prime Minister Jawaharlal Nehru. So we sat around, the visitors and the lamas, while the Lhasa terriers growled and snapped their teeth at us, and the revealed lama tuned in. Suddenly film music from Bombay was heard. A man's voice was singing a love song, the voluptuous voice fragmenting the enchantment. I noticed that the monks, young and old, sat down, crossed their legs, closed their eyes and a look of beatitude came on their faces. The meditation session lasted till the music ended and the radio was switched off. Then they all arose and resumed their chatter. On enquiry we were told that to the lamas of Ladakh all music was sacred and a call to meditation. The sense of the vulgar or profane played no part in their consciousness. And so we took leave of the divinity of Hemis and the monks. Some years later I heard that Stag-Tshang-Raspa, our young friend of Hemis, had been sent by his religious teachers to Tibet to study under a renowned *siddha*, and that he had been killed at the time of the Chinese occupation of Tibet.

I revisited Ladakh in 1976, travelling in a limousine, along the metalled roads, between the high rock bound passes, skirting precipitous gorges. I paused in quietude before the soaring statue of the Bodhisatva Maitreya and watched the bearded men and bejewelled women of the Aryan tribes dancing. I passed Lamayuru and visited the Alchi monastery, six miles off the main road to Leh. *Gumphas* of enchanted splendour where guilds of painters from the 9th to the 12th centuries, from the Kashmir valley, braved the rigours of the formidable passes to paint in splendid miniatures on the walls of the Alchi *gumphas*, the compassionate song of the Buddha. With eyes that had drunk in the vast palette of colour provided by the subtle tones of rock in that treeless, no-colour landscape, the painters, the inheritors of the traditions of Bagh and Ajanta, illuminated lyrical yet sensuous curves of female divinities held within aureoles of gold, flanked by the glory of the remembered flowers and birds of the Kashmir valley.

The moving landscape and the many travellers and warriors who passed along the main trade routes were also reflected in some of the paintings. Of particular power and magnificence was the Central Asian chieftain, arrogant, fierce, with turbaned head, the ends streaming behind, wearing a rich brocaded coat woven with a design of dragons. The horse and the rider were defiant, posed, erect, the lines of their bodies tightened to express surcharged energy. Cracks had started appearing in some of the *gumpha* walls, but a number of frescoes retained the freshness and luminous quality of their first painting.

I could not recognise Leh. Concrete extravaganzas of the Central PWD had replaced the sun quenched tones of the adobe and stone. Many of the buildings had electricity and modern plumbing. Water was more plentiful, brilliant flowers were to be seen and in the special farm nurtured by the Army, lush green plants gave promise of a great vegetable crop. The landscape was transformed. The women had ceased to wear their magnificent turquoise jewellery, possibly sold to the many tourists or curio dealers from Sikkim, Kalimpong, Nepal who swarmed the bazaar. People from Europe, the United States, Canada, Japan had flocked to this undiscovered tourist paradise, stripping it of its splendour. The monasteries were empty husks. I noticed that some of the most splendid frescoes of the 16th century from the Thikse monastery had been brought in panels to Hemis and set into the courtyard wall. One panel showed a levitating monk, floating through white foam like clouds, with the grace and ease of a bird in flight, while two people gazed up at this phenomenon with wonder. In another panel mysterious beings were held in curving dragon-like clouds as they looked down at a *siddha*, entangled in plants and creepers, his lean body and eyes taut and fixed in formidable meditation. Another panel (shown in Madanjit Singh's book, *Himalayan Art*) was of Godhara, the mendicant, holding his prayer stick, while he walked amidst a landscape of lotus blossoms and water cranes. The gilded bronzes were no longer to be seen in the shrines of Hemis. The Lhasa terriers, fierce little watchdogs of the *gumphas*, who had gnashed their teeth in the open courtyard, had disappeared. The 16th and 17th century frescoes had vanished except for a few solitary examples. Some of the walls were bare, while others were painted over by modern masters with copies

42. A monastery
in the distance, with
chortens in the
foreground.

of the traditional divinities, the *dvarapals*, the dancing *dakinis*, the
siddhas and the great symbolic image of the male and female dancing
in eternal union. But the scenes from the birth, life, renunciation
and death of Gautama, the Buddha, were still there, further darkened by smoke and grime.

The bright eyed, revealed Lama had been replaced by another in-
carnated one, a fat cheeked youth with vacant eyes. The essence of
Hemis, and the mystery, fantasy, and splendour of Ladakh were
slowly ebbing away. A highly inbred, esoteric culture and civilization
was being exposed to a materialist attitude of mind and heart. New
values were taking over mutilating an archaic grace and dignity.
The vast silence lay fractured. A linear materialistic sense of time as
progress was replacing a sense of time as cyclic flux, symbolised by
the Buddha in the symbol of the *chakra*.

Kutch and Kathiawar

ROBERTO OTTOLENGHI

Kathiawar and Kutch, coastal regions of the State of Gujarat, have always been a human crossroad. Cultures have intermixed as traders and travellers of all types, pilgrims, foreign settlers, invaders and nomads have come in various periods of history, to stay or to vanish as the case may be. The sense of these diversities is the most exciting feature of this land. Their continuing presence or just their memory is one of the greatest sources of interest for a traveller of today.

Entering Kathiawar from the north east, the first the traveller meets are at Lothal, the Harappans themselves, travellers par excellence. The ruins of Lothal, built around 2000 B.C., as well as the many remnants of Harappan settlements along Kathiawar and the Rann of Kutch, inevitably prompt reflections as to why highly sophisticated societies fade away. For Harappan society, slow economic collapse coincided with the superimposition of the nomadic-pastoral pattern of living of neighbouring clans, while major ecological changes undoubtedly hastened the process of decay. The presence of the Portuguese, who appeared in Kathiawar some 3,000 years after the Harappans, was by contrast wiped out virtually overnight by a sudden shift of fortune.

Diu, built on an island, or rather a long stretch of sand, in the waters of the Arabian sea, carries the imprint of their presence. Deserted by its original founders, Diu is still a very evocative place. The creative values which inspire colonial architecture have been the subject of enough literature. The buildings meant to symbolise and give dignity to the imperial institutions are often pompous and, in an era of decolonisation, they come out as a display of excessive vanity. The process of analysing the roots of most colonial architecture becomes inevitably a pitiless task and generally little is regarded as of architectural value.

Not perhaps in the case of Diu. Here one feels that it is possible to take nostalgia as the main motive of inspiration. Generations of colonial Portuguese were born in a little understood country and the images which to their fathers were memories became dreams to them. Diu grew in almost complete detachment from the mainland and from a world which its settlers regarded with apprehension. The Portuguese empire was not interested in a hinterland, but in sea bases as a support for its trade routes, so the muddy stretch of sea, which nowadays one crosses on a metal road after going through a check post, must have looked in those days a disturbing barrier.

Once across the canal and heading toward the small town at the eastern corner of the island, one encounters derelict traces of a past wealth, a cathedral, a palace, villas, all surrounded by lush vegetation, in contrast with the barren landscape of the Kathiawar coast. The town is mediterranean, built in narrow streets opening into piazzas. The residential architecture is imaginative, often bizarre—imposing three storeyed mansions with vast terraces and porches, floral motives and coloured stuccos. There is nothing just like this in Portugal, not even in the late Baroque. Diu's architecture is evidently not merely a repetition of motifs from the homeland; it is rather the nostalgic memory of them coupled with local elements. The result, even if bizarre, is moving.

The network of streets leads to a vast piazza on the sea shore and from there to the fort. Two deep moats, sunk in rocky terrain, stand as defence on the mainland side, the steep conformation of the coast forming a natural defence from the sea. Entry to the port is controlled by a fortified tower built in the stream; at night a chain used to be stretched between the tower and the fort at the surface of the water, preventing all access to the bay. The fort is practically abandoned, only the jailhouse still functions; the policemen still speak Portuguese among themselves and the inscriptions on the walls are in Portuguese. The police force is and was manned by Harijans with whom the old rulers traded status against loyalty. Bushes and crumbled walls, rusty cannon and old inscriptions—ruins stimulate the imagination and one can almost see the Portuguese descend from the fort toward the seashore in the evenings and stroll in front of the shops or sit at the *casa de luxo* (luxury house) which still serves the brandy and the arrack distilled locally.

All that came to an end suddenly in a morning of December 1961. The Portuguese fled as Indian troops crossed the canal on motor launches and the local police mounted a meaningless and, by all accounts, bloody defence, down near the moat. Today the small town waits in silence, probably an economic silence, for administrative integration in the State of Gujarat which will not be long in coming. Then, the incoming boom of activities and people will wash away the suggestive patina of memories.

Only a hundred miles away lives another set of people whose memory of the motherland has dwindled even more than in the case of the Portuguese settlers of Diu. These are the negroes from Abyssinia who still inhabit the edges of the Gir forest. The tourists who come in flocks to the forest to watch the celebrated "lion show" mostly miss the village of Sirvan, just inside the bush, where about two hundred of these people live. They are poor and dejected, illiterate and unaware of the technology which, in a few years, has so deeply changed the agricultural conditions of the Kathiawar country-side around them.

Still, the elders have stories of splendour to tell: how they came along with Mahmud of Ghazni as part of his army, which is pro-bably not true, or how they came by sea to form the special body-guard of the sultans of Gujarat, which is more likely. But many of them may well have come as slaves, as part of the big trade that the Arabs of the Persian Gulf ran as far as to the Muslim kingdoms of Gujarat. Warriors, bodyguards or slaves, they were one day discarded, when their growing number might have created a pro-blem, when the purpose for which they came happened to be no longer viable or simply when the ruler decided he wanted to.

43. A seventeenth century map of the city of Diu.

They were given land where they remained as an insular society, kept aside by the local population, neglected by the administration. Today they are like any Muslim backward community in the country. The people gather around the visitor when the elder of the village tells the story of their roots. He is sitting under a straw porch of his mud hut, barren and lacking even the simple but well cared for possessions which in many Gujarati village communities differentiate poverty from misery. When he mentions Africa and Abyssinia silence falls. There is no doubt that these words trigger emotions; no images or real references, here nostalgia is almost mystical. Some little girls start a dance which they accompany with singing; to our disappointment, the song is in Gujarati. The negroes of Sirvan may soon become a tourist attraction. The bush land in which they live has been both their confinement and their shelter; one does not know what may happen once the shelter is lost.

Travellers, strangers, and pilgrims of all sorts cooperated in creating and building up Junagadh. Junagadh is pilgrims' land, one of the most intense points of the religious path that stretches through Kathiawar down to Dwarka, Beit, to the localities of Koteshwar and Narayan Sarovar in Kutch and up to Inglaj, now in Pakistan. The structure and the atmosphere of Junagadh are the typical ones of most pilgrimage centres; its economic *raison d'etre* can be read in the thick texture of its architecture, in the animation of the bazaars, the lights of the hundreds of places where the pilgrim considers he has to be rewarded for his long journey: sweet shops, lodges, restaurants, rest houses of all sorts and categories, *dharamsalas,* shops, markets reward as they do in Benares, Hardwar, Puri, Ujjain, the pilgrim who, in his turn, pays because, being a city for pilgrims, Junagadh is mainly a place for spending.

The place was sacred to everybody even before the town came into existence. Hindus, Buddhists and Jains have taken over one another and encroached upon one another, have flourished and languished, have climbed mountain peaks and dug caves. If the richer Jains had an edge over the others in terms of splendour, the Hindus were building higher and higher. On their part, the Buddhists, long since gone, left some of the most astonishing examples of rock temples.

The holy mount Girnar stands a few miles apart, lonely, surrounded by a bushy amphitheatre of which the edges are thin and sharp as if sliced by a blade. The climb is long and hard; one can be carried by a *dholi,* a small chair held by two coolies, after having been weighed and charged accordingly. Till a place called Dholi Deri, at about 1,000 feet, the path winds comfortably through the forest, and at both sides are small shrines and images of divinities.

From this point the real climb starts; Anthony Burgess ascended the mountain in 1897 and gave this description of the trek: "The ascent now (from Dholi Deri) becomes more difficult as the path winds under the face of the cliff to the third rest house 1,400 feet up; stairs of sandstone then commence and taking advantage of every ledge on the almost vertical scarp, wind up the face of it, the *dholi* frequently grating against the rock on one side of the narrow path whilst its occupant looks down into an abyss on the other."

Nowadays the trek is broader and smoother, nevertheless the climb is breathtaking. Watch the elders, starting slowly at sunrise, refusing the *dholi*, taking every step as a trial, carried by the determination to accomplish what may well be the last and ultimate proof of devotion of a life. At approximately 2,500 feet, at a sharp turn on the edge of a vertical fall, stands a huge, isolated rock, the Bhairava-jap or "leap of death", otherwise known as Raja-melavana-pathar or the "desire realizing rock" from which devotees used to jump to death to attain salvation. "Laying a coconut on the dizzy verge of this rock, the deluded victim attempts to poise himself on it and in another instant he is beyond humanity's reach and his body a prey to the vultures that soar under the lofty cliff."

From this point it is the steepest climb, the silence broken only by the noise of the sticks of the *dholiwalas* on the stones to mark the rhythm of the walk. At the Jain temples of Neminath, Tejpala, and Vastipala, the devotees will bathe and change clothes. The temples are widely renovated; the descriptions given by history books don't match any longer, since new proofs of religious zeal and community status matter more than preservation of architecture.

The Hindus have gone higher up; at 3,300 feet stands the temple of Amba Mata, a form of Uma or Parvati. From there onward the path is the one of renunciation. Through a narrow stretch of rock, with the abyss on both sides, the pilgrim heads toward the small shrine of Gorakhanatha, leaving a shred of his cloth on a bush as he reaches the summit in safety.

It is an even harder climb to reach the topmost height, sacred to the Digambara Jains, named after Neminatha who became a Tirthankara and attained nirvana after meditating for seven hundred years on this peak, so narrow that one can hardly move, a solitary rock pillar, surrounded by void and seemingly suspended in the air. From here there is the sight of endless forests and a lower peak nearby, with the shrine of the goddess Kalika, where the Agho-

44. Facing page. Young boys from Kutch.

45. *Village architecture of Kutch.*

ras, Shiva devotees, used to take shelter "feeding on carrion and even on human flesh".

If the Girnar is still challenging to the pilgrim, Dwarka, which lies on the sea coast at the extreme north west of Kathiawar, in the district of Okha, was till recently even more difficult of access. The road from Jamnagar crosses a barren land with hardly any vegetation, territory of the Wakhars, a Rajput warlike clan who engaged the British authorities in endless skirmishes and made the journey to Dwarka somehow adventurous for the pilgrim. Nevertheless, people kept pouring in by the thousands since Dwarka is one of the seven holy places in India, having been the capital of Krishna after his flight from Mathura.

In front of the port of Okha, in the gulf of Kutch, the island of Bait is an exciting place and a pilgrimage centre too. The place catches the attention to a greater extent for being since early recorded history a starting point for adventurous sea trade with the

Persian Gulf. A commercial port of the Harappans once, its people have always crossed the Arabian Sea both ways. The Sumerians gave various accounts of these intrepid travellers also for the reason that most of their cities were built with stones shipped to the Persian Gulf from the coast of Kathiawar on the rudimentary boats of the people of Bait. Along with construction materials, another item of trade was the onions which the sailors traded for dates. Nowadays small motor launches leave Bait regularly on the usual sea routes— four days to Muscat and six days to Bahrein. Moreover, to prove that certain local economies defy the logic of time, the disappearance of civilisations, and technological changes, the people of Bait still found their prosperity on the same historical items of trade: tiles and bricks have substituted the stone, onions have remained, which may explain why this vegetable is at times for sale in the markets of Delhi and Bombay for as much as eight rupees a kilo.

The sanctity and the beauty of the island have always attracted a number of pilgrims and, as it appears, a great deal of wealthy ones, who have built in the last two centuries imposing and luxurious mansions along the coast. These palaces, in the style of the Marwari and Rajasthani *havelis*, are now deserted. Through the cracks of the bolted gates one has a glimpse of the carvings in the courtyards. Tourism in this place has been confined to this archaic dimension of a few Marwari families.

The Krishna temple is also an eighteenth century *haveli,* which encloses various worship halls entirely built in wood and painted in bright colours—an unusual combination of religious and civilian architectures. The land of Kutch is just across the bay; it is a three hour journey to the port of Mandvi on the same boats which sail to the Persian Gulf. If, on the contrary, one prefers to enter Kutch by road, going through the old princely town of Moorvi and crossing the bridge on the Little Rann, one gets the stunning view of an expanse of mud extending for miles in place of the ocean, whose waters cover the area only during monsoon; this very first sight will convey the fact that culturally and historically and for all practical purposes, Kutch has to be regarded as an island.

The Little and the Great Rann of Kutch were well known in history since Ptolemy gave his account in the *Periplus of the Erytrean Sea,* describing the perils they represented for sailors: "...both these seas are full of shoals and of eddies that are rapid and close to one another and stretch far out from the shore, so that frequently when the mainland has been lost sight of, vessels run into them and being carried forward into the inner circle of the vortex are destroyed".

46. *The lone caravan.* Caravans and nomadic groups have always crossed the two Ranns in the dry season and they still do, at least within the Indian territory, since the closure of the Indo-Pakistani border has interrupted the flow to and from Sind and Baluchistan.

The Great Rann stretches away to the horizon in different coloured patches of mud and sand; scanty vegetation and tiny mounds break the monotony of the landscape; cranes, flamingoes and wild asses are the only inhabitants. Since the days in which the Harappans, scattering their bases along the perimeter of the Rann, built a civilisation with only the existence of the small shepherd clans around them, there have always been two sets of people in Kutch, the nomads and the settlers.

The ecological changes which have occurred have left visible traces; settlements and cities have disappeared; Harappan mounds stand in a desolate countryside near dry riverbeds which suggest images of a lost fertility. The nomads seem to have remained unaffected throughout. Their caravans are a common sight all over Kutch, their women with their elaborate jewels and their costumes in which black, red and mauve seem to prevail, each pleated shirt a specimen of embroidery.

Still no one can match the elegance of the camels, in whose blankets all the craftsmen of Kutch seem to have put their best skill, homage to the vanity of the animals which are so much part of their lives. Everybody seems to be a skilled craftsman in Kutch. The Muslim nomads of the Benni district use a rudimentary foot-operated lathe to manufacture wooden items which they later coat with a coloured laquer. The Khatris of Khawda are masters in block printing. Every village, specially in Benni district, seems to have developed a school of embroidery of its own, every clan has its distinctive colours and patterns of design. The villages are generally hidden in dense bushland in the sandy terrain; south of Bhuj the sand and the bush change into a rocky and hilly terrain where the various colours of the stones create effects of unusual beauty. The womenfolk of the villages are remarkable for their *chunam* work which covers the walls of the houses with a light layer of coloured cowdung and mud, painted in glittering white with mirror work.

The urban pattern of life in Kutch is by no means less interesting than the nomadic one. The few urban settlements to be found in Kutch are examples of military power, strongholds along caravan routes, in a land often subject to invasion. Bhuj is dominated by a massive fort set in an amphitheatre formed by the perimeter of the hills. Its rajas, thanks to the size of their holdings, easily out-shadowed in terms of wealth most of the rulers scattered through Kathiawar and the rest of Gujarat.

The town, reached after the long approach journey through deso-late plains and desert landscape, offers an incredible show of busi-ness and wealth. The bazaars, winding through a network of narrow lanes within the city walls, are brought alive in the evenings by the trading activities of the picturesque folk from all parts of the district. The prosperity of the cities is often short-lived, dependant on un-predictable events, on the economic viability of a trade route, on the sick fantasy of a ruler.

At the extreme west of Kutch, facing the Pakistani border on the shore of the Great Rann, lies the city of Lakhpat, built 250 years ago by one of the rajas of Bhuj, to be a military stronghold and a compulsory halt for all the caravans en route to Baluchistan. It ought to have been a capital of splendour, but the dream was never fulfilled; the town was abandoned before completion. The city walls, several kilometres in perimeter, are majestic but nothing more than a barren backdrop: once through the main gate, the scene is of an almost empty esplanade with a few decayed buildings scat-tered here and there.

The settlers have almost totally vanished, leaving behind structures in disarray and the grotesque skeleton of the ramparts. A few deserted *havelis*, masterly carved, the roofs on the verge of collapse, bear witness to the unaccomplished dream of the ruler. Tombs of Muslim saints built in the 1800s, an example of late Muslim style, stand among the ruins. From the top of the ramparts overlooking the muddy immensity of the Rann, Lakhpat, silent and motionless, seems the last outpost before nowhere.

Perhaps the most impressive sight around Kutch is the *pallias*, memorial stones scattered in the countryside, near the village well, or the temple, or in the courtyards of the houses, often just in the open, lost in the wasteland. Erected in the memory of heroes, they are not bigger than normal tombstones, but because of the images carved on them, they could well be the most relevant record of the social history of Kutch. A hero is a warrior killed in a battle against an opposing clan and he is portrayed mostly while riding his horse; or he might be a villager who died fighting a lion, or a sailor who perished at sea, as shown by the *pallias* found in the coastal areas.

The inscriptions on the *pallias* generally bear a date. If one pays attention, one may find the same date often recurring, bloody landmarks of the history of Kutch, as, for instance, when in 1761 Rao Godaji of Bhuj lost a hundred thousand men in the war of Zeera against the rulers of Sind. Often sad arrays of *pallias* winding through small villages render the dimension of the public grief. Men and women on horses, holding bows, shields, and spears testify the tribute paid by the community in the hard process of building and strengthening a clan.

The hero becomes a superman, then almost a god. The *pallias* become objects of worship. The hero is then anybody who dies according to the ethos of the clan, like the man who commits ritual suicide and is depicted in the *pallia* while cutting his throat, because that too is bound to increase respect for the clan. Scattered among the others, many *pallias* bear the image of a woman's arm with open hand: this is a *sati* stone erected for the widow who lets herself burn to death on the husband's pyre. In the outskirts of Bhuj, among rocks and thorny bushes, the funeral monument of Rao Lakhpatji shows the *pallia* of the riding ruler and at its sides the fifteen *pallias* of his wives who followed him into the fire.

Pallias of anonymous village wives stand everywhere in Kutch and if the attribute of heroism is to be used, these widows may well deserve it, irrespective of their *sati* being voluntary or not. Unwillingness becomes willingness and fear becomes determination through family pressures and social coercion; thus reluctant women are made heroines.

Economic reasons probably more than religious ones were behind the ritual of *sati*. But along with these, it is interesting to consider a theory recently formulated by western researchers which suggests that among the witches burnt in Europe through the centuries, the most were widows. The "widow-witch" is an outrage to the society so far as her independent female power remains unchecked, following the disappearance of her man. Her very existence as woman independent of a man triggers feelings of tension in a male dominated society. The society meets the challenge by burning her.

If this theory applies here too, the *sati* may find an explanation in the sexual taboos rooted in human psychology as well as in the economic compulsion of the members of the clan. The logic of existence in a harsh environment is severe. Kutch is a harsh land and its people are used to a hard struggle for survival. This island surrounded by mud is culturally and socially remote from the rest of Gujarat. Its beauty is immense and practically untouched. A journey into Kutch is still accompanied by flights of ducks and cranes, deer and foxes crossing the path and nomads in caravans slowly gliding aside.

The Wonders of Ellora

JOHN B. SEELY

(1825)

In commencing my journey to the temples at Ellora, three unpleasant circumstances presented themselves. First, in bidding adieu to a body of excellent men, with whom I had been in the habit of daily and friendly intercourse for a long period of time; secondly, a long and dreary journey before me, through the Mahratta country, of nearly three hundred miles; and lastly, in writing an account of my peregrinations.

Before embarking in our boat for Panwell, the first town on the continent, it will not be amiss to offer a few brief observations on the island of Bombay. The climate of Bombay is preferable to most parts of India, having a refreshing sea-breeze, commonly called, from its healthful effects, *the Doctor*. There is now very little wood on the island, no marshes, and but few large pools of stagnant water. To those causes much of the sickness that prevails in other parts of India must be attributed, and the salubrity of Bombay causes it to be resorted to by invalids from the other presidencies and the interior.

Nothing can be more delightful than the rides and drives in this island: they extend twenty-one miles, and communicate to the neighbouring island of Salsette by means of a causeway. The prospect is as grand and as beautiful as can be imagined—the mighty range of the Ghats towering in the clouds and extending as far as the eye can reach; the bold views on the continent; the diversified objects on the island; old ruinous convents and monasteries erected by its former conquerors, the Portuguese; the noble country-houses of the Europeans; Hindoo pagodas, Mahometan mosques; the remains of Mahratta forts and buildings: these, with the rural appearance of Hindoo villages, where every patch of ground is richly cultivated or ornamented, and interspersed with groves of date and cocoanut trees, afford a prospect of luxuriance and beauty to be met with nowhere but in the Concan (the population, under the government of Bombay, is estimated at 2,500,000/Square miles 11,000).

As we turn our eyes towards the sea, we are presented with a fine hard beach, running on to the high and romantic spot called Malabar Point which promontory is studded with neat villas, while the city and fort are seen in the background, with the ships securely at anchor in the harbour. Nor must we forget the isthmus called Colaba (probably Cal-ab, or black water), running for about two miles in a straight line from Bombay, from which it is separated at high water. On this small island, which scarcely exceeds a quarter of a mile in breadth, are several good houses and a range of barracks. At its farthest or western end stands a noble signal and lighthouses from the top of which is a very fine view of the island.

Before stepping into our fishing-boat from the dock, *en passant* I may just remark, that the Bombay docks are inferior to none in England. They are built of a fine firm stone, capacious, and every way convenient, and do the highest credit to the abilities of the military engineer, Captain Cooper, of the Company's service, who built them. Ships for the East India Company of 1,400 tons burthen have been built here, with the wood of the country called teak, procured from the neighbouring forests of Canara. These vessels are found remarkably durable. The workmen and architects are entirely native Parsees—a very numerous, useful, and industrious race at Bombay. These docks have likewise furnished several very fine ships for his Majesty's navy, from the rate of a sloop of war to an 80-gun ship, and their qualities have been found admirable.

The sea-breeze sets in at about ten o'clock in the morning, and keeps gaining strength till the meridian, at which time a fine breeze usually blows directly up the bay. At this time we embarked in our fishing boat. Our party consisted of five persons: four gentlemen wishing to accompany me as far as the first stage on the continent. None of the party had attained the age of 23, but were in the prime of youth, hale and strong; neither of them were free livers, but, unfortunately for themselves, they were great sportsmen. Of these gentlemen, one was the best linguist in the Bombay army in the Mahratta and Hindustani languages. The second was a pure philanthropist—he could not do too much good. The third was a good singer, and the best amateur comedian we had: the last was an inveterate sportsman—tiger, hog, wolf, jackal, or bird, all the same—the rifle or double barrel was scarcely ever out of his hand. With the scenery, as far as the eye can reach, grand, beautiful, and picturesque in the extreme, an excursion of this kind, with agreeable companions, after a few months' grilling in the interior, makes the mind joyful and the soul glad. On one side, as you proceed up the harbour, you have the mighty range of mountains stretching away

47. A view of
Bombay harbour
and islands.

their cloud-capt tops in every fantastic and romantic shape; peaks, cliffs, and hollows indented here, and thickly wooded there: the busy and noisy suburbs of Bombay lying on your left, where handsome English mansions, rural-looking native huts, monastic buildings of the Portuguese, with large Mahratta houses, inhabited by wealthy natives, denote opulence and splendour; while the whole scene is embellished with a variety of cultivation and foliage.

As you pass on is an extensive and handsome range of barracks for the king's troops; a little farther on brings you to the town of Mazagaum, chiefly inhabited by Portuguese and natives. Many pretty views present themselves on the shore in passing up the harbour, while the city and the shipping are gradually receding from sight. In front is a large old-fashioned house, built by Governor Hornby; beyond that is a large, handsome, white tomb, conspicuously placed on a promontory, containing the mortal remains of a distinguished Mussulman. The curious looking hill called the Funnel, from its similarity of shape, rises abruptly in front, while on the right a Mahratta fort, called Shoon Ghur (probably Arzoon Ghur), raises its romantic turrets in solitary grandeur in the heart of the mountains, surrounded by jungle, in all the wildness of nature.

On the left the view is bounded by the hills of Salsette, which afford an agreeable background to the whole of this magnificent scenery.

Considerably to our right, and almost in mid-bay, is Butcher's Island, where is a large range of buildings used as hospital barracks for the seamen of his Majesty's navy in time of war. In this place I have spent several pleasant days. One of our amusements was snake catching: these reptiles are here very numerous and large, but I believe not very venomous. Many a brave British tar has at this spot found his final resting place—"*Till he hears the last whistle/ When he'll jump upon deck.*"

On quitting Butcher's Island, called by the natives Deva Devi, or Island of the Gods, not far up the bay stands the celebrated Elephanta Island. It is of considerable elevation, and famous for its caves hewn out of the solid rock from the face of the mountain. These caves are very much injured by the action of the sea-breeze, and from not having drains cut on the top of the mountain to carry off the rain water. Nor has any care been taken to have trenches made at the foundation; so that in the periodical rains they are often inundated, and abound with reptiles, particularly snakes. The view from the caves is very fine, as they are situated about 350 feet above the level of the sea. Here is the famous colossal figure of the Tri-murti—Brahma, Vishnu, and Siva—the creating, preserving, and destroying powers of the Hindoo mythology.

After passing Elephanta (Gharri-pouri) for three or four miles, we approach the left-hand shore about Billapore, the land, fort, and villages belonging to the Mahrattas. The swift sailing of our boat, and fine sea-breeze blowing directly up the harbour, with four pleasing companions, made our excursion very delightful. The boats used on these occasions are generally the common Mahratta fishing-boats. They sail remarkably fast, are built sharp at both ends, have a very broad beam, and about a third of the keel-piece is deep, but slightly hollowed out in the centre; the latteen sail appears disproportionally large, and it is a good deal peaked; the foot of the sail is almost fore and aft, as the tack is made fast to the stem of the boat, and the sheet in the centre abaft the midships; while the extreme point of the sail at the upper part projects far aft, there being nearly four times more canvas abaft than forward.

Tigers are very numerous; nor are alligators wanting in the water, as I have heard, although I never saw any of the latter. There are various modes of destroying these formidable and ravenous beasts. In the upper province of Bengal, the peasants at night place themselves in a tree, at the foot of which is tied a dog or a kid. The noise that these poor creatures make attracts the tiger, and those keeping watch, as he approaches, soon level the monster with the ground. On these occasions I have seen them use a match-lock gun, with a barrel of more than the usual length. The balls are in general of iron, of an irregular form, and a good deal jagged. There is some little danger in the above mode of destroying wild beasts. Leopards, which are very common, on their being fired at will instantly climb the tree, and would wound, if not destroy, the assailant.

On Salsette, I have seen cages used for decoying the tiger. The cages are on small wheels, for the purpose of being more easily transported from place to place, and are formed of two apartments, one larger than the other, and divided by strong wooden railings: in the smaller apartment is placed some unfortunate pariah dog, or worn-out milch goat. The bleating of the animal is sure to bring the tiger: finding he cannot get at his prey, he enters the door of the larger apartment, which the cunning workman has made so as to fall down the moment the beast enters. When the tiger finds he can neither get at his victim, nor retreat from his narrow confinement, his bellowings and roarings are terrific. The midnight forest echoes and shakes with his lamentations and fury, and his former wild companions flee away stricken with fear.

These cages, on Salsette, were constructed by order of the government. They were about nine feet high, and about nine feet square. I believe ten rupees were paid to the natives for every tiger they shot. The decoy animal in the cage, occasioned by fear, was generally found dead. I was once accompanying a native Portuguese priest into a rather gloomy cave on Salsette, and had proceeded some distance, when we discovered a tiger lying asleep. The poor padre was horror-stricken, and instead of quietly turning round and sneaking away, he put the hollow of his hand to his mouth, and was beginning to cry out, *bah!, bah!* when, for our mutual preservation, I was obliged to give him a kick, by way of rousing him and silencing his vociferations. For, assuredly stupefied as he was by fear, had I not, by this violent proceeding and dragging him away by his cassock at the same time, both of us would have become the prey of the tiger.

Pits are sometimes used for the purpose of destroying tigers. These are constructed like the common pit-falls—but only narrower. At the bottom are driven in stakes, generally of bamboo, the upper parts sharpened and hardened by fire. In the pit is placed a dog or kid; this of course draws the tiger, or leopard, or wolf to the spot, and in eagerness to get at his prey, he is at last tantalized to make the

fatal descent; and when transfixed on the stakes, his agonies and exertions are better conceived than described.

The fort of Billapore stands rather high, and on a commanding situation. This being the great thoroughfare from the Deccan to Bombay and the towns to the northward, it formerly must have been of importance to the Mahratta government, and they still make a show of bringing boats to. We landed, but the old *killedar,* with a superciliousness that would better have suited the former days of Mahratta power, would not allow us even to approach his castle. We purchased at the village, not knowing but we might be detained by shooting or other causes, four fowls, rice, yams, onions and spices sufficient for five persons, with fire-wood for cooking, for about 2s. 9d. English money, and this was dearer than a native would have

49. Royal
Necropolis,
Golconda.

paid. Our precaution was not needless; for with loitering, stepping on shore at times, shooting, and a few frolics in *our* managing the boat, we lost the flood-tide, and the fine sea-breeze had gradually declined in strength, till we brought up for the night by making the boat fast to a large wooden peg driven in the bank, alongside of which we lay. At daylight we cast off, and, what with rowing and occasionally sailing, we arrived at Panwell in time for breakfast.

The town is distant from the landing-place about half a mile. It consists of a few irregular streets; the houses in general are small and a few only are tiled. The bazaars are well supplied, and most commodities of Indian manufacture are sold in the shops. Around the town are tracts of rice land, which at that time were nearly in full ear. Panwell, from its proximity to Bombay, and being the most convenient and populous thoroughfare to the Deccan, as a central mart, carries on a good trade.

Our horses had arrived during the day via Tannah, which is a long day's journey from hence by land. There are three modes of conveying luggage from this place to Poona: *viz.* coolies, *tattoos*, and oxen. The hire is settled by a native officer appointed for that purpose by our government. His duty is to see that you are not imposed upon either by bad cattle or overcharges; and, moreover, it is his especial duty to use every exertion that the traveller may not be unnecessarily detained. Without this officer's assistance much inconvenience would be experienced. For the information of the traveller that is passing this road, I shall subjoin the established rates of hire:

A *cooly* (porter), to carry 50 lbs.

	Rupees	Qrs.	Reas
From Panwell to Poona	2	0	0
Seroor	3	2	0
Ahmed-nuggur	6	1	0
Toka	10	1	0
Joulnah	16	3	0

A bullock, to carry 160 lbs.

From Panwell to Poona	3	0	0
Seroor	5	0	0
Ahmed-nuggur	8	2	50
Toka	14	2	50

The hire of the *tattoo* is, on all the above stages, half a rupee dearer than the ox. Considering that they walk somewhat faster of the two, the *tattoo* is the most preferable animal for baggage. Every day that you make an extra halt, an allowance of a quarter of a rupee is to be paid to each cooly. It is ordered, likewise, that an advance amounting to one half of the hire is to be paid to your coolies, or to the owner of the cattle. There is no danger of their absconding on the road, as their houses and families are well known to the officer who procures them for you.

After a pleasant evening with my friends at Panwell, at daybreak my baggage moved on. As the cavalcade may be new to the English reader, I subjoin a list. Three bullocks to carry a tent, twelve feet square, consisting of inner shell and outer fly, and two walls. Three bullocks for clothes, provisions, books, & c.; two porters for camp-cot and writing-desk; one ditto, for breakfast utensils & c.; one *tattoo*, or pony, for head servant; two ditto belonging to my servants, of whom I had four with me. There was an escort of six *siphauees* and a corporal. Several native travellers accompanied my people for their security, as the country was sometimes infested with robbers. Although so near to Bombay, yet the neighbouring mountains in the Peishwa's territories afforded them safe and unknown retreats, whence they decended at pleasure to the plains of the Concan, or the lowlands above the Ghats.

To Choke, fourteen miles. After leaving Panwell, the road is rugged and very rocky; in some parts a great want of cultivation appears where the land has a fertile appearance. Crossed the Panwell river, called the Pen, or Pan. From the sea having run out, the water was clear and sweet. Two stony *nullahs* likewise lay in the route, having fine clear streams running to the westward. These are supplied either from springs in the Ghats, or else drain through channels from unknown sources. About one-third of the journey on, the country assumes a very mountainous appearance. The brows of the mountains present singular and romantic views. Frequently, around those of a great altitude, clouds float along their summits.

The village of Choke is small and rural. The cottages are neat and well thatched with chopped straw, and the environs of the village are well laid out in rice-grounds. At this stage the traveller will find the best lodgings that are to be met with between this and Aurangabad: it is a Hindoo pagoda, built of wood and stone, standing on a terrace. The part of the pagoda that the traveller occupies is a large convenient apartment. Towards the night it is rather cool, as the front is entirely open and exposed: the breeze at night is very chilly. Robberies are not very frequent, the Patel of the village having within these few months inflicted a summary punishment upon some Bheels who had begun to infest the neighbourhood. Two of them being detected in plundering, he had them hung up by the heels, perfectly naked, and exposed to the fury of the mid-day sun till they were dead. Two *siphauees* are placed in the village for its protection, and for the assistance of officers who are passing.

At daylight, having taken a final farewell of my three friends, who intended returning to Bombay, after remaining two days at Panwell with my late host I proceeded on my journey, having the preceding night sent off the breakfast utensils and supplies by my servant and a *cooly*, and one *siphauee*, with an order to halt, after nightfall, at the first hut or village he might come to. By precautions of this kind, your servant, &c. being in advance of you for four or five miles, after your arrival on the following morning, fatigued and tired with bad roads and a hot sun, you have not long to wait for breakfast, for it is ten to one if the remainder of your baggage or servants arrive till ten or eleven o'clock, as probably they do not get everything packed upon and moved off the ground till half an hour after your departure. In the rainy season, with the execrable state of the roads, rivulets or *nullahs* running impetuously, and large rivers without bridges, the miseries of travelling, regulated by a heavily laden ox's pace, are most intolerable. While sojourning after his fatigues on muddy ground, his baggage wet through, and his servants exhausted, the most lonely hedge alehouse in Cornwall would appear to him a palace.

The distance from the last stage, Choke to Capooly, is fourteen miles, the roads very bad, at times winding, and over several rugged ascents. The view all round is limited by mountains and hills. In front is seen the great range of Ghats peeping above the clouds in one continued chain of precipices, naked rock of inaccessible heights; but little cultivation during the journey, although the soil appears rich, and fit for agricultural purposes.

Now, kind reader, lest I, a poor half-pay captain, should undo myself in your critical opinion, or weary your patience, we will, with your kind leave, arrive at once at our halting ground at Capooly, a mean, dirty little village, situated at the very base of the great barrier wall of rock that supports the tableland of the Deccan, propping up an immense tract of country, some large rivers, several millions of people, and many cities, towns, and villages.

This enormous chain of mountain is securely fastened by iron-bound buttresses of primeval granite, as naked and frightful to look on in some places, as they are romantic and singular in appearance in others. From the wretched state of the roads, my poor servants did not arrive till past the meridian hour. But one whom I had sent forward overnight had prepared my breakfast, after which, as I was often wont to do after the perspiration produced by walking about the village had subsided, I jumped into a tank, clothes and all, which, without apprehension of danger, I left to dry upon me. It was insufferably hot at this place, situated in an amphitheatre of mountains, the naked face of each burning with heat, and reflecting the rays, while every breeze was excluded. All the heat was concentrated, as it were, in a focus. The thermometer was at 104° in the shade.

Not wishing to give my servants trouble after their long march, I did not pitch my tent, but occupied the house, or rather hovel, mentioned in the subjoined public document. In an adjoining house, belonging to a Brahman, a lady of quality of the Poona court, on her way to the fort to Bassein, had taken up her abode. She was accompanied by a numerous suite, guarded by thirty horsemen and ten match-lock men. In her retinue were several females: her tents and baggage were carried by two elephants, eight camels, and several led horses.

At Capooly is a very large tank, exceedingly well built, the sides lined and the banks paved with a fine stone; there are several flights of handsome steps leading to the water. It was excavated by the wisest and best of men, the celebrated Mahratta minister Nana Furnavese, at an expense of about 12,000*l*. Nana, though a Mahratta, and a person of the highest power, paid for both labour and materials. The tank occupies a quarter of a mile of ground. In this tank several young females, both beautiful and innocent, were bathing and playing, quite unconcerned at my near approach. Had they been spoken to they would have fled like the timid deer, or if only on a probable chance of pollution, they would have drowned themselves instantly, or stuck a dagger in their hearts.

A little before day-break we commenced our formidable undertaking, of what appeared to be nothing less than scaling the mural sides of towering mountains. The road, after going some little distance, becomes very steep, lined with high banks, and interrupted by large stones and fragments of rock. In some parts of the road the passage is guttered by little streams of water that run gurgling down the precipitous fronts of the rock, affording a pleasing, soothing sound, as we trace our course through these sequestered spots. Not quite half way up is a small patch of tableland where the traveller is sure to halt and take some refreshment, not more for the purpose of recruiting his strength than regaining his wind. For, what with clambering, slipping, and proceeding up a very steep ascent, great personal exertion is required.

At this spot I halted for nearly half an hour, enjoying the happiness of early morn amid some of the most magnificent and beautiful scenery that can be imagined, and which is only to be found in mountainous regions. The exuberant beauty of the vegetable world, a fine cool morning, the solitude of the pass, and the constant change in the character of the mountains, hills, rocks, and valleys, as I proceeded upwards, gave an elasticity to a youthful mind that may be felt, but cannot be expressed by a tame writer like myself.

It was near 9 a.m. before I arrived at the village of Cundalla, situated at the top of the defile. It was not until near 3 p.m. that the poor *coolies* arrived, dreadfully fatigued in consequence of the labour they had undergone. I gave to each man sufficient rice, vegetables, &c. to make a good, hearty meal, and for which they were very thankful. For two hours after nightfall they were singing and playing music in the most cheerful and lively manner. It would strike with wonder a stranger to observe a body of *coolies* conveying a pipe of wine, a 24-pounder, or an 80 gallon cask of beer, up the defile, at the top of which we had just arrived.

As the method of transporting so heavy and unwieldy an article as a pipe of wine, up a steep, narrow, and rugged path, may not be generally known, I will endeavour to describe it. A strong pole is used, to which is firmly lashed three stout slings, passing round the ends and centre of the cask. Across the long pole, which is placed lengthwise, are seven short poles, lashed on the top of the longer one. To each of these short poles are two men, who receive the end of the short pole on the back of their necks, where a large fold of cloth is placed. They move on, two and two, obliquely. When they require to relieve their shoulders, they move on, right or left, in front alternately. When the cask or gun is suspended, and the men walking, the cross-poles are about three inches distant and above the large one, which latter is about twenty-two inches above the article carried. They can easily rest by merely stooping and laying their load on the ground, and which is just as easily taken up again. This class of porters are called *nogunnees:* those who carry loads on the head are called *bigharees.* It is well known with what ease twelve (sometimes ten only) palanquin-bearers will carry a heavy palanquin containing the precious carcass of a sleek, well-fed, heavy Christian, with his writing-desk, over rivers and mountains and very bad roads, sometimes the distance of fourteen or fifteen miles, for a remuneration of seven pence sterling. The regulated allowance of weight to be carried by a cooly is fifty-six pounds.

The chain of mountains, among which we had now encamped, extends from Cape Comorin, opposite Ceylon, in one unbroken series (with the exception of an opening at Paniany in the Malabar

50. The indispensable dak ghari.

country, of about twelve miles broad), stretching away, in a northern line, to the province of Candeish, and not far distant from Surat. In no part do they exceed fifty miles from the sea, and in one part only do they approach closer than eight miles. The mountains of which we are now speaking decrease in altitude about thirty miles to the northward of Bombay. To the southward of Poona the passes, I am told, have a northern descent. Stretching along to the southward, they separate what is generally called Malabar, supporting the Mysore and Soondah countries in the form of a terrace.

Sept. 24. The previous evening I made arrangements to breakfast at the great temple of Karli, to spend the day there, and towards the evening to return to my tent, which was to be pitched at the village of Karli, about two miles and a quarter from the caves, and directly opposite to them. At daybreak, we moved on a distance of nine miles; the road is very rocky and bad for the first three miles. After descending a small steep pass, the country is more open to the left, possessing abundance of water and a rich soil.

I proceeded across the open country to the left, to the mountain of Ekverah; where, at a considerable height above the plain, stands a large temple hewn out of the solid rock. The path by which the temple of Ekverah (Karli) is reached is very steep and difficult, winding along the face of the mountain. In fact, it is little better than a water-course, broken, rugged, and precipitous; so that the traveller is well tired before he reaches the top. When he does get to the head of the path, he is highly gratified by the view beneath of an open, rich, and beautiful country, having the mountains at a distance, and the pretty rural village of Karli, situated in a grove of mango-trees, with a large tank near it, on one side of which stands a handsome Hindoo temple.

On the left of a terrace at the end of the footpath, excavated from the bowels of the mountain, stands, in solemn magnificence, the great arched temple of Karli, with its noble vestibule and entrance, and the sitting figure of Buddha. On looking into the temple, an object of wonder presents itself—a ponderous arched roof of solid stone, supported by two rows of pillars, the capitals of each surmounted by a well-sculptured male and female figure, seated, with their arms encircling each other, on the back of elephants, crouching, as it were, under the weight they sustain. At the further end of the temple is an immense hemispherical altar of stone, with a kind of wooden umbrella spreading over the top.

Towards the evening I descended the mountains, and proceeded across the fields to my tent. The dak, or post-carrier, having passed

51. Entrance of
the great cave at
Karli.

me on the preceding day, I dropped a letter into his leathern bag,
requesting a friend to send his horse on for me to Telligaum, a stage
fourteen miles distant. These dak-men, for a small pay, go in the
most inclement weather through the wildest parts, day and night,
at a quick trot. In the dry season, though the distance may be 800
miles, such is their regularity, that there is seldom half an hour's
difference in the time of their arrival. Should they be carried off by
a tiger, or fall sick, which frequently happens, the bag is generally
found and brought on by the following dak-bearer. They stop travellers on the road, that they may have an opportunity of inspect-
ing the bag. It is usual to direct letters or newspapers for travellers
outside the dak, that is, in the bag loose, but not in the packet. Not
a word is exchanged; you may take what packets you please and on
trots the poor solitary fellow with his flambeau and dirk, at midnight, through a wilderness, the horrors of which would appal many
a stout English heart. In the rainy season it is a dreadful employ.
A bag thus exposed would not go quite so safely in England.

Telligaum is nineteen miles from Karli: this distance, although
considerable in India, I purposed with the aid of the relief-horse,
performing in one day. At 8 a.m. I arrived at Telligaum, which has
been a considerable town; it still has a good market. Near the town
is a fine tank of considerable size, well stocked with fish, and close
by is a room built for the accommodation of travellers. It was at

52. *Departure from Poona.*

this spot, during the late war, that the two brothers (Vaughans) were barbarously murdered in cold blood by a body of Mahratta troops, at the instigation of Trimbuckjee. At Telligaum a sheep might be purchased for about 2s.2d.

The roads leading into the city of Poona are in good repair. One route proceeds by the British residency at the Sangam; the other by a good substantial stone bridge over the Moota river. It was near sunset as I entered Poona, the setting rays of that glorious orb reflecting its beams on the venerable roof of the Parbutti temple, on turreted walls, large white terraced houses, lofty shining spires, and on handsome-looking pagodas, intermingled with Moghul buildings, Hindoo palaces, castles, and gardens, afforded, on a serene evening, an imposing sight to a stranger, while a fine river running in front of the city added an interesting feature to the view. This was not lessened upon entering a crowded city, where the objects were as varied in appearance as the external view had been half a mile off, and consisted of large heavy houses, built of stone, more for defence than comfort, many of them painted with representations of peacocks, figures of Ganesa and Hanuman. Shops of all descriptions were seen, having open fronts, with the goods exposed on an inclined platform, the streets narrow and thronged with people, among whom might be discovered the sedate, decently-clad Brahman, the delicate and pretty-featured Hindoo female, the portly, dignified, and handsomely-dressed Mussulman, Arab horsemen completely armed, prancing along upon their fine chargers, *fakirs* in a state of nudity, and Mahratta foot-soldiers.

In this diversified moving mass we must not forget a few Jews and Portuguese Christians, and occasionally a British *siphauee* in his neat undress, on leave of absence for a few hours. The living picture has the addition of state elephants, splendid cavalcades of public officers decked out with parade and show, accompanied by richly caparisoned led horses, and camels trotting along at a quick pace, with rows of little tinkling bells suspended round their necks. If to all this we add crowded markets, religious processions, and bands of noisy musicians, some idea may be formed of the tumult and bustle of the capital city of the Mahratta empire towards evening.

There are on the Poona road two convenient and neat lodges, built by subscription, for the accommodation of travellers, and for the residence of sporting parties, who come from Poona and Seroor, sometimes for a week or ten days together. The neighbouring plains are plentifully stocked with antelopes, wild-hogs, hares and partridges. Tigers are sometimes found, but wolves, jackals, and foxes are constantly met with. Hog-hunting, however, was the principal sport followed. These lodges are at Lonee, eight miles from Poona, and at Shikarpoor (place of hunting), twenty miles from Seroor. At Seroor I had to relieve my guard, and procure fresh

53. Kailash.

coolies and cattle. I likewise bought a camel for about eight pounds sterling, as I intended to make long marches.

On my arrival at Ahmednaggur, I was greeted in the kindest manner by the officers. I was cautioned to keep my *siphauees* and baggage close at hand, as the Ghat was infested by Bheels. Some few I saw, but they did not offer to molest me, and I passed by quite unconcerned. The country at the foot of the pass is a fine cultivated tract. This the natives accounted for partly by the neighbourhood of our troops, and the proprietor of the village and lands being a Brahman, who kept in his pay thirty-five Arab soldiers. These men, being under his own immediate inspection, neither did mischief themselves, nor permitted the incursions of robbers. The next day I proceeded on my route to Toka, 15 miles away, the landscape for the whole distance one wild barren waste. On the right-hand side of the road were some quarries containing a close-grained blue stone: it had been worked but little, but the strata appeared to extend to a considerable distance. The country is not deficient in wood, many streams intersect the land; the soil is very rich.

I set out on the third day after my arrival to Shahpoor (or Place of Kings); which, notwithstanding its name, was a miserable little hamlet. After crossing the Godavery in a large unwieldy boat, a short distance on, the country is overrun with a thick jungle, in which numerous hordes of Bheels find a secure retreat, levying a certain sum on each passenger and on his cattle, and, if he has the temerity to resist, he is sure to be maltreated. During the journey, I could not have seen less than 150 of them in different parties. Several accosted me, but having three *siphauees* with me, their muskets loaded, and myself armed, they offered no interruption to us. But my servant, who had preceded me, rather than have an altercation, had paid a tribute of 4 rupees (10s), greatly in opposition to the wishes of the *siphauees,* who objected to any compromise with the Bheels. After getting through the jungle, which extends for some miles, the country becomes hilly, with a range extending from north to east. Daulutabad is seen bearing N.E. distant about 14 miles. Shahpoor is 16 miles from Toka; its inhabitants diseased, half-naked, and poor in the extreme.

At day-break I pursued my journey to Elora, 18 miles distant, the country becoming more open, and a little cultivation occasionally to be seen. Game appeared to be plentiful—several hares and partridges being seen during my route. It was not without emotion I entered the pretty little rural village of Elora, embosomed in a grove of trees, inhabited by Brahmans, and on account of the holiness of the spot, the troops stationed here were Rajpoots. The whole district then belonged to the Mahratta prince Holkar, whose mother was a munificent patroness to the Brahmans and devotees living in the neighbourhood. It was excessively hot, and as I could not expect my baggage for three or four hours, I sought shelter in a pagoda—a handsome building of stone, about 18 feet square. The pagoda where I had taken my seat stands in a beautifully romantic spot. Near this pagoda is a tank, the masonry of which, for beauty and uniformity, I never saw equalled.

About 1 p.m. my people arrived, and I hurried them on to Elora, distant about a mile, for although both tired and hungry I could not resist proceeding on at once to the glorious scene which awaited me at the eternal temples and houses in the mountain. No inducement could have prevailed on me to stop another half-hour.

Bruce's emotions were not more vivid or tumultuous on first beholding the springs of the Nile, than mine were on reaching the temples of Elora. I at once rushed into the wonders and glories of these immortal works. But it is totally impossible to describe the feelings of admiration and awe excited in the mind upon first beholding these stupendous excavations. The feelings are interested to a degree of awe, wonder, and delight that at first is painful, and it is a long time before they become sufficiently sobered and calm

54. Interior at Ellora.

55. Village of
Mahabaleshwar.

to contemplate with any attention the surrounding wonders. The death-like stillness of the place, the solitude of the adjoining plains, the romantic beauty of the country, and the mountain itself, perforated in every part, all tend to impress the mind of the stranger with feelings quite new, and far different from those felt in viewing magnificent edifices amidst the busy haunts of man. Everything here invites the mind to contemplation, and every surrounding object reminds it of a remote period, and a mighty people, who were in a state of high civilization, whilst the natives of our own land were barbarians, living in woods and wilds.

Conceive the burst of surprise at suddenly coming upon a stupendous temple, within a large open court, hewn out of the solid rock, with all its parts perfect and beautiful, standing proudly alone upon its native bed, and detached from the neighbouring mountain by a spacious area all round, nearly 250 feet deep, and 150 feet broad: this unrivalled fare rearing its rocky head to a height of nearly 100 feet—its length about 145 feet, by 62 broad—having well-formed doorways, windows, staircases to its upper floor, containing fine large rooms of a smooth and polished surface, regularly divided by rows of pillars: the whole bulk of this immense block of isolated excavation being upwards of 500 feet in circumference, and, extraordinary as it may appear, having beyond its areas three handsome figure galleries, or verandahs, supported by regular pillars, with compartments hewn out of the boundary scarp, containing 42 curious gigantic figures of the Hindoo mythology—the whole three galleries in continuity, enclosing the areas, and occupying the almost incredible space of nearly 420 feet of excavated rock; being, upon the average, about 13 feet 2 inches broad all round, and in height 14 feet and a half; while, positively, above these again are excavated fine large rooms. Within the court, and opposite these galleries, or verandahs, stands Keylas the Proud, wonderfully towering in hoary majesty—a mighty fabric of rock, surpassed by no relic of antiquity in the known world.

The Bengali Traveller

SANTI P. CHOWDHURY

The Bengali is a great traveller. Yet the concept of travel for pleasure is of comparatively recent origin. It is difficult to think of a Bengali Marco Polo. Dipankar Srigyan travelled to Tibet in the tenth century to preach Buddhism. There was, of course, travel for trade, but for most, travel was a pilgrimage.

Bankim Chandra's classic novel *Kapalkundala* describes events of late sixteenth century Mughal India. A group of pilgrims are on their way back from the Sagar island in the Bay of Bengal. Their boat is adrift in the sea in thick fog. The worst is feared and there is much lament. An elderly pilgrim complains about his business losses. Nabakumar, protagonist of the novel, chides the man, "Such journeys should not be undertaken by men burdened with worldly care."

"But one comes to the Sagar to honour religious vows. Why have *you* come?" the old man questions Nabakumar.

दुरादयश्चक्रनिभस्य तन्वी तमालतालीवनराजिनीला ।
आभाति बेला लवनाम्बुराशेर्द्धासनिवद्धेर कलंकरेखा ॥

Nabakumar recites from Kalidasa's *Raghuvansham*. This is how Rama saw the sea and the coastline from his aerial chariot after rescuing Sita on his way back from Lanka. Nabakumar has made the perilous journey to see the sea. He must have been one of the earliest Bengali travellers who had travelled for pleasure. He was an exception.

Travel for the sake of travel, for curiosity and discovery, for excitement and pleasure, came to India much later. Like so many things, the idea of travel is a gift of the British. Like the British, the anglicised Bengali *babus* took to travel by horse carriages even before the railways arrived in India. Their travels were made possible because of the institution of dak bungalows. Bholanath Chunder, travelling in 1860 from Calcutta to the Punjab, writes in his *Travels of a Hindoo*:

These dawk-bungalows are, in point of fact, miniature roadside inns on the European model. The principal building of masonry, one storey high, with a high-peaked roof of thatch or tiles, stands in the middle of a green plot. It consists of a suite of three or four rooms, one of which is appropriated to the purposes of a bath. In a corner of the compound lie the kitchen and the outhouses, and adjoining them is a well, generally of excellent water. There are beddings and furniture nearly as good as in the houses of decent townsfolk. The eatables and drinkables are good enough for nutritives in their way. The Asiatic has nothing to show like these bungalows.

Bholanath Chunder then proceeds to write about their halt in a dak bungalow in Bihar.

It was near nightfall—over the pure, cloudless sky was the glow of the last light. The breeze, bland and perfumed by the odour of the wild flowers, came in soft cool gushes. It was one of those calm and delightful evenings which we went out to enjoy by spreading a carpet on the green sward surrounding the bungalow. To heighten the enjoyment by a *sauce piquante,* we had each passed round to us a glass of that beverage, which was brewed not from the Vedic *soma* plant, but from the English hops—accompanied by that sovereign luxury, that never-failing source of refreshment to the weary—the invaluable *hooka.* Shortly after dark, dinner was announced...with white table-cloth, knives, forks, plates, dishes and napkins set on the table....

Of the various accounts of boat journeys, Iswar Chandra Gupta's "Letters of a Traveller Friend" serialised in his own newspaper, *Sambad Prabhakar,* round about 1850 are the most outstanding. He was Bankim Chandra's guru, pioneer editor, biographer, and the first Bengali author to live entirely by his pen. He made this boat journey through East Bengal to see the forests of Sunderban, and to get a taste of the sea. As far as I know this was the first bit of travel writing in Bengali.

Another great traveller was Debendranath Tagore. Rabindranath, writing about his father in *Jibansmriti,* tells us how his father was away most of the time, returning occasionally with a foreign servant. Foreign, of course, meant outside Bengal. Dalhousie introduced the railways in the 1850s and by the turn of the century trains made travel easy and romantic. Heroes of novels, including the ubiquitous

Devdas, were always taking trains to the 'West' at the slightest provocation. West, for some reason, always meant North India—the vast Gangetic plains and the hills beyond.

By the turn of the century, though travel became commonplace for the affluent middle class, it remained strongly hierarchic. First class was for the British or really rich Indians. The Maharajas had their private coaches and trains. Second class, one step down the ladder, was for the not-so-important sahibs and upper middle class Indians. The Inter class was for the salaried middle classes, specially those travelling with large families. The third was taboo for the *bhadralok*. One would rather borrow money than travel third.

Although the Bengali got anglicised in terms of education, ideas, etc., the majority did not change their life styles. A famous lawyer knighted by the British was travelling first class with his family. It did not take long before the compartment was transformed into their home. Relaxed, almost in undress, after a sumptuous snack, they were talking, dozing, reading, looking out of the windows. The train stopped at a station. A pucca memsahib walked in. The Anglo-Indian guard explained there was no room in the other first class compartments. Imagine the great lawyer's discomfiture (the memsahib wasn't actually very happy either) but there was nothing that he could do. A little before the next stop, he said something to his eldest son in Bengali. He was a rather hirsute young gentleman in his twenties. The train rolled to a stop at the station. The young gentleman was bare-bodied. He crossed over to face the lady, his arms upraised. The memsahib couldn't fail to see his body hair bursting into incredible luxuriance under the arm-pits. Swallowing a horror-stricken shriek, she got down from the coach never to be seen again. The young gentleman in time became a well-known Indian leader.

The institution of long vacations—the summer and the Puja holidays for schools, colleges, and courts—brought in the concept of a "change". This word in its special sense has now become a part of the Bengali language. Going for a change doesn't signify just travel or even a change of air—it means travel undertaken for the improvement of one's health. So the trek to the mountains and the sea-side started. Even if a Bengali is reasonably healthy, he generally believes that there is ample scope for further improvement of his health. More often than not, the yardstick is his capacity to eat and, having eaten, the capacity to digest the food unequivocally, so that he may eat some more. For the Bengali traveller, this is the most important aspect of his travels, particularly when such travels are presumably undertaken for a change. This is how Chotanagpur became a region of the Bengali mind. But more about that in a minute. Going to the mountains would mean one was going to Darjeeling, or the smaller, slightly lower hill stations of Kalimpong and Kurseong. These afforded a clear view of the Himalayan peaks of Kanchanjunga and Mount Everest—fleeting in summer but more reliably visible in autumn—lovely trees (all planted by the sahibs), superb vegetables, big red juicy raw cardamoms, succulent pork chops, ham and bacon, fresh butter and cheese. For the anglicised Bengali, there was nothing like Darjeeling, where a bit of riding and marvellous walks improved the appetite.

Affluent Bengalis built their bungalows. The shining blue dome of the Burdwan Maharaja's mansion, Cooch Behar's splendid lawn in the Jalapahar heights, comfortable homes built by C.R. Das and Sir

Jagadish Bose were landmarks in a place where the majority spoke Nepali. During the season, regular races were held at Lebong—one of the highest race courses in the country, where the ponies had their tails braided with gay ribbons. Buddhist pagodas, the red-hat and yellow-hat lamas, fluttering prayer flags, the somnolent chant and sombre religious music of drums and horns, the colourful processions and above all the pleasant poverty-defying gaiety of the hill people would rub off on the visiting babus, and their children would return to the city with cheeks pinked by the wafting Himalayan mists. There was Shillong—Assam's old capital—now Meghalaya's, the headquarters of the North East Council (currently India's biggest hill station) where Dr. B.C. Roy established the first hydel generation plant below the picturesque Bishop's Falls. Shillong was the setting for Tagore's *Sosher Kabita* (The Last Poem), a romantic but daringly modern novel for its day.

The sea-side invariably meant Puri in Orissa. The famous Jagannath temple was, of course, an added attraction. For the anglicised affluent there was the magnificent railway hotel on the beach. Now there are scores of small hotels catering to the Bengali palate. The average Bengali is averse to sea-fish, and though the white sands would glitter with the silver of fresh catches of sardines, mackerels, and sprats, he would only be interested in the prawns. In the old days the babus had their own bungalows just as in the hills. In fact, Abanindranath Tagore relates how, when his family decided to visit Puri, a bungalow first had to be built for their sojourn.

But neither the cool hills nor the splendid surf fully answered the Bengali traveller's search for a "change" in terms of miraculous digestive properties. This was found in the wells of Chotanagpur—especially in the Santhal Parganas. The water was absolutely incredible. As we say in Bengali, one could digest a stone. With its sylvan landscape, low hills, brooks and rivulets, cheap and fertile land, and salubrious climate, bungalows erupted all over the borders of Bengal and Bihar.

This time not only the affluents, but a much broader segment of the middle classes joined the fray. Scores of places with names like Mihijam, Jamtara, Karmatar, Madhupur, Simultala, Giridih, Jhanjha, Deoghar, Jassidih are dotted with pretty bungalows built by other generations. The bungalows always have names. Sans Souci, Hill View, Rose Villa—shades of British suburbia. Occasionally more pompous names such as Ghose Manor or Banerjee Castle. It is only fair to point out, however, that "Raipur House" in Simultala was built by Lord Sinha of Raipur (not to be confused with the Shukla

56. *The Esplanade,*
Calcutta.

fiefdom in Madhya Pradesh), the only hereditary peerage created in
India by the British Crown. But the most popular names—the names
that are engraved in marble in every other bungalow—are Matri-
Smriti, Matri-Sadan, Matri-Dham bearing witness to the Bengali's
overwhelming Oedipal drive.

Many of these bungalows have now largely fallen into disuse.
Today's travellers prefer more distant destinations and, in any case,
very few have the means to set up a vacation home. In more leisurely
times families used to visit with large retinues sometimes staying for
the autumn and a good part of the winter. There was much coming
and going, and relatives, friends, and friends' friends, all were
welcome. The bungalows would have large compounds—the
boundary walls dotted with elegant eucalyptus trees. Roses grew
easily and the ochre earth would be covered by a carpet of fallen
petals—white, yellow and all shades of pink and red. Dwarf papaya
trees would bend with the weight of fruit, and every bungalow had
a sort of orchard with guava, mango and custard-apple.

The permanent caretaker was generally a Santhal *mali*—like a
sculpture carved out of black stone. He made bows and arrows for the
children, slaughtered the chickens, looked after the garden. The San-
thals were like mythic figures—handsome, gracious and courageous.
Their neat villages, the beauty of their women, their simplicity and

The Bengali Traveller 177

order gave one a sense of well-being that somehow transcended one's discomfort at their obvious poverty. But there was something in their black skin, unrevealing eyes, the throb of their distant drums in the evenings that evoked a strong feeling of atavism for one's own tribal past.

The pride of the house was, of course, the well. In terms of digestive effectiveness, some wells were considered better than others, even though the distance between the superior and less superior well would sometimes be no more than a couple of hundred yards. Everyone drank a lot of water—to work up an appetite, and after meals as a carminative. There is a vast baroque house in Jassidih with an elaborate garden full of statues—nymphs and dryads lining the gravel paths. The well in this property is reputed to be one of the best in the area. Water from this well is sent regularly by train to the Marwari owner in Calcutta. They say the Nizam, one of the richest men in the world in his time, used to travel with his own drinking water from the Osmansagar lake.

With such water and with the Bengali's declared predeliction for good food, the major part of all activity would be predictably culinary. The first part of the morning would be spent searching for the day's food. Interesting variations of the walk to the daily bazaar would be to go to some nearby village market which generally assembled once a week. All these places provided easy grazing—so there was never any dearth of good milk, pure ghee, and a whole range of simple but delicious Bengali-style sweets. The initiative would always be taken by the menfolk—most of whom fancied themselves as expert cooks, although their cooking would always be limited to meat (goat) and chicken curries, or what they chose to call stews.

Incidentally, very few Bengali kitchens would allow the cooking of meat, specially chicken, inside the house. So the cooking would be done in the garden or some mysterious corner adding a festive atmosphere to the whole operation. The stew would be a more lightly spiced, watery version of the curry with whole onions and tomatoes thrown in. The chicken curry, however, was just a generic term for culinary self-expression covering the whole range from the barely edible to the divine. This would include *kormas, dopiazas, rezzalas,* and long would be the arguments in favour of squeezing the juice of ginger, garlic and onion rather than using them in the usual ground paste form. Each had his own approach to marinating with a general preference for sour curd.

But the chicken curry which swept people off their feet was a simple one deriving its inspiration from the cooking style pioneered by the sailors in East Bengal steamers. The best cooks in India were the Baruas from Chittagong. The Baruas ruled over the kitchens of the maharajas, sahibs, clubs, army messes, Jesuit Fathers —they were the last word in Anglo-Indian cuisine. Fragrant rice (Bengali rice is always light because the starch is washed off) and hot chicken curry—ask anyone who has travelled in East Bengal and he would probably tell you that he has never eaten anything better. The Santhal Parganas chicken curry is close to the steamer curry in flavour and texture except for the chillis. The steamer curry was irresistible and one kept on eating while tears rolled down one's cheeks. It was difficult to stop. There are some eats, such as roasted cashew nuts, *golgappa,* etc. with the same peculiarity—a kind of seductive, persuasive titillation of the palate that leads one to shameless gluttony.

The Calcutta *bhadralok* would never eat rice at night and his taste for chilli was nowhere near his more desperate brethren from East Bengal. The Calcutta babu would only eat what they called *maida* at night. Dainty triangular *parathas* fried in *ghee,* or more commonly, *luchis*—those fluffy paper-thin ephemeral *puris,* a kind of extremely small, white, blushing, flour puff ball fried in ghee. The Bengalis don't know how to make *chapatis* and *atta* has come to Bengal in the wake of rationing and PL 480 wheat. On rare occasions when they did eat *chapatis,* they were made of flour, liberally coated with *ghee* on both sides. So *maida* and chicken curry would be the culinary climax of the day. The hissing pressure lamps would be put out, and the jewelled vault of the sky would hold us rapt, listening to Tagore's lilting melodies.

There was romance in the air. If one did not fall in love with the girls in the neighbourhood, there was always the twilight promenade at the railway station (the equivalent of hill station Malls) where the girls preened and pranced. If one did not fall in love with a handy cousin, there was always some young aunt or other. The age of lust was yet to come and the language of secret love wove surcharged patterns through the indolent day—a deliberate mistake at a game of cards, the clever unnecessary sacrifice of a chess piece, a miraculous moment of togetherness at a picnic, glances, gestures and songs learnt from popular films. There was much reading and talking. Grown-ups would talk like characters out of Russian novels— enveloping the young in a nebulous vapour of politics, literature, philosophy, and above all, the meaning of life.

In memory, all the nights were moonlit and all the days offered shade. Dappled light, shade, *parchhainya*—fugitive from the hunting sun—the sun is there, you can see beyond the hills, lazy drone of the bees, sound of cattle-bells, yet the sun is not there under your tree—a peaceful balmy shade as mysterious as the shade you see on the faces of some of our women. Innumerable stories, novels, poems, films, plays have evoked the Santhal Parganas. For the Bengali traveller Chotanagpur is a region of the Bengali mind.

They used to fly Dakotas those days. We were on our way to Imphal. Doljatra in Manipur was supposed to be the most elegant festival in India. The plane had difficulty landing at the Silchar airport (miles out of town in the middle of nowhere) in squally weather. The small airport building (or was it a biggish hut?) was already jammed with passengers waiting for flights. The suspense was short. Soon all flights were cancelled including ours to Imphal. The rain was pouring down in thick sheets. If you want to watch rain, come to North-East India. Passengers scrambled to get into the small airlines bus. Soon several were standing. Irate males, querulous females, babies yelling with irritation at not finding the nipple. Everyone travels by plane in N.E. India. The bus arrived at the bank of the Barak river. Normally a ribbon, it now heaved, writhed and rolled like a mythical snake. The bus gingerly rolled on to the diesel ferry. The rain went as suddenly as it came, the monsoon was still more than a month away. We were all inside the bus. The ferry chugged to the other bank and stopped. A *kutcha* road snaked up the high embankments.

A truck was making its journey in groaning first gear. We waited. The truck disappeared around the bend. Our driver switched on the ignition. Before we knew what was happening, the bus was sliding back into the river. The iron chain at the edge had snapped. The moment is clearly etched in my memory—the smell and taste of that moment of certain death. Suddenly the bus was motionless. The front axle had got caught at the edge of the jetty, and the bus hung at a precarious angle half in the water and half outside. Passengers jumped into the water, a few swallowed a bit of the river, there was noisy panic, but by the time the bus went under (in a couple of minutes), all were home and dry. A few had minor injuries. A plump, elderly gentleman in a dazzling sharkskin suit had managed to save his huge box of cake from Flury's, Calcutta. I vividly remember his dazed and funny expression.

The point of this anecdote is not to tell a survival story but to stress the fact that even twenty years ago journeys into north-east India were quite frequently uncomfortable. In spite of a lot of change —you now get a Boeing from Calcutta to Imphal five days a week—the basic element of uncertainty still predominates north-eastern journeys. Recently I bumped into a friend at Gauhati airport whose flight to Silchar had been cancelled due to bad weather. We ourselves had arrived from Imphal nearly four hours late. The friend had been touring north-eastern India twenty days in the month, for two decades, selling cigarettes. Apparently there are fourteen air pockets over the hills between Silchar and Gauhati. So the Fokker doesn't take any chances.

Earlier in the year we were stranded at Agartala as some flights had been cancelled and we couldn't get any seats. We had to hire a station wagon and drive for two days to get to Gauhati via Shillong. A picturesque journey no doubt, but it plays hell with your schedules. How much of these difficulties are due to bad weather, how much due to the indifference of the Airlines (airfares in north-east India are cheap and highly subsidised)—I don't know. Dr. Bhupen Hazarika says Delhi's concern stops at Patna. Trains are almost non-existent. It is perhaps because of this that large areas in northeast India retain some of their traditional charm.

To go back to our accident-interruped journey to Imphal twenty years ago. Next day the plane flew over emerald hills which turned to a mineral red as we approached the Imphal airport. We flew down over the heads of grazing cattle and Imphal appeared very pastoral. There was a hotel of sorts where an American woman was staying permanently. She was already a fairly advanced student of Manipuri

dance. I believe she returned to the States with a handsome Manipuri youth, no doubt to continue her lessons in Manipuri dance. As far as I know, no foreigners are now allowed to visit Manipur. Be that as it may, the fact remains that the most striking thing about Manipuri culture is its dance. Dance not only as an expression of joy but dance as spiritual expression, dance as a whole way of life.

On the day of *Holi,* we woke early. In the east you don't get up by the watch. There was a slight chill in the air. Dozens of little groups were forming, presently to go in little processions to the Govindji temple, part of the palace complex. Grave-faced elders (a lot of them looked like Sachin Dev Burman) in pure white—flowing white *dhotis, kurta, chaddar* draped around their necks and graceful white turbans on their heads. Other groups were in vibrating pink and lemon yellow. Some of the women were in saffron. I wish some of the Hare-Krishna cultwallahs could learn from Manipur the grace and dignity of the Nam Sankirtan. Under a huge shed by the temple they gathered. A group would rise and sing, moving gracefully all the time. Others would squirt sprays of colour on them. Their spotless clothes, now polka-dotted with bright colours, would take on the beauty of abstract paintings. The strange wails and rhythm of the music would soon grow hypnotic, accentuating the contemplative trance on their faces.

They would visit relations. In front of the family elders, they would prostrate themselves on the ground—the whole scene as if unfolding in slow motion, a case of the ridiculous elevated to the sublime. It is easy for a Bengali to read Manipuri hoardings and newspapers as they use the Bengali alphabet. The language, however, is of the Tibeto-Burman group. The juxtaposition of the familiar alphabet and the mysterious phonetics, though highly surrealistic, is only but a part of the many cross-currents of this bizarre sub-continent. At some stage, Vaishnavism came to Manipur from Bengal, the king's proselytisation leading to Bengali culture heavily lacing the religious and cultural life of the valley. Even now, in spite of the political demands for an indigenous script, most people over forty speak Bengali. With the arrival of the British came the Christian missionaries who converted most of the tribal people in the hills. The majority of the valley people—the Meiteis—are devout Vaishnavs. The Vaishnavite sandal mark (*rasakeli*) is still very much a daily ritual, but pre-Hindu Manipuri culture exists with equal vitality and relevance.

By this time, I am, of course, tenseless—twenty-year old memories making an amalgam of various visits including the three I made this year—the images obtaining a pictorial autonomy almost free of time

and space. Thus a winter dusk of pale mist, a tall woman in white robe walking under a white umbrella (to protect herself from the dew), a few more in similar habit, some with white bundles on their heads—an image devised by Kurosawa. A procession of Manipuri Muslim ladies on their way to some village bearing gifts for relatives for some ritual. Again, a village road alight with fireflies—we followed the sound of music and arrived at an opening. Women were dancing in a big circle—from girls of four to white-haired ladies in their eighties (you don't see much grey hair in Manipur although people live long).

The dance was a part of the *Lai-haraoba* festival of the Gods—an elaborate ceremony spread over several days and nights. This is pre-Hindu. Each area has its own god and *Lai-haraoba* is Manipur's biggest festival. I have heard it said that there is no ceremony more beautiful anywhere else in the world. To come back to the summer evening. Everyone had that expression of beatitude, an expression that reminded one of phrases like "peace that passeth understanding" or "a touch of that which defies description". The movements were slow and simple as in all Manipuri dance but of almost unbearable grace. The *mayibi* (priestess) was, of course, the most graceful dancer. An elderly man dressed in rich clothes (reminding one of the dress worn by the kings of Siam and Cambodia), his turbaned head keeping time to his country violin, danced alongside. Horn loud-speakers sent out cascades of ululating song towards the hills. Soon the petromaxes were lit, dangling from bamboo structures, casting eerie shadows.

The grace was now gone, the music had grown a bit frenetic, the *mayibi* was in a trance. She had now become an oracle, a prophetess of doom. She would forecast what was in store for the village—the health and welfare of the people, the nature of the harvest. The hysterical wailing went on for some time. Someone handed her a decorative polo stick and a white polo ball. Still, totally in a state of trance, she moved, a strange tableau mostly in white. After a while she hit the ball. Anxious eyes watched the flight of the ball. It went wide over the heads of a group. They looked visibly relieved. If the ball hits someone, it is an evil omen. Someone would retrieve the ball and hand it over to the moving, dancing, entranced *mayibi* and this would go on. One knew it was all mumbo-jumbo, the metallic speakers had already introduced a shrillness that prevented one from soaring, yet the spell was binding. A little distance away people were selling snacks as they do all over the country, in the light of smoking kerosene lamps. It took the careful eating of fried *koi* (a fish which is

killed only just before cooking and has very tricky side-bones) and
the tartness of the sauce—a mixture of chopped onions, tamarind,
plenty of chillis and some herbs—before we returned to reality and
left for Imphal.

There is a legendary Manipuri tale where the dowager queen warns
the prince to be careful about people with sharp noses and large eyes.
Such people today are found everywhere in Manipur. On our way
back from the Subhas Bose memorial at Moirang, we stopped at the
bazaar for tea. The shop is owned by someone from a village near
Gorakhpur. The single-chair hair-dressing saloon next door was run
by someone from a village in Bihar. There is even a *dhaba* of sorts on
the Tiddium Chin Road at Churachandpur. The food was bad but
there were quite a few of the Central Reserve Police knocking down
dozens of *tandoori roti* with some nondescript *sabji*. You can buy

Ajinomoto from Thailand and a score of other imported (smuggled) things, including cane hats from Burma, if they are not suspicious about you. The main road is straight as an arrow lined by shops and reminds you of the American westerns. A powerfully built Kuki in dapper clothes stood in the sun picking his teeth.

After you pass Dunhill store and Apollo store, your eyes get locked into some unknown script on a signboard. Judean Photo Studio, the Kuki explained. The hieroglyphics are Hebrew. I remembered seeing a cottage up in the hills named Zion cottage. Yes, there are three hundred Jews. One Mr. Daniel had been the proselytiser. By this time, the proprietor of Judean Photo Studio had joined the conversation. "We are spiritual Jews, not physical," he said. I don't know what he meant but perhaps he was trying to tell us that they were not circumcised. There is no synagogue but there is a prayer hall. We moved next door to the Great Eastern Book Store. There were some religious tracts in Paite including the Bible. From Gutenburg to some lonely missionary in the Manipur hills, the history of printing is the printing of the Bible. To misquote Dostoyevsky: If there is Jesus, everything is possible. Some of the other titles I remember were by Agatha Christie and Erle Stanley Gardener (surely close competitors to the Bible), love letters, a lavishly produced book for executives based on the monthly bulletins of the Royal Bank of Canada, and J. Edgar Hoover's book against communism.

The place is full of Mizos—migrants from Mizoram—hard working, gay, secretive people. Some young people put up a show for us, the famous Mizo bamboo dance. The girls were very beautiful and sturdy—strong but extremely feminine. The dance called for perfect timing. Some girls squatted on the ground each with two bamboo poles, one group facing another. Two other groups sat similarly on two other sides, forming a square chequer-board pattern with the poles. A mod youth strummed on his guitar—the lilting song would start slow, the crouching girls keeping time building rhythmic patterns by banging the bamboo poles, the dancing girls weaving in and out of individual chessboard squares. The tempo would build up never losing its melodic lilt as the sure-footed girls danced with total concentration. One slip and the moving bamboos would smash their feet. A touch of danger always seems to improve the performance.

The hill people, owing to the missionaries, seem very westernised, at least superficially. Many of the young wear smart imported clothes, and their hair styles are also very modern. In comparison, the valley people are still strongly entrenched in their own tradition, though the narrow streets of Paonabazar and Thangalbazar in Imphal are noisy with current pop hits. But both in the hills and the valley, one is overwhelmed by the vigour of the women. Every house has a loom, every woman works. Yet they seem to have gone beyond women's lib. They have the rights but they remain so feminine. There is no coyness, only charm. The handloom bazaar, the main market at Imphal, and scores of other markets and stalls you see throughout Manipur are run entirely by women. Middle-aged women and elderly women, after they have raised their children, get a bit bored with housework and take to enterprise.

It is truly Chitrangada country and the Mahabharata story does indicate a society where women have enjoyed this autonomy for a long time. Chitrangada sings in Tagore's dance-drama of the same name "I am Chitrangada—not just an ordinary woman". In Manipur every woman seems to glow with the pride of being a special woman. In fact, at first glance it may appear that women do all the work. You will see them fishing in water-logged paddy fields using bamboo contraptions similar to the ones in Cochin, but much smaller in size. A gentleman with us from Delhi who had spent his childhood in Chittagong, got very excited remembering how he had caught fish with similar contraptions in the canals of the Karnaphuli river.

There is so much to say about Sikkim and Bhutan, Tripura and Nagaland, and the tribes of Arunachal. There is so much that provokes enquiry. Why do the Khasi in the Meghalaya hills and the Mundari in South Bihar happen to be languages of the Khmer group? Why is the Naga so dynamic? It is a many-splendoured world of infinite variety in the north-eastern hills. But like so many other places in India, this is a vanishing world.

The Bengali traveller meanwhile is alive and well. He is now a regular travel-maniac. Travel has spread to the lower middle classes, to the working classes in Durgapur and Asansol. After food, travel remains his next most important priority. He will merrily spend his hard-earned bonus money for the annual trip. Travel is now highly institutionalised. Package tours and reserved trains, some of them fitted with special kitchens for fussy widows, cater to the people's needs. You will see bent old ladies at the Kulu fair, rotund matrons riding ponies in Khilanmarg, cackling children in the caves of Ajanta. Outside the 5-star orbit, Bengalis today are the most gregarious travellers in India. Yet you will find only a very few of them travelling next door to their neighbours. As the poet has said, one roams all over the world searching for beauty, but one never stops to look at the wonder of a dew-drop on a blade of grass.

Sketches by Paritosh Sen

Assam: A Different Story

AMENA JAYAL

Sometime in early 1947, my father set off for Assam as its first Governor. The jet-age had not yet hit India, but it was, nevertheless, a far-cry from the age of gas-lit streets and hansom-cabs which today's young associate with my generation's improbable youth. I forget which British Viceroy was credited with saying he belonged not to the "hunting, shooting, fishing", but the "shunting, tooting, hissing" type of Englishman, who preferred laying railway lines to pig-sticking. But worthies like him were responsible for our very comfortable railway journey to Assam in a splendid white gubernatorial saloon, which must long since have joined similar other antiquities of the British Raj in some forgotten junk-yard. Even the British had been unable to lay a railway track from Gauhati up to Shillong, so this part of our journey was made in some shining vintage cars through some of the prettiest hill-country one could hope to see. But despite such prosaic modes of travel, interior Assam, particularly the remote and inaccessible eastern hills, had much to offer the intrepid traveller in his search for the new and strange.

Pre-Independence Shillong was like a small English county-town with its pseudo-Tudor houses, rolling downs, and true-blue pukka sahibs and memsahibs. Their dogs, all impressively pedigreed imports from 'home'—Great Danes, Golden Retrievers, Spaniels, Bulldogs and every known variation on the Terrier theme—paced the immaculate streets with their masters or with uniformed dog-'boys' who were usually as old as Methuselah, and romped with small pink children in trim gardens filled with utterly English flowers. There were tweed jackets and grey flannel 'bags', tweed skirts and wool twin-sets always worn with Mother's Brogues and Lyle stockings and a variety of scruffy, shapeless woollen hats. It was almost as if the British were parodying the British.

In strong contrast to this colourless conformity, like gorgeous butterflies among drab moths, strode the tribal people of the hills of Assam: Nagas, Lushais, Mishmis, Akas, Mompas, Apatanis, and

57. Facing page. Angami Nagas dancing.

many other tribes and sub-tribes. They came down to the plains for trade, supplies, and sometimes education, bringing with them their tremendous zest for life, their enjoyment of it patent in their vigorous speech and movement, and their fresh, spontaneous laughter. But I shall return to these stimulating people later.

I believe the beautiful mixed forests around Shillong are no longer as lush as they used to be, and that even the ubiquitous Khasi pine has had to give way to the pressures of overpopulation. But certainly until 1961, when I last enjoyed wandering through them, it was a different story. The forests then were rich and varied and made doubly fascinating by a profusion of many kinds of flowering shrubs and creepers that thrived in the fertile soil. Orchids of every description glowed like bright silk threads on an arboreal tapestry that sheltered many forms of wild life. There were butterflies and beetles and birds I had never seen before; panther, wild-pig and jungle-cat, racoon and snake. Wild hare abounded—unfortunately so did leeches, scorpions, centipedes and other less attractive kinds of wild life. I once arrived at a friend's house after a walk through the forest, with a very active leech writhing fatly at the base of my throat. I had no idea it was there and almost died of fright when she pounced on me with a loud yell and thrust the glowing end of her cigarette into it. The leech, disgustingly distended with my blood, fell off at my feet; then *I* yelled. One's first leech is rather unnerving.

Contrary to our somewhat apprehensive speculation, we found the Governor's house at Shillong was not the cold, forbidding, gigantic stone pile so beloved of the British Raj. On the contrary it was more like a large, rambling, country-house radiating warmth and charm and blending perfectly with the gently undulating terrain. It was set in a perfect jewel of a garden landscaped by the man who designed Kew Gardens in England, and it even had its resident ghost! The original building had collapsed during a particularly severe earthquake in 1897, and was rebuilt on the old foundations with the tilting capacity of a double-decker bus! I never really got used to sitting down to meals in a seemingly normal dining room, only to see, somewhere between soup and dessert, the beautiful Burma-teak panelled walls begin to sway from side to side with the angle becoming now acute, now obtuse until we felt as I am sure bugs would feel in a matchbox squeezed in the same way! I mention the dining-room particularly because, although the whole house swayed, it was only this centrally placed room that took on this distorted diamond shape during the many earthquakes that plagued Shillong.

The only really formal room in the house was a large banquet-hall, cool and white and lofty and elegant, with a parquet floor laid over hundreds of carriage-springs which made it marvellously buoyant for dancing. It was less than marvellous for committee meetings! If the popular Indian sedentary sports of foot-waggling, leg jigging and knee-flapping were indulged in with the customary gusto by even *one* member, it shook the entire floor, the long table with everything on it, and all the other members sitting on their chairs as well! This could be very disconcerting.

One of my father's earliest official visits was to the north-eastern border district of Lakhimpur in Upper Assam. If Shillong was 'County-England', this was 'Birmingham, Manchester and Leeds'! While most Europeans retired from government service soon after Independence, they lingered on in Jorhat and the Lakhimpur District towns of Dibrugarh, Margherita and Digboi, held captive by their rich interests in tea, coal and oil—the last white islands in a rising tide of brown!

We spent some time on the Brahmaputra during this pre-Independence visit, cruising along on board a floating luxury hotel thinly disguised as a river flat-boat. Consuming vast, gourmet meals in the opulent dining-room, or lolling around in deck-chairs sipping long, iced drinks, we watched people and temples and towns pass before us like scenes from a film on Assam's 'glorious past'. It is curious how unreal everything looks when seen from a moving boat. We would stop at some of the towns and wave good-bye to my father as he set off with Johnny Walker, his adviser, to toil and sweat while his family canoed off to some quiet sandy beach to laze and swim, or went ashore to see the sights. What a life! What a perfectly marvellous life!

58. Wanelio carving of a man singing.

Somewhere along the river was a very old *ashram* which was said to have been established around 1662 to serve an even older and very sacred Nag temple by one of the Ahom kings. The visit of a Muslim Governor to a Hindu shrine would be a graceful gesture in keeping with independent India's secular objectives, and so my father decided to pay his respects there. It was, however, *such* a sacred place that only male *brahmacharis* were considered pure enough to live there. The incredibly decrepit head-*brahmachari*, who had come on board to invite my father to the *ashram*, said that in all but really exceptional circumstances women were taboo there as they banished peace and subverted sanctity! For some reason my father found this deplorable male chauvinism hugely diverting. A mad young Ahom princess had established a sort of precedent by visiting the *ashram* to be cured of her malady prior to her marriage to an extremely elderly prince—my sister and I felt his senility may explain her madness, and wondered what the cure might have been. Apparently my father's visit was an equally exceptional circumstance, as he was permitted to bring his "*phemale phemily* members" with him provided we did our best not to furnish the starving *brahmacharis* with tempting evidence of all they were missing.

At the appointed time we followed him to shore wrapped in shawls like Egyptian Mummies, looking as unappetisingly neuter as we could. We might have spared ourselves the trouble! Not a single *brahmachari* could we see who might be in the least likely to be troubled by anything more disturbing than the infirmities that accompanied extreme old age. Perhaps celibacy was no longer the in thing with Assam's younger set. Could the more vulnerable ones have been packed off somewhere out of harm's way for the duration of our visit? It must remain, forever, one of life's tantalising little mysteries! But what a lovely spot it was, timeless, almost dreamlike, as such ancient places always are.

The temple-complex lay not far from the river in the middle of a large grove of mango trees. That these trees were of great antiquity was clear from their unusual height and girth. The temple and the cells in which the *brahmacharis* lived flanked an old stone tank that was said to date from pre-Ahom times. They ate in a long community dining hall with woven cane walls and a reed-thatch roof, adjoining a large stone kitchen, which was kept supplied with vegetables from its own well-stocked garden. Several sleek cows and one tremendous bull promised a plentiful supply of milk and manure! I have often wondered if these good people and their carefully tended animals had the time to flee to safety and a new home, or whether they had perished with their idyllic surroundings when the raging river engulfed them, along with so much else, in its relentless course.

What has never ceased to amaze me is the phenomenal increase in ceremonial paraphernalia that a man is expected to acquire in direct ratio to his rise in government service or the political hierarchy. This is a colonial legacy that the passage of time has in no way devalued; what it *has* devalued is *style,* now sadly missing from the "conspicuous consumption" of their successors.

At that time, the north-eastern frontier tribal areas now united as Arunachal Pradesh were somewhat differently administered from what were known as the Excluded Areas comprising the Khasi/Jaintia, Naga and Lushai Hill districts, and the states of Manipur, Tripura and Cooch Behar, but they shared a feeling of uneasy distrust of the coming regime, which was particularly strong in the

59. Facing page. A village on the Patkoi range.

Lushai Hills district, now called Mizoram. This name was evolved due to the modern Lushai's preference for the name 'Mizo' or 'inhabitant of the hills' rather than 'Lushai', as this was said to have been derived from the words *Lu,* or 'head' and *sha,* 'to cut', although the clan name is Lushei and not Lushai. A regular air-service now connects the capital with Assam, but in those days you had to make the journey to Aijal, the District Headquarters, on foot. If you were lucky you could risk almost certain disintegration—as we did—by rattling up the glorified cattle track of a link-road in a jeep or in one of the ricketty old army 'Dodges' that continued to ply as civilian trucks long after they should have. Accommodation, both en route and at Aijal, had been declared either 'tight' or 'unfit', so we transported our own!

The huge, over-sumptuously accoutred governor's 'Swiss-cottage', several smaller tents and their cumbersome 'camp' furniture, bedding, crockery, cutlery, kitchen equipment and an army of servants in scarlet and gold livery were brought down all the way from Shillong in large, Government House lorries. At Silchar, everything was transferred to several Dodges and sent on ahead up the cattle-track with the servants, so that camp could be set up, baths laid, and dinner prepared before we arrived. When you consider we spent a total of six days on the road with a two-day halt at Aijal providing the only break in the tedious routine of setting up camp in the evening and striking camp in the morning, I find it remarkable that only the "thunder-boxes" cracked under the strain!

Tension had been mounting for quite some time before this visit, owing to resentment at the autocratic rule of the Lushai chiefs. The British government had for many years exercised only the most nominal control over administration in the district, preferring to use the Chiefs as their agents in village affairs in all but the most serious matters or in cases of murder. Thus, to the already great powers and privileges enjoyed by them as their villagers' traditional overlords, had been added the useful advantage of government support of their authority, which some of them had grossly misused and exploited. They had, for years, been abusing their privileges, exacting illegal taxes and enforcing labour from their villagers, whom they often used as personal servants to carry loads or make their purchases from far-away markets. Something clearly had to be done, and so the Mizo Union was constituted to prevent further exploitation and put an end to the Chief's oppressive and unlawful demands. Finding their authority threatened they retaliated by electing a council of their representatives to introduce strong measures to counter the

activities of the Mizo Union, which then decided to boycott the Chiefs altogether, urging the villagers to defy their orders and refuse to pay them any taxes.

In the meantime, a third combatant had entered the lists: the United Mizo Freedom Organisation. This resounding title stood for a party that ostensibly supported the Chiefs' Council and opposed the Mizo Union. It in fact did neither but was rumoured to be busily engaged in trying to break away from India and establish links with the Chinese across the Burma border. By its tacit support of the Chiefs' authority, the government had also invited the angry censure of the Mizo Union which threatened to erupt into a full-scale Civil Disobedience Movement if their grievances failed to be redressed through peaceful means.

But suffering and ferment were not all the Lushai Hills could offer —*far* from it! Having shot their belt at heated meetings during the day, all the warring elements united in friendly camaraderie at sundown, giving themselves up to feasting, drinking rice-beer, dancing

60. Wanelio carving of a boy and girl singing, which is attached to a basket on head hunting expeditions.

and singing. Cowboy songs and familiar Christian hymns provided the melody of many Lushai songs, so my sister and I found no difficulty in singing along too—though we had to make do with la! la! la! and deedle! deedle! de! in lieu of words. Our instrumental accompaniment comprised an accoustic guitar and a large drum, and we all sat singing on long benches swaying from side to side to their rhythmic beat like poplars in a gale.

My father died two months after his fifty-third birthday, in December 1948, when his work had only just begun in a province where many tribal areas were seething in ferment.

But memories, now a little jaundiced by regret for what might have been, are only half the story. I shall never forget the night we heard a group of beautiful young men and women sing Handel's Messiah beneath the pines in Charles Pawsey's garden, with the purple hills in the background, the moon and stars above, and a captive audience of spell-bound Nagas wrapped in the varied and magnificent shawls of their different tribes, lit by the flames of a tremendous bonfire. What followed was a delightfully absurd descent from the sublime to the ridiculous, in the shape of two little girls splendidly beribboned and befrilled in satin and starched white muslin. With solemn gravity and a loudly vocal attention to rhythm, jerky hand-movements and determined tinkling of ankle-bells, they performed an 'Indian dance' to the tune of 'Oh! Danny Boy', picked out with martial precision on a guitar.

Sketches by Amena Jayal

Notes from the South

EDWARD LEAR

(1873-75)

Aug. 12.   When the 11 p.m. train came in and no ladies, I thought I might get to bed, but then I heard that a Madras train would come at 2 a.m., so I had to sit on, upon two chairs, pretty well half dead. At 2, "no ladies" was called out, and we thereon removed to the ladies' waiting room, where Giorgio instantly made up the two beds, and I soon fell asleep, after barricading the doors with a washhand-stand. I decide to go on to Arkonam and the line has run through beautiful hill country, perfectly green, and often reminding me of Corsica. But this child is knocked up and depressed and demoralised. Nothing surprises me so greatly in this southern journey as the beauty of the scenery on the line hereabouts, whereas I had expected to find it hopelessly contemptible. It seems to me that no process so de-moralises me, body and mind, as railway shaking. Country now pervaded with jungle; bamboos also, but not so beautiful as those of Darjeeling, yet they are becoming finer as we go on. The Strontian brilliancy of the young green rice is a wonder; it is provoking to be unable to draw these things.

Reach Arkonam at 4.30, a large divided station at the junction of the Bombay-Madras and the Madras-Malabar lines, with a gents' waiting room, refreshment room, etc., so we soon get settled, the whole state of things a great comfort after last night's misery. How-beit, the shrieking of railway engines forbids repose. State afterwards and talked to Giorgio who has been very silent all day. Beds is being made, but publicity is the necessity of this odious life, as some five or six trains are to come in before 6 a.m., and all wash and wait in these rooms. O! beastly row! O! hateful Indian travel!

Aug. 21.   At the station by 7. Gray gloom of weather ever, and gloom of heart, though health is tolerably good. But oh! this mon-soon travel is weary work; weary; weary! It was cold at starting from Bangalore, but is getting comfortable now. A Brahmin in white and another native in green are on the next seat of our compartment, and discourse in English, which fact provokes my curiosity, whereon

61. *Fort St. George, Madras.*

I learn that the green man only speaks Tamil and Telugu, the white only Maharatta and Bengali. So both understand English; that is their medium. "And, Sir," said the Brahmin, "you perhaps have not long been in these parts, or you would have learned that the English tongue is very much understood among Indian men."

Sky dappled, blue and silvery clouds; landscape generally interesting which about poor dear Bangalore it certainly is not. The Tamil green-vested native is from Colombo, a railway apothecary: he lends me a paper, by which I see Sir William Fairbairn is dead. The Brahmin repeats, "You see, Sir, English is fast becoming the language of this country." Madras at 7; very forlorn and benighted railway station reception: half tipsy official advises, but we mainly depend on our own exertions for getting all things into one *garry*. The drive along the sea, dimly seen afar by half moonlight, seemed endless. The chatter of a native close behind the carriage seat, driving me, already weary and worried, half mad. The only vacant rooms at the Pall Mall were too indescribably odious, all open and full of dirty furniture. I had rather have slept on the road than in them. So, off again, a fearfully long drive to Atkinson's, a hotel which I had heard spoken of in decent praise and extolled as newest and best. Here were two large rooms on the ground floor. One, an ante-room, did for Giorgio. But I do not at all know if I shall stay, even through to-morrow, so weary and cruelly disgusted do I feel. Got some dinner and soon to bed, where I might have slept from sheer fatigue but that the boards of the bedstead soon gave way, and let me down bumpily.

Aug. 24. Canal boat, covered, low, and not at all too comfortable. I doubt if I can bear being inside it for long, yet must go, now I am here. A new boy to cook, etc., is with us. Off "tracking" at 7. Tracking along the canal is quiet work enough; as yet no sail is put up. Giorgio, who has a sulky fit, is gone up on the roof; I remain in recumbent posture below. There is no beauty in this canal that one should desire her—a distant line of coco-trees, flat green fields near at hand, twice or thrice a sailing boat, but those not over-picturesque. We ourselves are sailing now; breakfast was sumptuous, to wit: boiled prawns, prawn curry, cold mutton, bread and butter and plantains. Of the two boatmen, one holds a sort of helm, t'other cooks bread, which the smoke of ain't pleasant. Quiet folk, but it seems to me not as interesting as Arabs was. O Nile! O beautifully endlessly endowed Nile! O weary and stupid India!

Noon, and very much better scenery; broad now, with beautiful parrot-green foliage of coco-trees and bamboos to the water's edge. This, however, soon ceases, and we relapse into commonplace canalism. The noise made by the older boatman drove me almost mad, coming as it did after bad thumps on the head. Moreover, the boat leaks and creaks; very nearly I am on the point of ordering it round, when a fair wind would carry me soon back again. A most detestable day of passive suffering! A large gray mullet offers himself as a voluntary sacrifice by leaping on board. Arrived at Mahabalipuram after a very miserably uncomfortable journey and too tired to eat, except a bit of bread, but some beer made me a little better.

Sept. 2. Heat at night something "by common"! Yet I feel pretty generally well, though I mean to take some quinine as a precaution. Walked to the temple of Little Conjeeveram and beyond it, hoping to get some general view, but found that quite impossible. Myriads of long winged ants fill the air, and falling, were picked up into small tins by children, which are legion here. Beautiful as is this long line of village buildings and coco-palms, there is hardly a spot to draw in out of the blazing sunshine, but even in the shade, such rivers of perspiration ran from one's face as presently spoiled the paper. I came, therefore, to the conclusion that to see the two Conjeeveram temples is all I can attain to, without attempting to draw them; a mortification, but one yet to be remedied. So I get back to the station and give up all drawing till I go, if indeed I go, to Mysore.

Half asleep and reposed till Giorgio announced breakfast, eggs, sardines, tea and bread. The boy, who is like a buffalo, puts water for six cups when we order two, and not enough for two when we order

62. Cape Comorin.   four. The heat increased terribly later, and I have not felt anything like it in India as yet. Slept, and at noon resolved to make a last trial to get something out of this very picturesque place. So I went out alone with a small book, and got two drawings, but such crowds came about I was obliged to give it up, as they followed me and increased like a snowball. So I came back and went to the Inspector of Police who gave me a cheerful constable, with whom I set out once more. But then ensued another difficulty. For, after a short shower and cloudiness the sun came out with fury, and it seemed impossible even to walk, and yet more so to stand still and draw. Nevertheless, perhaps foolishly, I persevered, and actually got two more sketches so that I can really express the characteristics of the Conjeeveram villages pretty well; the broad roads and multitudinous walkers, the beautiful coco-palms and tamarinds, and the endless way-side temples. Giorgio has made a truly wonderful pilaff, so we dined really well. Good evans! if any of my old friends could know how much beer and brandy and sherry this child consumes, would they recognise me? The most amazing event, or rather negative lack of event here, is the utter absence of fleas and bugs, and all vermin, save a few, very few, ants. There are not even flies! Conjeeveram has been rather a difficulty in many respects, but a broad notion of the condition of religion and politics in India can only be, however slightly, obtained by visiting such places.

No Place Like Home

ABU ABRAHAM

Till the age of seventeen, Kerala was the only world I knew. And I imagined that the whole world was like Kerala—sea and lake, rivers, mountains, coconut palms and rice fields. I was, of course, aware of the existence of desert and snow and wildernesses of sorts, but these were just geography book abstractions. Such places were in any case aberrations, I thought. The natural order was coconuts, lakes, sea. In the beginning there was the sea, and God said, "Let there be coconuts."

And then one September I went on a trip to Madras and Vijayawada to spend my fortnight's university vacation with my uncle who lived in Vijayawada. That was when I first saw 'villages'— groups of huts with clumps of desert palms, once every few miles of rail. The landscape, once the train crossed the western ghats (with their forests, waterfalls and monkeys) was flat, dry and monotonous. I marvelled that people lived in such places. It would be difficult, I thought, for a Keralite to live in a village like that. For one thing it would be hard for him to find enough water for his twice-daily bath—without which he would get itchy and irritable.

Water makes an important cultural division between the Malayali and his neighbour, the Tamil. Malayalis are water-oriented, fish-oriented. Tamils as a rule aren't. Even on the Coromandel Coast of Tamil Nadu not many use the sea for a swim or bath— except the fisher children, of course. Most Tamils don't know how to swim, whereas most Malayalis do. In Kerala there is water everywhere, so one learns to swim early.

It was in the sea that I taught myself to swim. Sea water being heavier, it's easier to float than in a river or lake. My first fifteen years were spent in a harbour town called Kollam, which the British, with their usual perversity about foreign names, changed to Quilon. It is still called that, though Kollam is the accepted name in Malayalam. Quilon is forty miles north of Trivandrum, which again is an English aberration, because the original name of the town is Thiruvananthapuram (Lord Anantha's town). Trivandrum, the capital of Kerala, was the capital of the old Travancore State. Trivandrum is where the famous Kovalam beach is. Kovalam's fame comes from the fact that it was made famous. What was in my university days a fishing village is now on the world tourist map.

Such misfortune has not yet struck the people of Quilon. Here there is a bathing beach the kind of which I have not seen anywhere else in all my travels round the world. This beach is as picturesque as Kovalam, but the sea is very different. It is a lively sea full of surf and immensely safe diving into most parts of the year. Because of reefs in the distance, the water is shallow and the waves broken up into manageable sizes. This beach is known as Thirumullavarum. There are two other beaches—Kochupilammood and next to it Thangasserry. The first is where people go to sit on the sands in the evening and watch the sun go down. Ships pass in the distance. Occasionally a merchant ship anchors a mile or so away and puts out its cargo into small boats. There is not much of a harbour, but history had made it one, because Thangassery belonged to the Dutch, the Portuguese and the British. It was a small foreign enclave of about a couple of square miles. A community of Catholic Christians live in cottages around an old lighthouse. This and a large church are the only monuments here. This coastline is full of rugged black rocks against which the powerful waves lash themselves into glorious white foam, spraying the graceful coconuts that lean out to the sea.

In Kerala there is an elaborate network of waterways, particularly along the coast. Canals connect the numerous lakes and rivers in the area. One can travel from almost any place to any other (except to the mountains) by boat. Some of the most breathtaking scenery in Kerala can in fact be seen only by boat. Tourists don't have the time but hippies do. It is strange, however, that the waterways have not been developed yet for pleasure cruises. There are a large number of trips one can take by ordinary motor boats, but the most enjoyable journey—though I have not done it since childhood—is by one of the country crafts. These long tapering vessels are spacious inside and a large one can take a family and all the household articles. Two boatmen at each end use poles to navigate the boats. When there is a wind the sail spreads out. It is a slow journey. What takes four or five hours by motor boat can take two days in one of these. The boatmen cook, catch fish, wash clothes. At night, the deep silence is only broken by the dull thud of the bamboo pole touching the side of the boat. If the sky

is starless or without a moon, the journey can be, as I remember, somewhat eerie. But then, as a child I was frightened of the dark and of deep waters. Generally these boats keep close to the shore; accidents are rare.

I left Quilon when I was fifteen, when I went to Trivandrum University to get myself a degree. After Trivandrum I went off to Bombay in search of a job, then arrived in Delhi, and later went to England where I spent sixteen years. It was in England, about the time I turned forty, that I began to realise what Quilon had done to me. I felt that Quilon was not just a town I lived my early years in, but something which had become a part of me. A sudden nostalgia gripped me and I realised that I still carried somewhere inside me the sights, smells and sounds of the town. The temple bells, the bells on the cart bullocks, the clanging of the coppersmith, all these sounds rang in my ears. The smells came into my nostrils as if a box of assorted scents had been opened before me. There were smells sweet and smells foul. The smell of fresh earth after the first monsoon rains, the smell of grass, the smell of hay. When the soil is parched by the scorching heat of the summer, the first rain wets it without soaking, so that the scent rises upwards with the warm air. With the later heavier rains, it is washed away.

The smell of grass was another intoxicant. As a child I used to put my head in the long bundles of freshly-cut and washed grass which the tribal women brought to our house every evening at sunset. We gave it to the couple of goats we kept, but not before I had had a good roll in it. The goats too had their own special smell. When they had kids my whole life centred around them. I hugged and kissed the little ones.

The smell of the sea. The big beach where people went to stroll in the evening was only a mile away from my house. Here the sea was powerful, the sands warm, dry, and plentiful. There were shells, big and small, by the thousand. Fishermen sat between the rows of cutamarans, knitting and repairing nets. Drying fish were spread on one side. The air smelt a mixture of all these—shells, fish nets and boats—and it was not unpleasant.

In Quilon there was also a lake, Ashtamudi (it had eight branches like an octopus), which joined the sea, and there was a canal running through the town. It was always crammed with long, tapering boats carrying coconuts, coconut husks or coir. Once they released themselves from the canal, the boats spread out their sails and slid gracefully over the expanse of the lake. On lazy week ends I have spent hours gazing at these boats from the jetty of an old palace

of the Maharaja of Travancore. The boats smelt of shark oil and seaweed. Oil is smeared on the body of the boat to preserve the wood.

The coconut palm is perhaps the most versatile of all trees. In Kerala no part of it is wasted. The beams of our houses are made of its timber, the leaves are used for thatching. With coconut shells our kitchen spoons are made; from the husk are made coir and coirmats. Tender coconut provides a good thirst quenching drink; coconut kernel and coconut oil are used in much of our cooking.

Come to think of it, coconut is the major producer of smells in Kerala. The most sensual smell I can remember from my youth is that of freshly washed and groomed girls. In the capital town of Trivandrum (forty miles south of Quilon) where I spent my four university years, the college girls moved in batches in the evenings. I suppose numbers gave them security, though one of them could knock down a dozen young men with her fragrance alone. When auch a group had passed you by on the street, the smell lashed you s few moments later, sending ycu into a daze. The smell was a combination of coconut oil and jasmine. Strings of fresh white] jasmine in their hair were an important part of the armoury of college girls.

Jasmine to me is the sweetest of all smells. We had a jasmine bush in our garden. Early in the morning the smell in the courtyard was overpowering. There is a saying in Malayalam that one jasmine bush is enough to spread its smell throughout the garden, meaning that one good man can spread his virtue throughout the community. Jasmine to me is warm Indian dawn; Kathakali, Carnatic music, temple bells, festivals, annual days at school.

But childhood and youth in Kerala were not all beauty and joy for me. There was always a certain sadness in the atmosphere. Darkness came suddenly and menacingly in those days. After watching the sunset at the beach, I would rush home, fearful of the black night. Apart from a short stretch of well-lit shops, the way was full of danger. I was frightened of rowdies, of snakes. The road was poorly lit by dim kerosene lamps. In the thatched huts on the

way wick lamps flickered. Boys and girls sat close to them, reading their lessons or reciting prayers. There was also wailing from little children, hungry before their mothers had cooked the rice. Occasionally there were also scenes of tragedy, like when a little girl bringing coconut oil, salt and chillies from the shop, had dropped it all on the road and stood weeping bitterly beside the broken bottle, afraid to go home.

In the primary school I attended, most of the boys wore only a *dhoti*, and no shirt. Many came late because they had to come walking from homes as distant as five miles. On rainy days, some of them came totally drenched because they only had half a banana leaf to hold over their heads. Most were underfed. A common reply to the teacher's question, "Why are you late?" was, "The rice gruel was not ready." Such dismal poverty does not exist today. You will not easily find undernourished children in Kerala. Economic improvement together with a comprehensive health service that covers the entire state has made a tremendous difference.

Until the early sixties, Kerala's per capita income and calorie intake according to statistics, was the lowest in India. Today they are distinctly better. But statistics cannot convey the sense of well-being of the common people. The common people are better looking and better clothed than they were even a decade ago. Look at a line of girls going in the morning to work in the ricefields. The straight, lithe bodies, the bright blouses and *mundus* can't be described by statistics. No sociologist has measured their bosoms, nor examined their healthy teeth and long tresses adorned with flowers. There are no statistics to measure the per capita smile on the bright faces of children going in processions to schools in the morning.

Above all, there is a dignity among the people, a total absence of servility. Education and political awareness (and action) have given them a self-confidence which they didn't have before. This is why every time I go to Kerala it is like a dream fulfilled. This is why every Malayali's dream is to settle in Kerala, after making money in the Persian Gulf or in Ludhiana.

Breathes there the man whose soul so dead....

Sketches by Abu Abraham

Journey into the Interior

MULK RAJ ANAND

I often journey into the interior. From the time I played at puff-puffing like an engine with other boys, I have loved to make journeys, specially by train.

The last one I undertook was because I was going to a seminar on Nandi Hill. Unfortunately, the connecting trains were late. So I missed the fast nonstop train from Bangalore to Mysore at 1.45 p.m. and had to take a Janata Express two hours later.

As soon as the engine brought the shabby looking train on the platform, the people, who had been waiting patiently, rushed towards the doors of various compartments, struggling, straining, pushing and shoving, with their bundles acting as cushions against being hurt. It seemed to me that the peasants believe the train will run away as soon as it arrives and leave them behind, and no one wants to be left on a platform after a long wait.

I walked by one or two compartments, found them full, then saw a man getting up from a seat and coming out on to the platform. I rushed in, along with the lady student who had come to guide me to the seminar, and occupied the vacant seat, pretending it had been kept for me. Actually, I presumed that the man who had walked out was the servant who had kept it for someone who had not turned up. Of course, my occupation of the vacant seat provoked displeasure among the neighbours. Some stared at me. Others made side glances at each other. And one, who seemed to be a literate fellow, raised his eyebrows. I pretended to be unconcerned, made room for the student and buried my head in a novel entitled *Samskar*.

The heat of early summer mixed with the stale breath of many people in the compartment made me perspire and feel slightly dizzy. I craned my neck to see why the train was not moving. But just then there was a whistle from the guard somewhere behind. With a jolt, the compartment pushed forward.

Movement brought relief, so that my neighbour, a pious Muhammadan with a rosary in his hand, smiled contentedly and gave me a few inches more. I in turn yielded a little more space to the modest girl student.

The generosity of the Muslim seemed to arouse the ire of the Brahmin opposite, with the three lines of white paste on his high forehead. He glared at me. His sharp nose breathed out fire. His twisted mouth suppressed a curse. His ears burned.

I dipped my head into the book before me.

There was coughing and spitting, sniggers, whispers, and the cry of a child.

I remained absorbed in the novel.

As the air blew in from the green land I lifted my head to survey the scene and inhaled deeply.

I could see segments of mouths, heads with tuft knots, some with Gandhi caps on, others with Astrakhans after the fashion set by the film star Chief Minister of Tamil Nadu, Ramachandran, and huge turbans sat squatly on other heads, with a ready-made gold braided turban cap here and there.

The bundles, trunks, small bags of the passengers lay anyhow, anywhere, obstructing movement, so that the whole compartment seemed jammed into a solid mass, the congestion now relieved somewhat by the breeze.

The Brahmin sitting opposite the girl student, Kumari Meera, asked her something in Kannada, which I did not understand. I looked at her enquiringly and she wrote in a scrapbook the words: "He says he is a Hoysala Brahmin and asks me what is my caste. I have told him I am a Mahadeva Brahmin."

I put down my note below hers, asking: "What is the difference?" She wrote: "It is very complex and difficult to explain. But we are opposed to each other for generations."

I wrote back: "Opposition will get you nowhere. We must discover things on which we agree."

At that juncture I see a ticket inspector come pushing through the crowd from the connecting passage between our compartment and the one behind. He did not advance beyond the first knot of passengers, who stood cheek by jowl, as it were. Soon there was an altercation between him and a smart young fellow with longish hair, and a shirt with a Byronic open collar. I guessed that the young man was "without".

The T.C. stood doggedly, facing the young man. The young man raised his head defiantly. The T.C. pronounced the word: "Police". The young man hung his head down, put his hand in his pocket and slipped something into the T.C.'s hand. The T.C. moved on and the young man became pale. He seemed to accept his defeat, and looked away from everyone.

I wondered whether he had tried to cheat deliberately or just could not get the ticket as he had come late to the station.

The T.C. advanced further and had similar furtive altercations. I saw that most of the faces turned away from him. One man tried to bury his head like an ostrich hiding his face in the sand. A couple of young people pushed ahead towards the latrine.

I felt the circumference of my vision closing into my mind.

All these people, I imagined, have come from somewhere and are going somewhere. They were separate. The T.C. is going to inspect each one and check whether they have paid the cash for the fare. He is the representative of the distant money god who must extract dues. If they have no money and have not bought the ticket, they are guilty of cheating the money god. They have no other existence apart from the cash nexus. In fact, they are bundles of flesh and blood tossed about on the surface of life and are the property of the invisible demon who has sent the Ticket Collector there.

I saw that the Muslim gentleman was also perturbed by the presence of the T.C. He closed his eyes and began to move the rosary in his hands. I turned my gaze towards the Hoysala Brahmin. He was not disturbed, but folded his legs in the lotus posture and began to whisper a prayer. I wondered why they had suddenly taken to con-

63. Interior of a railway compartment.

templation. Anyhow, the T.C. could not enter into the complex where we are. Giving one glance towards us, he moved on.

I noticed that he looked like the younger brother of a notorious politician with a black round face, the whites of his eyes tinctured with yellow, his nostrils sniffing the air with contempt for the passengers. Might he not be an incarnation of one of the demons in hell?

My eyes swam in a kind of vague pity for the victims of his vigilance. But there was no way of transferring my affection to the half-dead. Each one was isolated beyond my reach, cut-off from me, the only northerner. If I talked to anyone I would not be understood. Nor could they communicate with me, except through the young girl.

I turned to her and asked: "Are they peasants or merchants or clerks?"

"Mostly peasants," she said.

"Will they be going all the way to Mysore?"

"Yes," she says. "It is our New Year's day, and they will all go to the temple at Nandi Hill."

I realised that there *was* something common between us all. We were all going to Nandi Hill.

Growls, grunts and shouts. A quarrel had broken out at the far end of the compartment. I looked towards the T.C. and found him unconcerned as he invigilated, notebook in hand.

Soon there came the sounds of a more vociferous exchange, as the group at the further end seemed to have joined in fisticuffs. I looked to the girl student for an explanation.

"Probably a leper has touched a Brahmin," she said.

"Are lepers allowed here?" I ask.

She did not answer.

I presumed that though quarrels may break out about pollution, there was a vague acceptance of everyone by everyone at one remove or the other. Uprooted from heaven and consigned to hell, we all know that there are *others*. But each one is a stranger. We have multiplied from the same stock, but lost contact in the oblivion of the world.

I asked myself whether I too am not judging everyone from the outside.

The quarrel subsided, but the frayed tempers persisted. As ripples in a sea, there are whispers, deep breaths of relief, and gossip about the incident from the centre of anger.

The train stopped at a station. A shoeshine boy crept in. He spotted me as the only likely victim. I don't know why.

I looked at his small shapely face, shrunk by hunger, and there was an appeal in his eyes.

I can never resist these open mouthed apertures of indigence, innocence and want. I took off my brown leather shoes and gave a sign with my hand, indicating I will pay twenty-five paise only. The fellow opened his kit from a broken tin box and began the operation.

The Hoysala Brahmin shunned him like the plague and sat up on his haunches.

The little fellow showed tremendous alacrity. I was constrained to give something of my affection to him in my smile. The shoeshine boy responded with greater alacrity, as he polished my shoes vigorously.

I felt that, deprived of contact with others, I wanted to touch him, so that I may know I am not out of touch, and he may understand he is not forgotten. In the state of suppressed pain, with agitation of nerves among the afflicted, I dreamt of distributing love. But the way the little boy put his hand out, I realise that he wanted twenty-five paise and no sentiment. I looked for the twenty-five paise piece and then dug into my pocket for another five paise and put it in his palm. Instead of the glee at getting a baksheesh, he adroitly manoeuvred himself out of the circumference of my hand and made his way between people's legs to the next pair of leather shoes.

I brooded on the situation. I have to accept this universe as it is. In this world, I am. Therefore, I fell. And whether the others wish it or not, they are in me and I am in them. I contain multitudes—that is the truth I must realise.

The shrubs and the plants and the trees past which we are going are all different, but take colour and form and smell from the earth. And if we were separate, it was not always so. In that sense, I must accept the hell of this compartment as the universe to which we are condemned and relax.

I became aware that four people in the next enclosure are playing cards. It is a good way to pass the time and forget the irritations of the journey. They did not seem to be very well off from their clothes, and yet I saw that they were counting the number of marks on a piece of paper. The concentration they seemed to bring to their cards, hiding these from each other, the manipulation of the numbers, the adroit calculations, indicated a mystique of which the secret is known only to the players.

I remembered seeing that someone invented playing cards in this area, with symbols which are not understandable now. I suppose each set of people, in each generation, invents mythical games to while

away time, because—isn't our journey, like all journeys, not only in space but also in time?

64. The Decauville locomotive, built 1902.

There is another halt, with the screeching of brakes and the grinding of wheels and the grunt of the padding between the compartments.

And in between the stop and the departure, there came a ventriloquist. With a brief whistle on his flute, he invited the attention of the passengers and then announced in Kannada the various acts that he was going to perform. I recognised the names of Indira Gandhi, Morarji Desai, Devraj Urs.

The very first impersonation of a speech by Indira was tantalising. The imitation of the thin feminine voice in Hindi was masterly. And at the end of the speech with the shriek of *"Jai Hind"*, he just about summed up the clever populism of the ex-Prime Minister.

He changed over to the dull intonation of Morarji Bhai, in the slow drawl, of a speech on prohibition. The repetition of the English word "prohibition" brought smiles to many faces, and the "don't! don't! don't" made for laughter. The ending with the English words "non-violence! non-violence! non-violence!" emphatically said was a reference to Morarji's inner violence. Then the superb actor interpreted the words, in Kannada, of Devraj Urs. Soft, sibilant and evasive, with emphasis only on *'harijan'*, the tone of voice was so cleverly manipulated that it aroused subdued smiles.

The mimester now passed a little bag around into which two people put ten paise each, while some passed the bag without putting in anything. When it came to me, I put in a rupee note as a token of my appreciation of the actor who, I felt, should go to the capital and debunk the other men of the hour. I was confirmed in my view that, within the universe of discourse of politics, the only way to oppose slogans is by defeating them. And as the mild humour of mime does not betoken hatred but satire, it may be the only way to demonstrate the chicanery of the suppression of freedom through a leader's evasive talk.

I looked out of the window and wondered whether the rulers of the past also told lies to the people.

I saw the *gopuram* of a temple and wondered if the donations given to shrines by the old kings were not bribes offered to the Gods to appease the sin of killing enemies in war. By deflecting the minds of people to the unseen, and the declaration by each dynasty of descent from the God King Rama, or the God Surya, or Vishnu Bhagwan, the feudal chiefs were able to reach the subconscious and make patriarchy acceptable. In the darkness of the jungles, it was possible to conquer everything by radiating divine light, as nowadays every pseudo-Gandhian masks himself with the spirituality of Mahatma Gandhi to cultivate the love of people.

I don't think, however, they realised that you can't cultivate love the way peasants cultivate plentiful paddy by throwing organic manure on the soil.

My thoughts went into a void. I found myself opposing myself. And from the conflict in me arose a sudden anger in my being. I felt that my face was flushed with inner turmoil, bad nerves, and the warmth of the sun which had percolated into the compartment, mixed with the breath of mouths and noses and the smell of sweat. I was perspiring under the neck and felt I could do with a drink of water. Fortunately, the girl student was carrying a thermos flask in a big cloth *jhola* bag. I indicated my need to her. She willingly filled up a cup for me with the elixir of life.

Still another halt.

And I heard the chant of a *sadhu*—"*Tat Tvam Asi*". The man appeared with the skull bowl in his hand, his body ash-smeared, his hair matted and brown by copious accumulations of dust. A brief *dhoti* covered the vital part of his nudity.

"*Tat Tvam Asi*" he shouts again. And then he tried to make his way into the compartment across the few people who were descending from the train. As the train moved again he repeated "*Tat Tvam Asi*".

This reminder that the "other is yourself" makes me recognise myself as the ascetic's counterpart, if he really means what he says. But I know he means by the 'other' that in himself which is ultimate wisdom and the highest joy, God.

I am full of fear of that 'other', if he exists, because of salvationists like the ascetic, the Hoysala Brahmin and the Muslim divine. They seem to be too exalted in the pride of their transcendence to consider their neighbours as part of themselves. And yet there is a resonance in the cry. *"Tat Tvam Asi"*, the *sadhu* shouts again.

Surprisingly, quite a few passengers dropped ten paise pieces into his skull bowl. An old woman emptied some roasted gram into the vessel. A young peasant put a bunch of bananas into the ascetic's hands. It seemed to me, then, that the resonance of this ancient cry had touched the hearts of others. I marvelled at the survival of this memory in the populace.

Those of us who have emerged into the new world wonder why we are here and not there, and who put us here, and where we are going —and we have no answer.

I wondered if the journey through space has not so blunted our minds that we had lost our sense of direction. We didn't even remember the station from which we bought the ticket. Our minds were adrift, as we were just going, going, going. And the heat of the journey created a torpor in which we floated as in the proverbial ocean of hell.

I wondered if the passengers, who were going to the temple on Nandi Hill for the New Year festival, were aware of the reminder given to them by the ascetic's cry *"Tat Tvam Asi"*.

It seemed to me unlikely from the concern for the luggage that the passengers were carrying, that they had given a thought to the end of the journey. And as I had been reading the novel *Samskar,* I too was involved in the distracted talk about the conflicts which arise from the separation of man from man. I was disturbed by the anxiety about what I would say at the seminar on Ananda Coomaraswamy. This sage was converted to the Sanatan Dharma, or the perennial philosophy. He believed that *Satyug,* or age of truth, was over and that we were now in the *Kaliyug,* the age of darkness. He rejected all the knowledge piled up by the discoveries of five hundred years of experimentation in the west. He was against the machine, even more so than Gandhi, who conceded travel by railway. Of course, it was easy for this Englishman, converted to the Hindu faith, to live safely in the closed shell of tradition as a Boston Brahmin. But I have the sense that the mystery of existence has not yet been solved. *Neti!*

Neti! (It is not this, it is not that) is no answer. We are on this planet Earth. And as yet we do not know whether there is life on any other planet, and what will happen in the future to man and all his works.

To be sure, the ascetic shouted *"Tat Tvam Asi"* and those who believe in the transcendence to the highest self, will always dismiss those who want to look both ways inside and outside. They consider that they are the only ones who are awake in the darkness, while those who admire the flowers and the sunshine are sleep-walkers.

After meditating in the void, when I saw that my feelings were disturbed by the question-mark in my head, I looked out and saw the beautiful old trees with their roots spread out.

And I felt that I was between two trees, the holy tree whose roots are in heaven and whose branches spread into my nerves and tendons, and the tree of life whose roots are in the earth and whose branches stretch out towards the sky.

I was lost in my sense of wonder.

I felt that my journey will never end. I shall always go on travelling.

After getting to the seminar I shall again be in a train, in a compartment with a crowd similar to the one surrounding me.

And I shall be always going somewhere, everywhere and nowhere, catching butterflies in Kangra Valley, watching birds in Bharatpur sanctuary, warming to the embraces of lovers in Khajuraho, and writing a poem every day to create the whole world afresh, on that day, for myself and others.

Notes on the Authors

Romila Thapar is Professor of Ancient Indian History at the Jawaharlal Nehru University. She is the author of several books, including *Ashoka and the Decline of the Mauryas, History of India*, Volume I, in the Pelican series, *Past and Prejudice*, and *Ancient Indian Social History: Some Interpretations*.

Reginald Heber was the archbishop of Calcutta and travelled extensively in India between 1824 and 1826, leaving us a detailed narrative of his journey from Calcutta to Bombay to Madras and the rest of the South. The extract is taken from *Narrative of a journey through the upper Provinces of India from Calcutta to Bombay 1824-25, with notes upon Ceylon; an account of a journey to Madras and Southern Provinces 1826, and letters written in India*, 3rd Edition, 3 Vols., Murray, 1828.

Akhilesh Mithal is a *Dilleewaallaa*.

Edward Lear, landscape painter and children's writer, came to India at the age of 62 on November 22, 1873, and remained here until 1885.

Louis Rousselet was a French writer who spent six years travelling through India. His specific interest was the life of the Rajas of Central India. "Across the Desert on Camel-back" has been taken from *India and its native princes: Travels in central India and in the presidencies of Bombay and Bengal,* revised and edited by Lieutenant Colonel Buckle, containing 317 illustrations and 6 maps, Champman, 1875. Plates 2, 4, 7, 8, 17, 18, 19, 20, 21, 22, 23, 25 and 49 are taken from his book.

Krishen Khanna is a contemporary painter.

Henry D'oyley Torrens was the author of *Travels in Ladakh, Tartary and Kashmir,* 2nd Edition, Saunders, Oatley and Co., 1863. Plates 26, 27, 28, 29, 30, 31, 32, 33 and 36 are taken from his book.

Pupul Jayakar is the author of *God is Not a Full Stop, Textile and Ornamental Arts of India,* and *The Earthen Drum.*

Roberto Ottolenghi teaches Italian at the Jawaharlal Nehru University.

John B. Seely was Captain in the Bombay Native Infantry, and author of *A Voice from India, in answer to the Reformers of England,* as well as *The Wonders of Elora,* extracts of which are reproduced in this volume.

Santi P. Chowdhury is a documentary film maker.

Amena Jayal is a free-lance writer and illustrator.

Abu Abraham is a cartoonist and journalist.

Mulk Raj Anand is a novelist, art critic and editor of *Marg* magazine.